Grow Your Family Tree Online

Getting Started,
Valuable Websites, and
All the Basics, Tips, and Tricks You Need to
Build Your Family Tree Using the Internet

Ryan Elson

Connect with the author online at the following sites:

Homepage:
http://www.ryan-elson.com

Facebook:
https://www.facebook.com/RyanElsonAuthor

Twitter:
https://twitter.com/authorryanelson

WordPress Blog:
http://ryanelson.wordpress.com/blog/

This book is also available for Kindle.

To my family,
for not being overly difficult to locate,
and my 7th-grade teacher,
for making me complete
my first family tree.

Table of Contents

Genealogy Basics, Tips, and Tricks

For the first-time genealogist, it can be difficult to know where to start or how to overcome stumbling blocks in your research. Thankfully, there are lots of resources to help with these problems, even if you don't live in the same city or state as your ancestors. Research isn't a word that has the most enjoyable connotations, but think of your genealogical research as a scavenger hunt or a giant jigsaw puzzle. You're hunting for clues and putting together the puzzle. If you don't like research, scavenger hunts, puzzles, mysteries, or the like, then I suppose that you'll just have to keep reading to find out whether genealogy appeals to you personally.

A few things to keep in mind when reading the book are the differences between records, databases, collections, and indexes. The easiest way to tie these items together is with an example. My great-great-grandparents, Wesley Elson and Matilda Woods, were married on September 18, 1878. Their marriage record is part of a larger collection (or database) that includes marriages which took place in Martin County, Indiana, between 1877 and 1886. And since an index was put together for that collection (i.e., someone took the time to put together a list of all names in the collection), it was easy to locate. If the collection hadn't been indexed, I could have still looked for their marriage record, but I would have had to scan the collection visually instead of jumping directly to their record.

In an effort to keep things simple, I've broken the discussion down into short sections for easy digestion that, when taken as a whole, should help your research immensely. In this chapter, we discuss the types of questions to ask your relatives and how to start a family tree, before discussing how to find specific details you're missing or how to support details you already have with source documents.

Now, without further ado, let's get started with the initial, and most important, step, talking to your family.

Talk to Your Family

This is an obvious starting point, but not everyone takes the time to discuss family history with his or her parents and grandparents. And it's understandable because some families don't take the time to discuss anything at all, let alone family origins. If, however, you are on speaking terms with your kin, I would urge you to find out everything you can from them. In addition to simple information like your mother's and grandmother's maiden names, some families have written or oral histories that may include dates, names, children, and even unusual anecdotes, all of which can be helpful in putting together the puzzle that is your family tree. Remember that in addition to your parents and grandparents, you should ask your aunts, uncles, great-aunts, and great-uncles what they know or possess. After all, original written content can only be handed down to one descendant, so your aunt or uncle may be in possession of the family bible, not your parents.

When discussing your lineage, here are some things to consider, ask about, and take note of:

1. Talk to parents, grandparents, great-grandparents, and anyone else you think may know anything about your family--even your grandparents' neighbors might be worth speaking to if you can locate them. Once these individuals have passed away, any knowledge they had that wasn't written down will be lost forever. Or until we invent time travel. But if that comes to pass, then genealogical research will go the way of the dodo anyhow.

2. Write down the names of any and all family members that your relatives can come up with. You don't think you need the name of your great-aunt's ex-husband? Think again. You should take down direct ancestors, as well as siblings, siblings' children, brothers-in-law, and even widows' step-children from a second marriage. Take note of everyone you can. Any one individual might be the thread that ties your loose ends together.

3. Get dates to go along with all of the people you just recorded. These can be birthdates, death dates, marriage dates, dates of residency, or

immigration dates. Any date that you can tie to a specific event will be helpful. Even if you don't have an exact date, get a general one. Perhaps your ancestor's son was born sometime around 1832 or your relatives moved to Kansas sometime around 1855. That's good enough, at least to start.

4. Get locations to go along with your relatives and all of your newly acquired dates. Try to find out where people were born, died, and were married. Towns are great, but counties, or even states, are better than nothing.

5. Find out when your relatives moved to those locations, if possible. Relocation dates can be helpful for locating ancestors in all sorts of documents, including censuses, vital records, directories, land records, and more.

6. Ask about military service. Military records are another great way to find out family details and locate your ancestor in time.

7. Ask if there are any additional details that might be helpful. Was a town or schoolhouse named after your relatives? Were they the first settlers in a particular location? Were they experts in their field? What sort of work did they do? Did they immigrate to the United States? If so, from where and in what year? Have they written any books? Did they like to eat pudding? Okay, the last one probably won't help your research immensely. Unless your ancestor is Bill Cosby.

8. Call or email your family members and find out if any of them have already put together family trees. If so, this may save you from replicating their work and allow you to concentrate on areas of the tree that haven't been fleshed out yet. If you do locate a family tree, remember that there may be inaccuracies so you'll likely want to use it as a starting point without taking every bit of information contained therein as the gospel truth. Unless the tree already has source documents to back up the so-called "facts," that is.

Starting Your Family Tree

In the past, this was done mostly on paper. It still can be, and in some ways, a paper copy of your family tree is the most convenient way to look at things. However, without backup copies in another location, you run the risk of losing your work if, God forbid, your house burns down, floods, or the dog eats your files. Online family trees, such as those on websites like Ancestry.com, Archives.com, and others, help avoid these problems. Although you have to create an account, starting a family tree on

Ancestry.com is totally free. If you want to search the site's records, you'll have to sign up for a membership. We'll discuss this option and both of the previously mentioned websites in a later chapter, as well as alternate options. But for ease of modifying the facts (which sounds silly but it will happen; trust me) and the ability to add siblings and extended family members, an online tree is an easy way to go, and my preferred method.

In its most basic form, your family tree should contain you, your parents, grandparents, great-grandparents, and so on, back as far as you can possibly trace your lineage. Extended family is somewhat superfluous when looked at this way. However, don't make the mistake of thinking that they can be ignored. If nothing else, you'll need to consider extended family to help flesh things out--in fact, you'll come to rely on siblings and extended family in your research. That doesn't mean you need to research your great-great-aunt's first-husband's parents, but if you do, there's a slight chance, especially in small towns, that this information will prove useful somewhere down the line.

Once you build a family tree based on the information you now have about your ancestors (the information your family gave you), take a step back and look at what you've already accomplished. You've done a lot of work and should be proud of it. And what's more, you've got an excellent starting point for locating source documents and moving your family tree back even farther in time.

Determining What to Do Next

You've spoken with (or emailed) your family and you've built a family tree based on that information. Nice job! But where do you go next?

At this point, determining what to do depends partially on what you already have and what you want to focus on. There are really two directions you can go. First, you can start fleshing out the people you already have in your tree. And second, you can try to learn more about the past, adding as many additional generations to your tree as possible. Truth be told, these directions are one in the same--sometimes, that is.

If you have a wealth of information going back to your great-great-grandparents and you're fleshing out the life of your father, you probably won't learn much about relatives from previously unknown generations. Does that mean you shouldn't spend time on your father's history? Of course not. You still might learn a lot of worthwhile and satisfying information. In all likelihood, you just won't help move your family tree farther back in time.

As a personal example, although I already had information about my third-great-grandfather, when researching my great-grandfather, I learned about his first marriage and a daughter he had with his first wife. Although this didn't help move my tree any farther into the past, this was an interesting bit of information, especially since neither my grandfather nor his siblings knew about their father's first marriage or their half-sister. So in my opinion, this was a valuable find.

On the other hand, if your tree already goes as far back as your great-great-grandparents, and you start researching the lives of their children, this can be very beneficial indeed. Not only will you learn more about the children, but if you're lucky you may even stumble across additional details about their parents.

For any relative in your tree, even extended family and siblings of your ancestors, here are some details to look for and nail down. We'll discuss each at length after the list.

Name Variations
Date of Birth
Location of Birth
Date of Death
Location of Death
Is an Obituary Available?
Do They Have a Gravestone?
Date of Marriage
Location of Marriage
Maiden Name
Were There Multiple Marriages?
Names of Children
Names of Siblings
Names of Parents
Were you Adopted?
Locating Your Relatives in Each Federal Census
Immigration Date, if Applicable
Dates of Relocation, if Applicable
Military Service

I promised we would discuss each item in the list next. I lied. Although we could discuss each item now, we need to talk about conflicting information first. Then we'll get back to the list. I promise.

Conflicting Information

In today's society, we're required to write and use our names exactly as given. If we want to change our names, it's a process. If we want to get a driver's license or buy a plane ticket, we have to be very conscious that our name doesn't vary one iota from its expected value. It's okay to use a nickname with your friends or for school assignments, but when filling out government paperwork, we have a specific name that we're expected to use.

In times past, this wasn't the case. And this can be very frustrating for the genealogist. Not only did people go by different names and spell them differently from time to time, but relationships and exact birthdates weren't always required on each census or when applying for a marriage license. So in addition to conflicting names, you may find conflicting birth, marriage, or death information. Today, these dates aren't supposed to vary, but keep in mind that individuals didn't always know their own age and sometimes documents were filled out by someone with inaccurate information. As such, conflicting information not only occurred, but it was actually commonplace.

Now that we've addressed that matter, let's continue with our previous list of items. If pertinent to the discussion, I'll also address conflicting information in the context of each section below.

Name Variations

In my opinion, this can be one of the most difficult genealogical issues to handle, at least for the first-time researcher. But unfortunately, name variations were common in past centuries. There are several reasons for this.

Firstly, not everyone could read and write. If you can't read or write, chances are you won't know exactly how to spell your name, first or last. This means that it's up to the census taker, deed recorder, or church official to write it down based on how it sounds, something which can cause the spelling to change from one document to the next. This is true of both first and last names. Here are several surname examples I've run across and variations I've seen throughout my relatives' lives.

Elson
    Elston, Elison, Ellison, Eliston, Elsen

Rabideau
    Rabedo, Robidoux, Rabidoux, Robidou

Vanmeter

    Vanmeter, Vanmater, Vanmetre, Vanmatre, VanMeter, VanMater, VanMetre, VanMatre, Van Meter, Van Mater, Van Metre, Van Matre

Morlatt

    Malatt, Marlatt, Morlott, Molatt

Marszatek

    Marszalek, Marsolek, Marsatek, Marshall

And those are only some of the names for which I've found multiple variations. Although not all of my relatives' surnames have variations (that I know of), the majority have been spelled at least one or two different ways at some point in the past. The ones that I haven't found alternate spellings for yet? Names like Rider, Garner, and Miller, though alternate spellings for these surnames do exist (Ryder, Gardner, Mueller). First names can also be spelled more than one way (Lewis vs. Louis; Carry vs. Carrie; Wesley vs. Westley).

A second reason for varying names is that the government wasn't set up the same way as it is today, and we didn't need such naming precision. Social Security wasn't around before the 1930s, for one thing. And although many churches and counties recorded births and given names over the last two-hundred years or more, most states didn't require or start keeping official birth records until the late 1800s or early 1900s. Sometimes even when a birth was recorded, a first name wasn't. In these cases, the child may have been initially recorded as Infant, Boy, Son, or something similar, and since I've yet to come across an adult who was named Infant, Boy, or Son, we can assume these were placeholders and not given names.

In other words, names were given by the parents when the child was born (or later baptized) but could change as was deemed appropriate. Here are some variations and misrecordings of names you might not think denote the same person, when in fact they do.

Wesley Warren Elson, Wesley Elston, Warren Elson, W W Elston, Wesley W
    Baker

Mary Catherine Garner, Mary Garner, Catherine Garner, Catherine M.
    Garner, M. C. Garner, Polly Garner

Vanmeter Gabriel Rider, Gabe Rider, Vanmeter Rider, Gabriel Rider, V. G. Rider

Tim Detour, Timothy Detour, Mutty Detour, Mutty S Dutour

The bottom line is that, in census data and elsewhere, sometimes people went by one given name, sometimes they went by two, sometimes the middle name stood alone, sometimes they were listed by a nickname (e.g., Mutty or Polly), and sometimes census takers listed initials only. While Mutty is not a common nickname, there are lots of common nicknames to keep in mind when doing your research. Lists are easily located online, but several examples include: Polly for Mary; Betsy for Elizabeth; Sally for Sarah; Hank for Henry; even Jack for John. Abbreviations were also common: Wm for William; Geo for George; Chas for Charles; Jno for John; Thos for Thomas.

Another reason for naming differences is because your ancestors may have emigrated from another country. For example, I have Polish relatives whose given names are Franciszek, Katarzyna, and Wojciech. Not only might they appear in official records under these names (or an alternate spelling of them), but they also might have been recorded under an English equivalent-- Francis or Frank, Katherine or Kate, George or Albert. Yes, the English version of the Polish name Wojciech really might be either George or Albert. Last names were also sometimes translated into English. So my Polish relatives with the last name Marszatek might appear in official records with the last name Marshall (or with a spelling variation of either name in either language). Try to take advantage of wildcard searches online when you're looking for multiple spellings. In this case, if the website you're searching accepts wildcards, try searching mars* or marsz* instead of Marszatek. And simply do an online search for "Polish names in English" to find common translations (or whatever languages you're attempting to translate between).

Along these same lines, it's important to keep alphabetic characters that are unique to a given language in mind. Although I'm still working on my Polish lineage, it appears that the "t" in Marszatek may have originally been the letter "ł." Usually, this would convert into the letter "l" in English, not "t," but in my relatives' case, it appears they went with "t." Compounding matters further is the fact that the letter "ł" in Polish has a pronunciation similar to the English letter "w," which may help explain why I'm progressing more slowly on this line than many others in my family tree.

A final reason why you might run into variations of your ancestor's name is due to transcription errors. Handwriting in old documents can be faded, smudged, or just difficult to read. In addition, some letters looked like each other, even though they don't seem to today. For example, the letters "s" and "f" appear very similar in many old documents. While these transcription errors may not be actual recording errors on the source documents, if you're searching an index or database that's been transcribed from the original collection (an immensely helpful and time saving option), it's something you'll have to contend with. Transcription errors are sometimes so hideously incorrect that your ancestors' names won't come up in your searches at all, no matter how many name variations you try. Think of trying to find the Dutour surname, when it's been transcribed as De Tom. The odds are against you.

Date of Birth

As mentioned earlier, most states didn't require that an exact date of birth was filed with the state itself until the late 1800s or later. For more information about when filing birth records with a particular state became compulsory, please visit that state's official vital-records-department website or read the pertinent state write-up in "Chapter 4 - State-by-State Resources" to locate other resources with this information.

Thankfully, even before each state began keeping its own records, many churches and counties recorded this information. Churches recorded baptismal dates but didn't necessarily record exact birth dates. Don't worry if you're only able to locate a baptismal record, as for some of your relatives, this is probably as good as you're going to do. These records will generally list parents, and possibly godparents or witnesses. Along a similar vein, family bibles can provide lots of valuable information. Obituaries also provide birthdates (much of the time), and older obituaries, which regularly provided lengthy biographical write-ups of the deceased, may even provide these dates for parents or spouses. Death certificates (either through state or county records or the Social Security Death Index [SSDI]) can also provide birth information.

In the late 1800s and early 1900s, many historians wrote books detailing the history of particular towns or counties. In these books, biographies of prominent citizens are often given. While your ancestors may or may not have made the cut for inclusion in these books, if you do find a write-up for one of your relatives, you'll likely find a birth date as well. We'll discuss how to locate these books online in a later chapter.

Military records often list birthdates of males, especially World War I and World War II draft cards. Other military documents, like pension papers, may include birthdates of the serviceman or even his dependents (i.e., wife, children).   Gravestones usually have exact dates or at least years, and numerous websites are dedicated to indexing tombstones.   Finally, census records can be helpful in determining birth year.

Census records provide different information for different years. In some censuses (for example, the 1900 Federal Census), the birth month and year were both requested. In others, only the person's age was requested (for example, the 1880 Federal Census). In the latter case, one can estimate a year of birth based on the age provided, but this doesn't impart overly precise information. Additionally, if an age couldn't be provided by an individual, then census marshals were allowed to enter an approximation. As you may have surmised, information recorded in these instances might have introduced another source of error.

No matter where you find your ancestor's birth information, be aware that it may be conflicting.   Hopefully you'll have some agreement, and at a minimum the birth years should be semi-close to each other. If you locate a record for a man named Everett Leroy Elson who was born fifteen years before you think he should be, the chances are he might be a different Everett Leroy Elson than the one you're looking for (this actually happened to me).   Look around a little bit more before you make up your mind and start adding the wrong information to your family tree.   If you're unsure about the source/data but decide to add it anyhow, make a note so you can recheck it later. That way when you revisit that section of your family tree at a later date, you won't mistakenly assume that your questionable information is one-hundred-percent accurate.   A couple of years in either direction shouldn't be cause for concern, at least not initially.†

---

†A caveat is if your ancestor has a common given name and a lot of family in the area. In this case, there may be a lot of individuals with the same name and similar birthdates running around. For example, a man named Abraham Vanmeter has a large family with ten or more children (very common in past times). If a large number of these are sons, when they start having kids of their own, they may all choose to name a son after their father. In this way, there might be numerous Abraham Vanmeters born around the same time and living in the same area. Just something to consider.

Location of Birth

Most of the records listed in the above section, "Date of Birth," also apply to this section. Of course, sometimes a record may only provide a birth date but not a location, and vice versa.

You can also have conflicting information with regard to place of birth. Again, there are several reasons for this. One is transcription errors. For example, if a census taker used state abbreviations and your relatives are from Indiana, you would expect to see "IN." However, in the past some census takers used "IA," the current abbreviation for Iowa, as the abbreviation for Indiana. In these cases, the record might have been mistakenly transcribed as Iowa, when the state recorded was, in fact, Indiana.

Parts of some states also became other states. Parts of Virginia at the time of its initial statehood are now located in both Kentucky and West Virginia. And the southern tip of Nevada was previously part of the Arizona Territory. As such, individuals born in Virginia when it was, in fact, Virginia might have listed Virginia as their state of birth even if that land now belongs to Kentucky. In these cases, records generally reside in the actual location of birth, regardless of what state the land used to belong to.

Sometimes these things change for no apparent reason. In one census, the birth location for a relative may be Ohio, and in another it may be Pennsylvania. It's possible that these are actual errors because the family member providing the information to the census marshal has the facts mixed up.

Another reason for discrepancies is that border conflicts between states and colonies were fairly common. As such, a relative born in a disputed area might claim to be from one state, while pertinent records actually reside in another.

Census records are an easy starting place to determine birth location, but in my experience they are probably one of the least reliable records. Plus, census records only provide the state of birth and, while helpful, a town or county will get you much further. If your relative was born immediately before a census (several months or less), there's a good chance he or she was born in that enumeration district, though this isn't always true.

Date of Death

Much like the "Date of Birth" section, there are a lot of resources for determining date of death. Death records from the church, county, state, and SSDI may be the most helpful types of resources. Again, the availability of these records, prior to the SSDI, depends largely on where your relatives lived and county record keeping at that time. If your relatives died in years when federal census mortality schedules were taken (1850, 1860, 1870, 1880), then you might be able to locate an accurate federal death record. Some states also compiled mortality schedules for additional years, though all of these additional mortality schedules were recorded in the same general time period.

Obituaries, even of a spouse, sibling, or parent, can give you a date of death for your relative. If not an exact date, you may be able to determine whether your relative was still alive at the time of writing. For example, an obituary for your grandfather's brother may state that he is survived by two sisters and one brother preceded him in death. If this is the case, at least you know your grandfather died before the date of his brother's death. It may not be the homerun you were hoping for, but it's better than nothing.

The county history books mentioned earlier may or may not be helpful. Since most of the biographies in these publications are of living county residents, they won't usually include death information for the subject of the biography. However, they may include death information for the subject's grandparents, parents, spouses, or children. Searching websites like FindAGrave.com is also helpful, but be mindful that gravestones may have deteriorated or broken over the years, so you may not be able to locate every relative's headstone.

Once again we come to census records. Since only living individuals are enumerated, there won't be a record for your deceased relative. What there might be is a record of your deceased relative's spouse. If your relative shows up in one census record but not the next, you should try to find his or her spouse. If the spouse shows up as a widow (most census records list whether the person is single, married, or widowed), you know that your relative died sometime in that ten-year span between censuses. What can complicate your search is if the spouse was remarried in the interim. For example, let's say your great-grandfather shows up in one census but not the next. If he died shortly after a census was taken and his wife remarried before the next census, she will never show up as a widow, only showing up with her new husband's name. This can lead the researcher to believe that the missing relatives have relocated, when in fact one died and the other remarried. We can try to get around this, but that's a discussion for the section on "Multiple Marriages." On the plus side, if you are able to identify a remarried spouse, then you've narrowed down the deceased's date of death even further, since it had to occur before the widow was remarried.

Wills and probate searches are also of great importance, but to date I haven't found many of these resources online. State Archives, discussed in a later chapter, often have information on how to locate these records, though as I just stated, I haven't found many of these indexed or available on the Internet. In all likelihood, as more vital records are digitized and indexed, wills and probate records will eventually get their turn. Until that time, you may have to search in person or hire a researcher if you don't live near the pertinent record repository itself. If you find your ancestor in a collection of wills and probate records, either online or in print, you'll probably be able to learn or confirm a great deal about his or her family. If a wife or child isn't mentioned in the will, these family members may have died before the husband/father. If they are mentioned, then it's likely they died afterwards. Not an exact date, but this information is helpful in a similar manner to the discussion on obituaries several paragraphs prior. A more detailed discussion on how to use wills and probate records is located in a later chapter.

One additional place to look which you might not think about is in city directories. Many directories from the late-19th and early-20th centuries list the name and address of each adult male in town, possibly listing the wife's name in parentheses. If the husband passes away, then the following year the wife will be listed first and her name may be followed by the word "wid" and her husband's name, indicating that the woman is the widow of the named male. Thus, you can use directories to find the year when your ancestors go from living together to one of them living as a widow after the death of their spouse. If your ancestors go missing entirely, that might also indicate a year of death. Or it could just mean that they've relocated to another town or state.

Location of Death

Again, this information is readily obtained from most of the same locations as discussed in the "Date of Death" section above. However, there are some things to be aware of. Sometimes, the SSDI information will conflict slightly with state-recorded death information. In addition, some ancestors may be interred in a different state or county than the one they died in (i.e., they died in one state or county but were buried in another).

Is an Obituary Available?

There are two directions from which you might approach your search for obituaries, either with the date and location of death already in hand, or without having that information.

Either way, if an online obituary index exists for the location in question (or a guess at the location if you don't yet know it), that should be the first place you check. The simple reason is because it's probably the easiest way to locate an obituary. If you already know or have a guess at the location of your relative's death, try consulting that state's subsection in "Chapter 4 - State-by-State Resources" to find out if a statewide obituary index is online. Alternately, if you know or have a guess at the specific town or county of death, you can search for indexes specifically held by a local library or at the county level. An obituary index located through any of these channels might prove useful in locating your ancestor even if you don't know exactly when or where he or she died.

If you do know when and where your relatives passed away (easier said than done, but let's pretend you used the information contained in this book to come up with a date of death) and you can't locate them with an online obituary index, then you need to determine which local newspapers were around at the time. Websites like Chronicling America (see "Chapter 3 - General Internet Resources") have comprehensive newspaper listings online, or you can try contacting a local library or historical society, as they'll be knowledgeable about the area in question.

While some newspapers are available on the Internet, through both free and subscription sites (discussed in a later chapter), older newspapers aren't always searchable online. Fear not, because you have other options. Use an online search engine (Google, Bing) to find the town or county library associated with the location of your ancestor's death. They will often have microfilm of old local newspapers. For a few dollars, most will take your ancestor's name, date, and location of death and check their newspaper microfilm holdings for obituaries. You'll probably still have to pay if nothing is found, but if you don't live in the area, this is a much cheaper option than hopping on a plane and flying to the appropriate location to do the research yourself. Local genealogical or historical societies often have access to newspaper archives too. The most readily available online obituaries tend to be for those people who have died since the Internet became pervasive to our society.

If you don't know the date or location of your ancestor's death, you can make a couple of guesses. If a relative goes missing after being recorded in a particular census or other official document and you believe that he passed away, it's reasonable to assume that he died in the same state in which he was last recorded. If your relative lived in a border town or county, you may want to search surrounding states as well.   This assumption won't help narrow down an exact date, but you can take your assumed location and follow up with a local genealogical society, library, or even the state archives to see if any of them hold an index that isn't available online.

Remember that in addition to newspapers from the location of death, if your ancestors moved from one county or state to another, their original place of residence may have an obituary also.   This is especially true if they were prominent in the community or still had relatives in the area.

Do They Have a Gravestone?

Searching websites like FindAGrave.com can help fill in the missing pieces if you don't have complete mortality information for your ancestors.   Search for your relatives, being sure to account for spelling variations, the fact that maiden names aren't always listed, and realizing that dates may not have been entered by the submitter of your relative's memorial record.   If there is a listing for your relative but no image, you can submit a free request for a picture to be taken and uploaded.   Local area volunteers can claim your request and fulfill it, uploading an image of the gravestone to the online memorial.   Although records with images may indicate "Unknown" for a date of birth or death, sometimes the date wasn't transcribed but is clearly listed on the gravestone.

Many older gravestones don't list birthdates at all.   However, they may indicate that your relative was *Aged 82 y, 3 m, 18 d.*   If you back calculate 82 years, 3 months, and 18 days from the time of death, you'll have a reasonable estimate of the birth date.   Tombstones don't normally list a location of death, though the majority of individuals are interred in the same town or county in which they lived.

One additional piece of information you might come across is with regard to relatives.   Abbreviations are often used, so if you see something like, *Susan Rider, w/o John*, you'll know that Susan was the wife of John Rider.   Similarly "d/o" and "s/o" mean "daughter of" and "son of," respectfully.   These two notations normally only show up if the person passed away before they were married.   Sometimes parents' or spouses' names aren't spelled out either. Initials may be good enough to confirm identity, however, so don't get discouraged.

Another thing to consider is whether there are other interments associated with your relative.   In other words, if you find a centralized Rider tombstone, are there other Rider family members buried around the main stone?   If so, they are probably all related in some way. This is a little harder to determine online and may be easier to visualize if you get a chance to visit the cemetery in question.

What you *can do* online is search for other interments with the same last name as your relative, especially those in the same cemetery or the same county. Just because you don't yet know a particular given name doesn't mean the individual is unrelated. Let's say my relatives are William James and Martha A Allhands (they are), and I know which cemetery they're buried in (I do). If I then look through all of the other Allhands in the cemetery, I may find some helpful information. Looking at a record for Horace Q Allhands, I find that his tombstone indicates *s/o WJ and MA*. This may not seem very helpful by itself, but this means that Horace Q is the son of William James (WJ) and Martha A (MA) Allhands. Since he was born after one census and died before the next, he was never recorded in a Federal Census. Official birth and death records weren't kept at that time either, so there was no way to locate Horace through a birth or death index. Ultimately, Horace didn't help move my tree backwards in time, but his inclusion does help flesh it out and make it more complete.

The same type of search can be performed with birth or marriage records by searching for the same surname in the same county or state and seeing if you're able to tie the resultant records to individuals you already have in your tree.

Date of Marriage

Surprisingly enough, this can be an easier nut to crack than finding someone's birth date. The reason is because records were usually kept for marriages long before they were for births. Depending on the age of the bride and groom (and the state and county of marriage), parents might even be listed in the documents. Or if they're not explicitly listed, you may get a clue by seeing who gave permission for a son or daughter to marry. There's a fair chance this will be the father, even if that's not expressly stated. Some marriage documents list those individuals who are responsible for the marriage license fee, and as these individuals aren't always the bride and groom, be sure to follow up and see if you can determine how everyone is related.

One thing to keep in mind is that you'll often have to view the original documents (or an online image of) in order to find these extra details. When marriage, birth, or death records are indexed and made searchable online, the indexes often leave the details out. For example, when searching online, it's reasonable to assume that you'll find the bride and groom, location of marriage, and date all listed together. This may not always be the case, but if the information was available, it was probably indexed. However, other details from the original documentation probably weren't transcribed or indexed. It is for this reason that one must look at an original copy in order to check for additional details, such as place and date of birth, parents, witnesses, and sometimes even if this is a second marriage, either through divorce or death of a spouse. Regardless of if you find these extra tidbits of information, marriage dates were often recorded well in advance of governmental birth records, so these can be a great help in your search.

Another way to narrow down a marriage date is through census records. In more recent census records, a small amount of marriage information is usually provided. Unfortunately, the information presented varies from one census to the next, so it's very important to keep this in mind and read each document carefully. In some censuses, enumerators were asked to record the number of years a couple had been married. Based on this data, a reasonable approximation for the year of the wedding can be determined. In other censuses, the data might provide the age at first marriage. In this case, you have to consider how old the person is in the year of the census and subtract to find out when the marriage took place. The major problem that arises from consulting "age at first marriage" is that this could be the second marriage for one or both parties. To find out, look at both ages-at-first-marriage and see if the same number of years has passed for both the husband and wife. If you do the subtraction and learn that the husband was first married 23 years ago and the wife was first married 12 years ago, then it's probable that the husband had a previous marriage. This may also help nail down whether a child is from a first or second marriage. If the wife was first married 12 years ago, as indicated in our above example, but a 16-year-old son is living with the family, this is likely a son from the father's first marriage.

A less documentation-based though marginally helpful way to narrow down marriage dates is to look at ages of children. Unlike today, many families started having children shortly after marriage, so if you find that your ancestors' first child was born in 1852, it's likely that the marriage took place sometime shortly before then. This is by no means a hard and fast rule, but it's something to consider.

Obituaries and county histories may also contain marriage dates.

Location of Marriage

The location of a marriage is usually found with the date, so don't forget to consult the above section. One caveat is that census records don't ask for the marriage locations, so this information won't be available through census data. However, if you have already located census data prior to and after the marriage date and your relatives lived in the same county before and after the marriage, the odds are they were married in that county. If nothing else, the county of residence and the surrounding counties are a great place to start looking. If the location of residence was different before and after the marriage, you may have to check both locations. This doesn't guarantee that the marriage took place in either location, but again, it's a good place to start.

Looking at the original documents can also help. A transcription of the record may only indicate the county where the marriage took place, while the actual document may include a city. Whether this helps your research depends on your own unique situation.

If you've already figured out the date and county, or town, of marriage, you may be interested in finding an exact location within the county. In this case, it may be advantageous to look at old newspaper articles (microfilm, digitized, or paper). If you have access to a digital newspaper archive, all the better, but if not, don't worry. Since you already know the date and county, or town, of marriage, you simply need to find out if an old newspaper is available from that time. Libraries and county offices are great places to search, as they will likely have microfilm archives. Check the date of the wedding and a few editions of the newspaper before and after in order to locate a wedding announcement. This may indicate that the couple was married in a particular church, or at the bride's home, or some other such thing.

Maiden Name

So you've traced back your ancestors but are missing the maiden name you need in order to get another generation of research started. What now? This can be a challenging problem, and how easy it is to overcome depends largely on persistence and the era in which your relative was alive. I've found that from about 1850 onwards, it's much easier to find maiden names. Before that, it can be a bit more complicated. Let's start with the most obvious maiden-name indicator, marriage.

As discussed in the two previous sections, marriage records can contain a wealth of information. The odds are a marriage record will give you a bride's maiden name, and as mentioned, sometimes even her father. If you were only looking for a maiden name and you found the father's given name or even the mother's maiden name, you've just hit the genealogical jackpot. Well, at least one of the minor jackpot varieties; perhaps the *Daily 3* or *Daily 4*. If you don't find the father's name, the maiden name is still a great find. This will allow you to look for wills, land records, birth records, possibly find siblings, and maybe locate your relative in a previous census.

Death records can also be helpful. These might list the deceased's maiden name outright, and possibly the parents' names, in which case you may come away with the mother's maiden name also. Information found in death records varies, but if there's a section for the "informant," this will often be a close relative, whether you recognize the surname or not. Small-town-newspaper obituaries often included a lot more information than they do today, so old obituaries may be particularly helpful in the maiden name puzzle. Historical publications from the late 1800s and early 1900s regularly included biographical sketches of prominent county residents, so these may have similarly detailed information.

Census records don't pay off often, but they may. Starting in 1880, census records indicated a person's relationship with regard to the head of the household. If you're searching a census record for a married female, you might find her listed as "Wife" in the section that asks for relationship to head of household. If you also find a "mother-in-law" or "brother-in-law" listed in the record, you've just found the maiden name you need. Be conscious that the mother might have remarried since she gave birth to your ancestor, and her last name might not be the maiden name you want. This can work the other way too. Let's say you already have information on a mother in your family tree but don't know what happened to her daughter. If you find the mother living with a strange family and listed as "mother-in-law," you've just found her daughter, husband, and possibly kids. This trick doesn't work as well before 1880 because relationships to head of household weren't listed. However, if you find someone thirty years older than the head-of-household and wife, ask yourself why he or she is living with your ancestors. This may be a boarder with no relation to your family whatsoever. But it also might be the wife's father or mother, complete with maiden name.

Land records can also play a part in your search. If your relative was an assignee for someone's land, perhaps through a bounty land warrant, ask yourself how the two individuals were related. Similarly, if your relative sells or purchases land, follow up on the buyer or seller. This might be an in-law you haven't identified yet. Finally, you can look at the names of the owners of nearby parcels. If you follow up and search those names for marriage records, you may uncover hitherto unknown relationships.

Another long shot, but something to consider is that a woman's maiden name may have been used as a name for a child. Sometimes families gave a child the maiden name of the mother, either as a first name or a middle name. Nothing will indicate this, but if you're desperate, it may be an avenue to pursue. Other times women will take their maiden name as their middle name, so don't forget to follow up on these clues.

Checking biographies, obituaries, birth, marriage, and death records of all children can be very helpful. Wills can also be beneficial, though as mentioned earlier I've not found many of these records online yet. The missing maiden name, and possibly even the mother's maiden name, could be located in any of these records. The key is to research all close relatives. Let's say you're looking for your great-great-grandmother's maiden name. Rather than limit your search to her and your great-grandfather (her son; your ancestor) solely, expand your search and check all of your great-great-grandmother's children. This may mean you have to search ten individuals instead of one, but one of those individuals may have a record that indicates the missing maiden name.

Were There Multiple Marriages?

The multiple-marriage problem is related to the maiden name problem above. This is especially true of women. If you found a first marriage for your female relative and you're looking for a subsequent one, try searching marriage records with her married name, not her maiden name. If her husband died and she remarried, her surname didn't revert to her maiden name upon the death of her spouse. So if Susan Van Meter married John Gardner, and John Gardner died first, a subsequent marriage for Susan should list her name as Susan Gardner.

Even if you don't know that your male ancestor died, if your relatives go missing, try searching for a marriage record with the wife's married name, in this case Susan Gardner. If you locate a marriage record for Susan Gardner that takes place after your relatives go missing, then it's possible that this is her second marriage after her first husband's death. This doesn't yet guarantee you've located the correct Susan Gardner, but at least you can look into it.

Finding additional marriages can help nail down all sorts of other details. Were there any half-brothers or sisters? Is this the correct sibling? Is this the correct son? If you know the name of a child and are able to locate a death record, even if it only has one seemingly correct parent, this might still be your ancestor. It's possible that the unknown parent on the record was a spouse from an additional marriage or the correct parent with a maiden name that you haven't uncovered yet. Or it might not be. Either way, if the other details match up, it's something worth looking into.

To complicate things just a bit further, you may have to move in the opposite direction to find a woman's maiden name (i.e., your lineage is from a woman's second marriage). Let's say you know that your relatives, Sanford and Melissa Stilson, were married around 1856 (perhaps based on the 1900 census). And when you search for their marriage, you learn that Sanford Stilson married Melissa B Gendron. Now you know that Melissa's maiden name was Gendron. Or do you? Unfortunately, Melissa might have been married previously so Gendron could be her surname from her first marriage, not her maiden name. If you're having trouble getting past Melissa and you believe she may have been married previously, try searching for men with the last name Gendron who married women named Melissa (her last name is unknown to you at this point). You might also run into this problem if a child's death record accidentally indicates a woman's surname from her first marriage instead of her maiden name. There are a couple of things to remember about this situation. First is that the middle initial in Melissa's marriage record, B, might be the initial of her maiden name. Perhaps Melissa Buchan married a man named Gendron first, and after her husband died Melissa B Gendron remarried. Alternately, her maiden name might actually be Gendron and you just haven't found the marriage record yet. In this case, the middle initial, B, might simply stand for a middle name, Melissa Belle, for example.

Names of Children

So far we've focused on census records for a lot of our information, but since the Federal Census is probably the most universally available and consistent item available nationwide, it makes sense that it should be an easy document to use in your research, regardless of where your relatives hail from. To locate children's names, we'll once again consult the census. In many cases, if you find your relatives, you'll find their children. Easy peasy. Before the 1880 census, relationships weren't listed, so you may have to make some assumptions and then try to prove them out through other documents. If you find other families with the same name living near your relatives in any census, try to find out how they're related. The odds are fairly good that if your ancestor, Jonathan Dickison, is living next to another Dickison family, then the two families may be related. Even if you find another family in the same county, you should try to find out if this family is related to your ancestors. This may not be practical with common surnames in big cities, but if your ancestor's surname was uncommon or he lived in a small town, you should follow up on similar or identical last names.

Birth and death records, as well as gravestones, can also be helpful. If you know your relatives lived in a particular county or are buried in a particular cemetery, check the vital records for that county and the interments for that cemetery. If you find people with the same last name, look a little closer. It's possible that they're related to family members you already know about.

City directories may also be helpful. If you know where your ancestors lived in a particular year, try to locate a city directory. Make note of the address and look to see if any of the other individuals with the same last name are living at the same address. These may be children, siblings, or even parents.

Land records can also be helpful in your search. If you find that your relative sold land to someone with the same surname, try to find out if this is a child, sibling, or other relation. Similarly, you can investigate owners of nearby property. If your ancestor, Adam Miller, is living next to a man named David Osborn, try searching marriage records for David Osborn. If you learn that he married a woman named Elizabeth Miller and the dates match up, there's a good chance that Elizabeth Miller is Adam Miller's daughter.

Additionally, obituaries, biographies, and wills often list children outright, sometimes their spouses, places of residence, and whether they are still alive or not.

Names of Siblings

Again, census records can be very helpful, but as we've mentioned them several times already, we won't dwell on this avenue any longer. Obituaries and biographies are also helpful. Wills tend to list family members, too, sometimes including siblings. Directories can also be helpful, although you'll probably have to confirm relationships on your own. For example, if you know your relatives lived in Marietta, Ohio, in 1910, then you can look for a Marietta, Ohio, directory from that time period. If you find your relatives, look at all of the additional people with the same last name. Are any of them living in the same house or on the same street? These may be siblings or relatives of some sort. Land records might indicate sales to, or from, siblings, and neighbors with the same surname could also be related.

Names of Parents

Much of the information already discussed applies to searching for the names of your ancestor's parents. As such, there's not a lot of new information to cover in this section without being redundant. Just remember that you may have to search laterally in order to find the information you're looking for. One option, that may or may not be time consuming depending on whether records have been transcribed, is to look at every biography you can find for the county your ancestors lived in. Let's say you're looking for the parents of Cornelia Myers. Well, although it may seem unrelated, a biography for Samuel Watson may indicate that his second marriage was to a Cornelia Myers, daughter of Jason and Eliza (Ezra) Myers. You may not be able to definitively say that this is the correct Cornelia Myers yet, but it's a good place to start. And if you already knew her last name was Watson, perhaps from the obituary of a sibling, then you've just confirmed her parents. We'll discuss websites that help with this type of search later in the book.

Land sales between individuals with the same surname might indicate parentage, and nearby residents should be researched to find out if they could be your ancestor's parents.

Remember when we talked about gravestones earlier? If you find that your ancestor, Jacob Allhands, is *s/o E.J. & E.F*, at least you've got some initials. Now search for the correct last name (and initials) on gravestones in the same cemetery, and you may be pleasantly surprised to find that Erastus James and Elizabeth Frances Allhands lived in the area and are buried nearby.

Were you Adopted?

When researching adopted relatives, whether yourself or a family member, you have a couple of options. Normally, you will know the names of your (or your relative's) adopted parents, so you should be able to track them down using the content presented throughout the rest of this book. You may not, however, know who the birth parents are. This can be problematic. The first thing to do is to ask yourself if you want to trace both birth and adopted parents, only birth parents, or only adopted parents. If you're most interested in family ties and relationships but hold a personal grudge against your birth parents for giving you up, then you may choose to focus on adopted parents. If so, there's no need to identify birth parents. If you're most interested in birth parents and direct lineage, perhaps for hereditary purposes (e.g., family health history, country of origin), then you will definitely want to identify birth parents and trace their roots.

Adoptions are very private matters, and each state handles them differently. As such, try consulting your state's vital-records department to determine what the laws are. Often, you can download the necessary order forms online, though, again, it depends on the state. In most cases, adopted children can request pre-adoption birth certificates once they reach a certain age. Some states allow children to request pre-adoption birth certificates for a parent, but only if the parent has already passed away. Other states may allow the adoptee's immediate family to request records. Basically, eligibility and how to request pre-adoption records depend largely on whose record you're searching for and what state that relative was born in.

Some states might have older adoption records online, though in my experience this is uncommon. The only collection of this nature that comes readily to mind is an adoption collection from Vermont in 1869 (see the Vermont section of "Chapter 4"). Although not many collections are online, try consulting the Archives for the state in which your relative was born. The Archives may have an old collection of adoption records that is now a matter of public record. If old church records have been made public, you may be able to find a baptismal record for your relative also. If the baptism took place before the adoption and wasn't amended, you may be able to determine birth parents' names.

If you don't have any luck with the above options, consider taking a DNA test (discussed in the next chapter). Assuming that someone else with the same lineage as yourself has taken the test, you might be able to fill in the gaps without any adoption documentation at all.

Locating Your Relatives in Each Federal Census

Although locating each census your relatives appeared in isn't strictly necessary and some censuses won't provide any new information, the more information you have the better. Perhaps a child only appeared in one census with his parents. Or perhaps a parent lived with an adult child for only one census. You don't know what you're missing until you find those records. Are you having trouble with a particular census? Sometimes online indexing isn't sufficient to find your ancestors. As previously mentioned, this may be due to transcription errors, incorrect spelling, or any number of things. The next question to ask yourself is if you know where your relatives lived during the missing census. If the previous (or subsequent) census indicates a street address, try locating that same address in the new census. If you found your relative in a directory, look for that address in the census records. Military, land, birth, and death records may also indicate addresses that you can check; if there is no address, try locating the same block or enumeration district as from the previous or subsequent census.

Have you found siblings or other relatives in the same town? If so, just scan a few pages forwards and backwards and see if you can spot your relatives. Oftentimes, relatives lived in the same part of town, or even on the same street.

If you're missing a child, he or she may have been living with extended family during the census in question. Try locating census records for extended family and seeing whether you can find your ancestor. Remember that he or she could have been recorded with the extended family's surname even though that surname wasn't actually correct. I've seen this exact situation happen several times in my own family tree. After his mother's death, my great-great-grandfather, Wesley Warren Elson, was living with his aunt and uncle during the 1860 census and was recorded as Wesley W Baker. And my grandfather's half-sister, Priscilla Marie Elson, was listed as Marie E Mooney in one census and Marie Seafler in another. Hers may be an extreme example, but in 1910 she was living with her mother after her parents were divorced (her middle initial, E, is actually her last name, Elson, and Mooney is her mother's maiden name). In 1920 she was living with her remarried mother and was recorded with her step-father's surname. Even her obituary listed her father's surname as Seafler, though when checked against birth records and other documentation, this information is clearly erroneous.

If none of the tricks listed above work, and you've tried searching all alternate spellings you can think of, you may have to use brute force. If you know, or are almost positive, that your relatives lived in a particular town during a particular census, you can flip through each page individually and look for them. This is a terribly time-consuming research method and if you don't have much to go off of in the first place, it can be difficult to make any progress. Name variations and misspellings make it even harder to locate your relatives, but at some point, this may be your last option. If you undertake this time-consuming task and are still unable to locate your relatives, you may have to consider the fact that they weren't recorded in the missing census. Either that or the names were recorded so incorrectly that you just didn't recognize them when they appeared.

Immigration Date, if Applicable

Obviously, not all of your relatives immigrated to the United States recently. But the odds are that if your research is successful enough, you'll trace back to a generation when at least some of them did. Recent censuses often list arrival dates, and naturalization dates can also be a good place to start. Border-crossing documents and ship manifests are also available, and many of them are searchable online. Ship manifests sometimes indicate traveling companions, family members either in the United States or in your relative's homeland, and perhaps an intended final destination complete with address.

Naturalization documents for some locations are also searchable online. These might include declarations of intent (the first paperwork in the naturalization process), as well as the naturalization itself. Sometimes you'll only find indexed information, so you'll have to request copies of the source documentation. Women and children didn't always have to file their own paperwork, so if you find the husband's or father's naturalization documentation, your search may be over. In this case, check the date of naturalization to determine whether you should keep searching for a woman's documentation.

Finally, biographies and obituaries can help fill in the gaps when you don't have any luck with the first few options.

If you find an immigration date in naturalization paperwork, try to follow this up and locate the passenger manifest from your ancestor's ship. We'll discuss where to find these manifests in a later chapter. If you're unable to find a manifest, simply do an online search for "immigration" and the date of arrival. Using this method, I was able to resolve a problem with one of my relative's immigration dates. His census data gave one immigration date while his naturalization paperwork gave another. After researching the date from his naturalization papers, I determined that one of my Polish relatives went back to Europe to fight in World War I as part of Haller's Army. His naturalization paperwork listed the date he returned after the war, not when he came to the United States originally.

Remember that although the majority of immigrants entered the country through New York, there were other immigration stations around the country. Some immigrants entered the country through places like San

Francisco, New Orleans, Baltimore, Boston, Philadelphia, and even smaller ports like Galveston, Texas, Providence, Rhode Island, and Charleston, South Carolina. Other immigrants landed in Canada before making their way into the United States.

Dates of Relocation, if Applicable

Relocation dates are similar to immigration dates, except when I speak about relocation, I simply mean moving from one town, county, or state to another, not moving to a new country. Biographies and obituaries (remember to research all children and siblings too) may provide this information, and sometimes census data can be helpful. In the 1940 census, there is a section for where each individual lived in 1935. Likewise, some state census records (Iowa, for example) and state death records list how long an individual has been a resident of a particular state.

If you search tax records or city directories forwards or backwards in time and find that your relatives go missing, the reason may be because they moved. This probably won't tell you where they moved, but you may be able to decide whether to keep searching within the same county or not. One Detroit city directory I found had a relative of mine listed up until 1897, and instead of him simply going missing in 1898, that edition of the directory still listed his name. However, in place of his address, it stated, "Removed to Chicago."

Land records, especially those federal land patents located through the BLM General Land Office Records website (discussed in a later chapter), can also be helpful. These patents often indicated where an individual hailed from, so if your ancestor, William Vanmeter, lived in Fulton County, Indiana, and you locate a land record in which a man named William M Vanmeter of Butler County, Ohio, purchased land in Fulton County, Indiana, then your William Vanmeter might be from Butler County, Ohio. The land entry case files that led to the land patents mentioned above aren't currently online. However, depending on the type of land purchase, these can contain additional genealogical information. Land sales records might also indicate when your relative arrived or left a particular location. There are lots of other types of land records to consider, though the BLM records are probably the most easily accessible online. We'll discuss land records in more detail in the following chapter.

Although you may not know that your relatives relocated, during the course of your research you might find that they were living in Illinois during one census and Kansas in the next. Assuming you have enough information (e.g., names, ages, children) to confirm that these two groups are, in fact, one in the same, then you know that they relocated to Kansas during the period of time between the two records. This isn't an exact date, but it's better than nothing.

Finally, small town newspapers discussed day-to-day happenings of most area residents. If you find a reference to your ancestors in one of these newspapers, it may indicate that your relatives were relocating to a particular town or county. Digitized newspapers may have this information online, though it may be difficult to locate these references in unindexed editions, especially if you don't already know when your relatives relocated.

Military Service

Military service records can be a particularly helpful avenue, though not usually for female relatives. There is such a variety of military information available that it would be difficult to cover each type of record in depth. We'll get into this subject briefly later, but for now remember that military documents can include enlistment records, casualties, bounty land warrants, pension records, as well as draft registration cards, veterans' gravesites, and more. Additionally, documents for most of these can be related to any number of wars: World War I, World War II, War of 1812, Civil War, Revolutionary War--the list could go on. Draft cards for WWI and WWII were perhaps the broadest reaching of these documents and included all sorts of information such as name, date and place of birth, nationality, nearest relative, physical characteristics, address, and even father's place of birth. Not all of this information was required on each draft card, but depending on which group your relatives registered with, these are some of the things you might find. If you find pension documents for your relatives, you might come across information relating to first marriages or even children's birthdates. If you find a bounty land warrant, it could indicate the regiment your ancestor served with, and it might provide an assignee for that land parcel. An assignee could be related in some way, so follow up on any names you come across, even if they're unfamiliar.

We've covered a lot of information already, but there's more to come. Although you've learned some of the best types of places to look for particular information and how it can help your research, next we need to cover some of the most common documents you'll run across. The following chapter discusses different types of readily available documents and what you might learn from them. Remember that many states, colonies, churches, and other countries have their own types of paperwork and documentation. As such, many hundreds of books could be devoted to different types of records and how to interpret each one. Unfortunately, there isn't time for this type of analysis, nor would you want to read such a lengthy tome even if there were.

As such, "Chapter 2 - Learning About Different Types of Records" deals, perhaps obviously, with different types of records, most of which are either federal in nature or are widely available across many states. We now turn to the particulars of each type of document, though the logistics of accessing each type of record is left for a later chapter.

Learning About Different Types of Records

Source documents are the glue that holds your family tree together. These are the immutable (hopefully) facts that you have to rely upon in order to make any progress.   Although source documents must necessarily be discussed within the context of their availability, in this chapter we'll attempt to discuss solely the documents themselves and leave access and availability information (both hardcopy and online) for the following chapters.

There are literally thousands, possibly millions, of genealogical collections out there, so it would be impossible to discuss every one of them in detail. As such, this chapter focuses on some of the most common, nationally available documents there are.

Some of the following types of records, like Federal Censuses and military draft cards, contain more or less uniform content across the country, while others must be discussed in somewhat general terms due to variations from one location or time period to another.   If you need more detailed information on a collection from a particular state, try the resources discussed in "Chapter 4 - State-by-State Resources." But before you do that, be sure to go over the following list, and each item's subsequent description, to ensure you are knowledgeable about the basics of the most broadly available types of resources.

Federal Census
Census Mortality Schedules
Social Security Death Index
Wills and Probate Records

Church Records
Military Documents
Land and Property Records/
Naturalization Paperwork
City Directories
DNA Testing

Federal Census

This is the big one. The granddaddy of them all. The crème de la crème. Okay, maybe not. The previous sentences actually refer to large earthquakes, the Rose Bowl, and possibly cream (the band or the dairy product?). But the Federal Census is very helpful in tracking down information about your ancestors. Although each census is slightly different, here are a few generalities to consider. Census records are released to the public 72 years after they are compiled. This is to protect the privacy of everyone involved. The most recent census available is the 1940 census, released in 2012. In 2022, the 1950 census will be released, followed by the 1960 census in the year 2032. The first Federal Census was carried out in 1790 and a new census is taken every ten years, with the most recent census taken in 2010.

Censuses include both states and territories, so in the 2010 census, not only was data collected from all 50 states, but it was also collected from American Samoa, Washington D.C., Guam, Puerto Rico, the Virgin Islands, and the Panama Canal Zone (according to Ancestry.com). This is important to remember because most states, aside from the 13 original colonies, were at one point part of another organized territory or state. As an example, West Virginia was part of Virginia until the mid-1800s, and Illinois was once part of the Indiana Territory. In other words, if your ancestors lived in present-day West Virginia in 1840, you should look at census data from Virginia, since West Virginia didn't yet exist. See each state's individual section for more information on border evolution.

Be aware that approximations were allowed for during census compilation. Instructions given to census takers, especially in the mid-1800s, ask that an exact age be recorded for each person but allow for approximations when necessary. So from census to census your ancestor's age, and thus year of birth, may change depending on if approximations had to be made. Additionally, census takers may have obtained information from a family member who didn't know where another person was born or how old they were. As such, this information may also be approximate. It's even possible that your ancestor is listed with the incorrect last name, a situation that I've run into several times in my own family tree and which was discussed briefly in the previous chapter. Situations that can lead to this incorrect data are things like a child born to a now-divorced couple or one living with extended family. For example, if your ancestor was born to a married couple who subsequently divorced, your ancestor might be found living with his mother and recorded with her last name. Similarly if your ancestor's parents died when he was young and he went to live with grandparents or an aunt and uncle, then he may be recorded incorrectly with one of those last names. If you think either of these situations might be the case and your ancestor is missing in a Federal Census, you'll have to search for extended family in that census and try to locate your ancestor living with another family.

If your relatives are missing in a Federal Census and you don't think the reason has to do with an incorrect surname, you can always try to locate them based on an address. If a document from around the same time as the missing census record recorded an address (perhaps a city directory or naturalization record), then you can try to find that address in the census in question. I've had trouble locating old census maps online, but consider trying Steve Morse's One-Step website (**http://stevemorse.org/**) for help. Not only does his website contain information on enumeration districts from one census to the next, but he also has links to a multitude of immigration and vital-records tools.

Finally, some states' data may be missing, especially from censuses prior to 1830. For example, according to a Georgia-Secretary-of-State website, census records for that state are missing up until 1820. And as everyone knows, the majority of the 1890 census was destroyed by a 1921 fire.

Now, on to brief write-ups for each publicly available Federal Census (assuming you're reading this before the year 2022, that is).

1790 Federal Census

Although the first Federal Census was taken in 1790, the U.S. Government didn't provide uniform census schedules until 1830. As such, each census taker (marshal) had to create his own documents for recording enumeration information. According to *Measuring America: The Decennial Censuses From 1790 to 2000*, a government publication put out by the Census Bureau, marshals were meant to tabulate the head-of-household's name, along with the number of free white males (above and below the age of 16), free white females, all other free persons, and slaves. However, the publication goes on to note that some marshals included additional information, owing to the lack of uniformity of census schedules. One benefit of the lack of uniformity is that some marshals have alphabetized their records. So if you know the location where your ancestors lived, you may be able to locate them in the records more easily.

The bottom line is that unless the marshal for your ancestor's enumeration district saw fit to include additional information, then you probably have only the head-of-household's name and a rough breakdown of how many people lived in the house. Keep in mind that not everyone in the house may have been immediate family. Something else to remember is that not all original records have survived for each state or territory. A complete description of which states' records have been lost can be found online.

Enumeration for the 1790 census was to commence on the first Monday of August, a cut-off date that stayed in effect until the 1830 census.

1800 Federal Census

This census was very similar to the previous one, with a few exceptions. First of all, the Secretary of State was put in charge of the census and marshals reported their results to him. Secondly, schedules had to list the county, parish, township, city, or town of residence for those enumerated. And finally, the age breakdown was different. The head of household was still listed, but free white males and females were listed as either under 10 years of age, 10 to 16, 16 to 26, 26 to 45, or 45 years old and up. There was also an area to enumerate slaves.

As with many older documents, uniformity wasn't always present. For example, in Marietta, Ohio (a territory at the time), it appears that online census records don't number everyone in each household, instead enumerating only those free males over 21 years of age. On the plus side, all free males over 21 appear to have been explicitly named, instead of just numbered.

1810 Federal Census

The third census was meant to include the exact same things as the previous one. Although additional manufacturing data was collected, it's not really pertinent to our discussion on genealogy.

1820 Federal Census

This was the last census before uniform census schedules were put in place. That being said, more categories were requested than in the previous two censuses. Free white males were also listed in the 16-to-18-year-old age category. And slaves and free colored persons were broken down by age and sex. Additionally, there were categories to enumerate the number of people engaged in agriculture, commerce, or manufacturing, as well as a category for the number of foreigners who had not been naturalized.

1830 Federal Census

Uniform census schedules were provided for the first time in 1830. These schedules were also more detailed than previous ones. Free white males and females were enumerated in five-year increments until the age of twenty (i.e., under 5 years old, 5 to 10, etc.), and in ten year increments from twenty to one-hundred (i.e., 20 to 30, 30 to 40, etc.), with a final category for those above one-hundred years old. Slaves and free colored persons were also enumerated by sex, though with less detailed age categories. Finally, categories were included for whether any of the previously listed people were blind or "Deaf and Dumb." Clearly, the designers of the census schedule were not worried about political correctness. Manufacturing data was not collected.

One thing to remember about this census is that instructions to census marshals set the cut-off date at 1 June 1830, regardless of when the enumeration took place. What I mean by this is that census takers were supposed to record the condition of life as of June 1, and not the actual date they showed up at any particular house. So if a census taker enumerated a house on August 26, then he was supposed to ignore any children (i.e., don't list them) that were born after June 1. Similarly, he was meant to list as living anyone who was already dead, provided they died after the June 1 cut-off date. This cut-off date stays in effect through the 1900 census.

1840 Federal Census

The 1840 census included the same information as the previous one but with several additions. In terms of health, a category for "Insane and Idiots" was added. Again, political correctness wasn't a paramount concern though it seems that between "Deaf and Dumb" and "Insane and Idiots," alliteration was of the utmost importance. In addition, occupational and educational information was collected, as well as information to indicate military pensioners, either from the Revolutionary War, the War of 1812, or other military service. This category can be helpful, as actual names are listed, even if the pensioner was not the head of household.

1850 Federal Census

The 1850 census is when things really get good. This is the first census that lists the names of all free members of each household. For each resident, enumerators collected name, age, sex, color, profession (males over the age of fifteen only), value of real estate, place of birth, and marked whether they were married within the year, attended school within the year, or were over the age of twenty and could not read or write. Finally, it was noted whether a resident was blind, deaf and dumb, insane, idiotic, a pauper, or a convict.

A separate census slave schedule was also compiled. Unfortunately, this schedule doesn't list everyone by name. It does, however, list the slave owner's name, along with a separate row for each slave that includes their age, sex, and race. So although names are not included, the schedule does provide a separate line and age for each individual. This is somewhat more helpful than the 1840 census.

In both cases, children under one year of age were enumerated with fractional ages (i.e., 1/12 if one month old, 2/12 if two months old). Personally, I've had the most luck finding relatives back to this census and slightly before, with less luck using online collections to get much farther back. I don't feel that this is for lack of available information overall, but rather a lack of available information presently online. For example, confirming a relative is the individual listed in an earlier census may require supporting documentation. However, much of the time-period-specific documentation (e.g., wills, probate, land records, family bibles) that would provide support isn't readily available online at this time.

1860 Federal Census

This census was basically the same as the 1850 census. However, female occupations were collected, and it broke out the value of real estate and the value of personal estates separately. Slave schedules remained unchanged.

1870 Federal Census

The main details of this census remain the same, but a few additional items have been added: if someone was married or born within the year, the month is asked for; occupations are asked for regardless of age; whether parents are of foreign birth (though not the actual location) is indicated. There are no longer any slave schedules since the thirteenth amendment was passed during the previous decade. Census takers are instructed to enumerate Indians only if they are living as any other citizen and exercising the same rights, and not in the context of tribal relations. Other Native Americans are considered "Indians not taxed" and are not counted in the normal census. "Indians not taxed" is meant to include free-roaming tribes in unsettled country, as well as those on government-supported reservations.

1880 Federal Census

This is the first census that lists relationships to head-of-household. This can be very beneficial because in the three previous censuses, although all free household members were named, their relationships were not. Most other items remain the same, or similar, with the exception of parentage. This census not only asks whether a person's parents are foreign-born, but asks where each parent was born. Thus, parental birthplaces (states, territories, or countries) can be found in this census record. An additional census schedule to enumerate Native Americans on reservations was also taken. Unfortunately, the collection of information was never completed, so the Native American enumeration is only a partial data set.

1890 Federal Census

Most of the original 1890 census records were destroyed by a fire in 1921. And by most, I mean MOST! Approximately 6,000 original records survived, out of a population of nearly 63 million. That being said, a small fraction of researchers may be able to locate their relatives. For the rest of you, consider looking at tax records, city directories, state censuses, and cemetery and church records to help fill the gap. If you have a relative who served in the Civil War, he may appear in the 1890 Census Veteran schedule. Although this isn't a substitute for the original records, unless someone invents a time machine (ahem, Doc Brown, I'm waiting for your DeLorean) and is able to prevent the fire, we'll never know what the rest of the records contained.

1900 Federal Census

As the first census record after the 1890 census (which was mostly destroyed), this is an important one. Combined with the 1880 census, if you know a few relatives, you may be able to bridge the twenty-year gap. For example, if your ancestor was born in 1881, there's a very real possibility that he/she was already married by the time the 1900 census rolled around. If you don't know parents or siblings, you'll probably have to resort to non-census records to put the pieces together. However, if you know the names of your ancestor's parents and possibly siblings, you'll be able to look for them in the 1880 census. Remember to consider second marriages also. If you lose a relative during the missing census, it's possible that they have remarried. If it's a female, she will have a different last name.

Several key items to note in this census include month and year of birth, birth places of parents, year of immigration to the United States, whether naturalized or not, number of years married, number of children and the number still living (females only), as well as information about whether the home is owned and whether it's free or mortgaged. In addition, there is a section at the left side of the census schedule to list the street name and address of each dwelling. This section appears to have been used mostly for those living in cities. Basically, this census has a lot of information. Not only do you get relationships and birth places, as in the past, but immigration and marriage dates are also provided, as well as the number of children a mother has given birth to. A Native-American census schedule was also taken.

This was the first census that included Americans living abroad (e.g., those in the military and civilian federal employees).

1910 Federal Census

Most of the information in this census is the same as in the previous one. A few new items are whether English is spoken, age is requested as opposed to birth year and month, and an individual can state whether he is a veteran of the Civil War. This census also asks for the number of years of the present marriage and should not include previous marriages. Another change is the cut-off date for recording ages, births, deaths, and marriages. Previously, this date had been June 1, but starting with this census the cut-off date is April 15. This cut-off date meant that census takers were trying to get the status of life on April 15 and not at the time of their visit. If a census taker visited a residence on April 24, he or she should not count marriages, births, or deaths that took place after April 15, even though they took place before the census was completed.   A special Native-American census schedule was also completed.

1920 Federal Census

Aside from another date change (January 1 is now the cut-off date for enumeration), this census doesn't provide any major changes from the previous one. The year of naturalization is requested, if applicable, and in addition to parents' birthplaces, their native language is also requested. Finally, the age of children under five years should include months when being recorded (e.g., 4 2/12 would be interpreted as four years, two months old). No special Native-American schedule was completed this year.

1930 Federal Census

Until early 2012, this was the most recently released census available. Requested marriage information was changed yet again and individuals were asked to report their age at first marriage, as opposed to the number of years actually married. Care should be taken as this field's content may be related to a previous marriage and not the current one. Special unemployment schedules were also completed (this was during the Great Depression), and April 1 was designated as the new cut-off date for enumeration.

1940 Federal Census

The 1940 census was released in April of 2012, 72 years after it was taken. All images were quickly posted on numerous websites, though it took a few months to complete indexing and errors will necessarily exist until users submit corrections. Found in this census is such information as where an individual lived in 1935, as well as expanded employment information. Immigration, naturalization, and parental information are no longer listed.

All of the above information has been noted through my direct experience or taken from U.S. government documents related to the census (e.g., laws enacted by Congress, summaries of previous census instructions). These government documents, as well as the census itself, are in the public domain and are freely accessible. We'll discuss where to access original census images in the upcoming chapter on Internet resources.

For copies of government legislation related to the census, see:
http://www.census.gov/history/www/reference/legislation/

For a good summary of census information from 1790 to 2000, see:
http://www.census.gov/prod/2002pubs/pol02marv.pdf

Census Mortality Schedules

In conjunction with the censuses from 1850 through 1880, the government compiled a series of mortality schedules. These schedules were meant to record everyone who died in the year prior to each census. However, it should be remembered that the census was based on a June 1 date, not January 1. So the year prior to the census was actually June 1 through May 31. For example, the 1850 mortality schedule should include anyone who died between 1 June 1849 and 31 May 1850. These records don't provide next of kin, but they do give the deceased's name, sex, race, age, month and cause of death, and even birth place.

Social Security Death Index

The Federal Government hasn't been keeping a close eye on death for very long. In fact, the Social Security Death Index (SSDI) really came into being in 1962. That's the year when people who passed away and had Social Security numbers (originally issued in November 1936) were first tracked, assuming their death was reported to the Social Security Administration, of course. Although some individuals who passed away prior to 1962 are listed in the index, this is usually only the case if their deaths were reported after 1962. In no case are deaths from prior to 1936 listed. Something else to keep in mind is that although most deceased individuals can now be located with the SSDI, this wasn't always true. According to FamilySearch.org, only fifty-percent of deceased individuals showed up from 1962 until 1971, and only eighty-five-percent showed up from that time until 2005.

The SSDI is considered a public document, and it is available to anyone who wants to search it. While the government and some subscription websites charge for queries, other sites provide free online searches, although you may have to register for a user ID.

Wills and Probate Records

As you might imagine, wills and probate records can be exceedingly useful, especially since one can sometimes locate these records from times when birth and death records weren't yet kept. If you do find these records, they can indicate spouses, children, and in-laws. In my experience, wife and children will usually be mentioned if they're alive, though the wife may not be mentioned by name, and married daughters will often be listed with their married names. Children who died young and before their father (or mother) have no reason to be mentioned. However, children who passed away after having offspring of their own may be mentioned in the will. For example, a will might say something like, "I leave one-fourth of my property to my wife, one-fourth to my son John, one-fourth to my daughter Margaret Walters (*this is likely her married name*), and one-fourth to the children of my deceased daughter Sally Stephenson."

Remember that just because someone wasn't mentioned in a will doesn't mean they didn't exist. For example, when a man's daughter was married, she could have received her inheritance at that time and may not be mentioned in her father's will. She might also be listed with her married name, as in the above example. Or a family member with whom there was a falling out might be left out of a will for that reason. Finally, someone who isn't mentioned might have died prior to the writing of the will.

In many cases if a wife isn't mentioned in a man's will, she has already passed away. Similarly, a larger share between two male offspring may indicate that the recipient of the larger share was the first-born. There were a lot of reasonably standard conventions used when writing wills, so once you have a will in hand make sure you read it carefully and understand how wills from that time period were written. Even if your ancestor died young, it may be useful to find his or her father's will since it may indicate surviving offspring or spouses, as mentioned above.

If you find that land was transferred to anyone in a will, try to learn who the recipient was since he may be a relative, by blood or marriage. You can also look for those particular parcels in land records for additional information. Sometimes wills indicate that a parcel of land was acquired from a specific individual or that a certain parcel of land is located next to land owned by other individuals. Follow up on these names even if they are unfamiliar.

A few websites have indexes online and if that doesn't work, then try searching the holdings of various institutions (such as State Archives or genealogical libraries discussed in "Chapter 4 - State-by-State Resources"), and you may learn where to locate the collection you desire. But you likely won't find every original record you're looking for online.

One institution that has a number of will and probate collections free online is FamilySearch.org, discussed in greater detail in the following chapter. At this time, collections are not available for every state, and some states with online collections include only a limited number of counties from a limited number of years. Other states have millions of probate images online, but they aren't yet indexed and searchable through the usual search feature. If you do find a collection of wills or probate records for an area you're interested in, look to see if any of the image sets are identified with the word "index" in the series' title. These indexes are often arranged in some sort of alphabetical order, at least by the first initial of the included surnames. Some of these indexes are also several volumes in length (usually indicated in the title), so you may have to search several places in the image set. For example, if you're looking for the last name Elston and you find a probate series called "Indiana, probate records 1845 - 1921 Vol. 1-3‡," then there could be three sets of alphabetized index material in the series. As such, you'll have to browse each set of letter-E surnames in order to perform a thorough search and not overlook anything. If there is no index but you already have a date, then you may be able to select the image set for the appropriate year and find your ancestor that way. The bottom line is that either of these methods will take some time, but this is an option for locating unindexed will and probate records online.

Hopefully once other collections like vital records have been fully digitized, more will and probate collections can be indexed and put online too. If you do find an online collection of wills or probate records and you need help making sense of the content, many websites, some discussed in later chapters, have write-ups on how to interpret the information you find. I would also recommend looking at the beginning or end of any will or probate book, even if the book isn't specifically an index. The reason is that these books sometimes have alphabetical indexes at the beginning or end of them. Remember however, that these indexes will be for the deceased individuals and won't include all of the individuals mentioned in a will. As such, you should look at each will that contains a familiar surname to see if it mentions your ancestors.

---

‡ This is a made-up series, or if it isn't, then I've gotten very lucky in creating this example.

Wills and probate records could be discussed at far greater length, but since the main objective of the book is to provide a level of genealogical familiarity sufficient to allow for online research, and in my experience there aren't many wills or probate records digitally available and indexed online, discussing in overarching detail seems unnecessary.

Church Records

Church records can be incredibly varied, so it's difficult to discuss specifics, but let's have a go at it anyhow, shall we?

One nice thing about church records is that items of note (baptisms, marriages, and even deaths) were sometimes recorded long before states required record keeping. This can be especially true in certain locations, like French-Canada and many parts of Europe. Unfortunately, like probate and land records, discussed above and below, respectively, many church records aren't yet easily accessible online. So you may have to do a little extra work, either ordering microfilm or contacting the church directly.

If you know the area your relatives are from but can't find any pertinent vital records, ask yourself if you know what religion they practiced. If you *do* know the religion but don't know what church they attended, think about contacting a local historical society to get some insight. Or just look around online to see which churches of the correct denomination were in the area during the timeframe in question. If you don't know where your ancestors lived, you may have to figure that out before church records will do you any good, especially if records for the church your relatives attended aren't yet indexed online.

Let's discuss what to do if you've already learned that church records for the area in question exist on the Internet. Some websites like Ancestry.com and FamilySearch.org have a limited number of collections that are already indexed and searchable. However, other online collections may not be indexed yet. If you run across a collection that is online but isn't indexed, you'll probably need to know the specific town or church to narrow your search and actually get started in the right place. Hopefully you can learn the location in question by using the hints and tips located throughout the rest of the book. Once you have a vague idea of either the location or church and the time period, you're ready to start looking. Similar to wills and probate records (discussed above), many church record books have a name index either at the beginning or end of the book (i.e., the first few or last few pages of the book [i.e., the beginning or end of the computer file {i.e., are you actually still reading this nested mess?}]). Simply open the file and look through the index, if there is one, for the surname in question. Keep in mind that separate indexes may exist for baptisms, marriages, and deaths, so remember to search all of these. If you find a relative of yours in a certain church, try searching previous and subsequent years for the same surname in the same church. Individuals often stayed in the same area and attended the same church for years, so you may get lucky. Also, remember to search for alternate spellings of your ancestor's name.

Okay, you've found a record online, but you don't speak the language. Now what? Thankfully, there are a lot of convenient translation programs online (Bing, Google, FreeTranslation.com), and some of them will even auto-detect the language and translate the content for you. The catch is that many old documents are written in cursive/script and they can be difficult to read in one's native language let alone one that you're not familiar with. My recommendation would be to do a quick online search for the nationality/language in question and something like, "how to read church records." Many types of records followed certain conventions that will hold for the majority of these documents. For example, the Drouin Collection pertains to Quebec-area vital records from various religious denominations, which incidentally is the best collection to use when searching for records that pertain to your French-Canadian relatives. Anyhow, many of these records are in French, but even if you don't speak the language, you may be able to discern the major facts. The records will usually start with a written-out date, and depending on the type of record (baptism, marriage, or death) they may go on to list the parents, whether they're still living, and perhaps their occupations. We could spend hours just discussing how to look at this particular collection, but the point is that most types of records, whether French-Canadian, Hungarian, English, or even American, follow certain conventions. So don't get scared just because you don't speak the language. Simply do an online search to learn what the conventions are, search for the basic words you'll need to know (e.g., dates, "daughter," "son," "father," "legitimate," "illegitimate," etc.), and see if you can put it all together. You don't need to know every term--simply enough to learn the type of record, dates, and relationships. A translation by a native speaker is probably worthwhile, as you may learn things like occupations or whether a relative was alive at the time of the record, but with a little patience you can likely figure out the basics on your own.

Military Documents

There are a lot of different military documents to consider. In fact, we could write a whole book on nothing but military records. Here we'll give a brief summary of a few of these items and list some others that are available. In the next section, we'll look for individual resources to locate them. Many of these documents are widely available, and some are even free. However, locating free versions may take significantly more effort than paying for access to a website which has copies of these files online. Keep in mind that, as with many early county records and the 1890 census, some military records have also been destroyed by fire over the years.

Compiled Service Records

This is a packet's worth of information on your ancestor. Information may vary based on any number of things, but potential records include information on your ancestor's rank and unit, biographical information, muster dates, and more. Many of these records are from the country's early military history, like the Revolutionary War, the War of 1812, and the Civil War.

Pension and Bounty Land

Pension application and payment records are available for armed forces personnel who served from 1775 through 1916. A pension application may contain a wealth of information, such as marriage documents, death certificates, or witness affidavits. Bounty Land documents might be combined with pension documentation. They relate to land that military veterans were able to apply for, and claim, as a result of military service from 1775 to 1855.

In my experience, pension records, bounty land records, and draft-registration cards, discussed below, often provide more genealogical information than other military sources. Some military land records can be located through the BLM General Land Office website, discussed in the following chapter.

Draft Registration Cards

Draft registration cards have been required at various times in the past. Both World War I (WWI) and World War II (WWII) documents have been digitized and are searchable online.   These cards included all sorts of information, such as name, date and place of birth, nationality, nearest relative, physical characteristics, address, and father's place of birth.   Not all of this information was available on each card, but depending on which group your relatives registered with, these are some of the things you might find.

Other Documents

There are many other documents to consider, but several noteworthy ones are casualty records, enlistment records, and veterans' gravesites records. Some of these are available from wars going all the way back to the Revolutionary.   Records from recent wars, like Vietnam, Korea, and Iraq, are mostly protected for privacy reasons, though casualty lists are readily accessible online.

Land and Property Records

Land records are an important, although sometimes overlooked (even by myself initially) source of genealogical information.   One reason they're so valuable is because property transactions were recorded from the very beginning of an area's settlement while vital records weren't always recorded until much later.   Even in the early 1800s and before, most settlers owned land, so as long as these records weren't accidently destroyed in a fire at some point, there should be a record of each transaction.   While a vast number of land patents issued by the Federal Government are now searchable online, this is only the tip of the iceberg.   Many ownership records are maintained at the state or county level, and, at this moment in time, the majority of these records are not yet available online.   There are exceptions for certain states and certain counties within states, but don't get your hopes up for finding comprehensive property-records collections on the Internet.

Try reading the following chapters to locate websites that have collections and/or indexes of property deeds online.   Otherwise, try using a search engine to find collections that relate to the state or county you're interested in. If you can't find the information online, you can always contact the county courthouse or the State Archives to see if anyone will perform research on your behalf.   If not, you might still have an option.   The Family History Library in Salt Lake City has microfilm of many deed collections and deed indexes from around the country, so check the FamilySearch.org website to see if it has anything you're interested in.   If it does, you can request to have microfilm sent to a Family History Center near you.

If you find a reference to your ancestor, online or in print, what do you do with it? Well, how helpful that reference is depends on what you've located. For example, the federally issued land patent records that you're likely to find online probably won't have much of genealogical value, at least not on the surface. Depending on the type of land patent, you'll probably learn the purchaser's name, county of residence, and what land was purchased. If it's a land record related to military service, you might learn which regiment your ancestor served in. Some military records indicate assignees or even spouses if the soldier has already passed away. While this information can help you learn where your relative hailed from or relocated to, unless you follow that information up with additional paperwork or deeds, then it might not be everything you hoped for.

The question now becomes *how* to follow up on the land patent you just found. One thing you can do from the privacy of your own home is plot your relative's piece of land and research who originally purchased the surrounding land. Remember that if you're searching for federal land records online, these will indicate initial owners only since subsequent land transactions, either through sales or wills, are usually found at the county level.

To plot your ancestor's land, you will need to know how the land description is written. For example, my third-great-grandfather, William Vanmeter, purchased land in Indiana in 1845 with the following description:

The North West quarter of the South East quarter of section nine in township twenty-nine North, of Range One East of the second principal meridian.

This may seem like a cumbersome, meaningless jumble of words, but this is the way land descriptions were written in Public Land States (i.e., states where land was originally part of the public domain before the Federal Government transferred it to individuals). Without getting into too much detail, the government created maps of principal meridians and baselines, and the second meridian in our example happens to be located in Indiana. Next, the state is broken into a grid pattern and for the parcel in question we have to move one township east of the meridian ("Range One East") and twenty-nine townships north of our baseline ("township twenty-nine North"). Within this township, the land is broken out into thirty-six separate sections-- we're looking for section nine. Finally, section nine is further broken down into sixteen smaller areas, each approximately forty acres in size. To find the northwest quarter of the southeast quarter, we first look at the southeast quarter of section nine. Then we take the northwest quarter of that smaller quarter, and bingo, we've located the land in question. These smaller sections of each section are called aliquot parts, in case you care to add a new q-word to your Scrabble game.

An easy way to plot you ancestor's land holdings without all the headaches of actually understanding what's going on is to use a free mapping tool available online; we'll discuss an option for accomplishing this in the following chapter.

If you think the parcel in question may be your ancestor's, you should next search the entire section (and possibly surrounding sections) indicated in the land patent in order to determine who the adjacent property owners were. In this case, use the BLM website discussed in the following chapter. The neighbors may be relatives you're already familiar with, new relatives or in-laws to add to your tree (once you figure out exact relationships), or they may not be related at all. But you won't know until you check.

Land Entry Case Files, the files that led to the previously mentioned land patents, often have more helpful genealogical information than the patents themselves and are held by the National Archives. According to the National Archives and Records Administration publication *Research in the Land Entry Files of the General Land Office*, the information contained in a case file largely depends on the type of land-entry case-file itself since "Over 40 separate legislative acts were used by Americans to make a land entry on public lands, and each act required different information from the entryman." It is beyond our scope to discuss each of these acts, but when you find a land patent you're interested in, make note of the act that it was attained under. Then you'll be able to determine what type of information the land entry case file should contain and whether you're interested in purchasing it for, at the time of writing, $50 per file. It should be noted that some types of files contain more genealogically relevant information than others, though it's difficult to say with one-hundred-percent certainty what any particular case file will contain until you actually have it in hand. While there's no guarantee what you'll find, it may be worth your time and money to order these records, especially if you've hit a brick wall in your research.

Pre-emption land claims, those claims pertaining to someone already living on the land prior to when the government started selling parcels in that area, and private land claims, those claims that pertained to individuals who already owned land under a previous government, may have a plethora of genealogical information, as the latter may diagram generations of ancestors to prove legal inheritance.

Finally, if you don't find birth dates, family information, or the like in the land records or case files you locate, don't despair. Now you need to look at the land descriptions you have and find additional transactions that pertain to the parcel in question; these transactions will likely be recorded at the county level. It may be that the land was bequeathed to family members upon your ancestor's death. Try to follow up on other names that you find associated with the transactions on your relative's parcel of land. These may turn out to be extended family members or relatives.

The bottom line with land records is that they're very valuable for early documentation, but you may need to get out from behind your computer to find them. It's difficult to say exactly how you should go about the process since the only true centralized land-transaction database is the BLM's General-Land-Office-records website, and even that helpful repository doesn't include every federally issued land title. If your ancestors weren't the first to attain land from the Federal Government or they lived in a non-Public-Land-State, this database won't help you either. Since many areas handled local transactions differently, I would start with the online searches mentioned in the following chapters, then search specifically for the area you're interested in. Even if a State Archive or State Library doesn't have a land-transaction-record index online, you might find out that they have collections of property records on-site.

If you don't find the information online or in the holdings of an archives facility, I would check to see if the Family History Library has microfilm or I would contact the county in question directly. Once you've found an index or an actual land transaction, remember to follow up on other individuals mentioned, on neighboring parcels, on additional transactions for the parcel in question, and on other transactions carried out in the same area by individuals with the same surname.

The previously mentioned government publication on land records, *Research in the Land Entry Files of the General Land Office*, can be located at the following URL:

http://www.archives.gov/publications/ref-info-papers/rip114.pdf

Naturalization Paperwork

Naturalization documents can be helpful if your relatives immigrated and then applied for citizenship. The first step in the process was to file a "Declaration of Intent." Then after a waiting period, one could actually complete the necessary paperwork for citizenship. I've found more indexes online than actual images of source documents, but if you locate anything interesting you can request the document itself. Remember that just because one filed a declaration of intent doesn't mean that the individual necessarily came back to complete the naturalization process. If the process wasn't completed originally, a second declaration of intent may have also been filed.

Depending on the filing date, naturalization documents may include information on family members, where the individual was born, and when he or she arrived. Generally, more information is provided on more recent documents. Remember to look for people with the same surname as your ancestor, especially checking to see whether the other applicants lived at the same address as your ancestor. This may help you locate additional relatives who immigrated around the same time.

The process has changed over the years, and in an effort to keep this section brief, we won't discuss each detail. However, here are a few items to remember. Some laws allowed for honorably discharged military veterans to apply for naturalization without first filing a declaration of intent. Women and children weren't originally listed in naturalization paperwork, even though they received citizenship when it was granted to their fathers or husbands. Women could also lose citizenship if they were born in the United States but married an un-naturalized immigrant. Married women didn't have to file their own naturalization paperwork until 1922.

City Directories

This might seem an unlikely source to consult in your research. I can assure you that it's not. Although you're unlikely to find exact dates for vital records, city directories can be quite valuable. For one thing, if you find your ancestors in a directory, you will likely find their address. You can then use this address to confirm that other records pertain to your relatives. For example, if you have an address from a city directory, you may find that same address listed in census or naturalization paperwork. If so, even if the names are spelled differently and seem at odds with each other, look closely and try to determine if the individual is your ancestor, or at least a relative of some sort. If you learn that your great-grandfather John Marszatek lived at 123 Washington Street in 1912, and you later find a naturalization record for a Jan Marsolek or a John Marshall living at 123 Washington Street in 1914, there's a good chance these are the same person even though the names don't match up exactly.

You should also look for other individuals with the same name in each directory. If there are multiple people with an uncommon name living in a small town, they may be related somehow. Even more helpful is when you find multiple people with the same surname living in the same household. These might be children, siblings, parents, or cousins though you will likely have to do further research to prove exact relationships. Another key is not to limit yourself to one particular year of a directory. Make note of the address you find and search previous and subsequent directories to see if your ancestors were living at the same address. If you don't find them, you might find someone else with the same surname living there. If so, then the odds are that these folks are somehow related.

One may also come away with names of spouses and might even be able to glean years of death or relocation from city directories. Depending on the directory and year, spouses might be listed in parenthesis, and after a husband's death, sometimes the wife is listed as the widow of her departed husband. Less common are listings that a family has moved, though I have come across directories that list an individual as a resident one year, and the following year, even though the resident has moved, the individual is still listed with a small note that indicates the city of relocation.

DNA Testing

If you don't have any luck with source documentation, either through the previously mentioned channels or the resources discussed in the following chapters, you might want to take a DNA test. Although you've no doubt heard that DNA can prove paternity, link someone to a crime, and write *The Hitchhiker's Guide to the Galaxy* (yes, Douglas Adams' middle name was Noel), you may not know much about its use in genealogy.

DNA testing for genealogy takes one of several forms--Y-DNA testing, mtDNA testing, and autosomal DNA testing. Although the first two are more limited than the last, all three can be beneficial. In all cases, individuals provide a DNA sample, usually a cheek swab, send it to a laboratory, and the laboratory provides results to the individual. These results are most helpful if other individuals of matching ancestry have also had a DNA test performed.

Y-DNA testing is a test that helps determine an individual's direct paternal lineage through testing of the Y-chromosome. Tests check for genetic markers, and the more identical markers two individuals have, the more likely it is that they're related within a certain number of generations. According to FamilyTreeDNA.com, if two individuals take a 37-marker test and their results are identical, it's likely they're related within the past eight generations. However, a 67-marker test with identical results will indicate a common ancestor in the past six generations. Tests that compare higher numbers of markers are more expensive but will probably prove more helpful in your research.

Since Y-chromosomes passed from father to son are identical, barring mutations, this is a valuable tool for determining your paternal lineage. Unfortunately, females don't have a Y-chromosome (actually, this is fortunate if you like females or the propagation of the human race), so they can't take the Y-DNA test. They can, however, have their father or brother take the test for them. Problem solved.

While this test only traces your direct paternal line, you can learn about your maternal grandfather's lineage by having him or a maternal uncle take a test of their own. Alternately, if you're interested in a particular ancestor, your father's mother's mother's father for example, and you've done enough research to locate a living direct paternal ancestor of that relative, you could have that living relative take a test and pass along the results.

One additional note on the Y-DNA test is that since Y-chromosomes rarely change, the test will also provide your Haplogroup, a genetic population associated with a geographic region of the planet.

The second type of test is the mtDNA test, which tests for mitochondrial DNA. Since mtDNA is provided by the mother and is passed on to each of her children (not only daughters), anyone can take an mtDNA test to determine their direct maternal lineage. Test kits may analyze only a portion of the mitochondrial DNA or more expensive kits may analyze the whole sequence. These results won't help pinpoint as close a relationship as those from the Y-DNA testing, since even a full sequence mtDNA match only provides ninety-percent certainty of a relationship within sixteen generations according to FamilyTreeDNA.com.

Although this test only traces your maternal lineage, if your paternal grandmother, father, or a paternal aunt or uncle is alive, you could have them take a test and learn more your father's lineage through their results.

Just like the Y-DNA test, since mitochondrial DNA rarely changes, the mtDNA test provides a Haplogroup on the maternal side.

The last type of DNA test is the autosomal test. This test is useful for both males and females, and it doesn't focus solely on paternal or maternal lineages. Autosomal tests look for genetic matches across hundreds of thousands of markers on all of your chromosomes, not just your sex chromosomes. By taking an autosomal DNA test, researchers will learn ethnic percentages of their ancestry (African, Eastern European, Native American), though which lines these percentages come from won't be specified. Individuals will receive matches with other individuals who have similar DNA results. These matches indicate the percent likelihood that the two individuals are related within a set number of generations. Again, these results won't indicate which line the relationship occurs on.

No matter what type of DNA test you take, how useful the test is will depend largely on how many people have already taken the test. This is because your results have to match up with someone else's to provide a positive match. If no one who's closely related to you has taken the same DNA test, then you'll have to wait for matching results to come in before you'll learn anything besides your Haplogroup or the percentage of different ethnicities in your family tree.

When you get your results, you should contact or look at the family tree of any matches you have. If you have a match with someone of the same surname from the same town as your ancestor, then you've made some excellent progress. And if your match has already done additional research, you might add generations to your family tree with relative ease. Even if your match's family tree doesn't contain any identical information to your own, you should contact him or her in order to determine how your research should progress and figure out how to tie your trees together in the future.

If you don't have any (or very few) matching results initially, you might still learn something. Perhaps you've traced most of your lines back to England, but you find that you've got a large percentage of Eastern-European ancestry in your results. If you have lines that haven't been fleshed out yet, the odds are that at least one of your underdeveloped lines is of an Eastern-European origin.

Quite a few companies sell test kits online, and depending on the company, type of kit, and number of markers tested for, these kits currently cost anywhere from about one-hundred dollars up to multiple hundreds. In all cases, more expensive kits usually test for extra markers, and some are actually combination tests which provide autosomal, mtDNA, and even Y-DNA results.

That was a quick overview of various nationally available source documents to consider. Documents like the Federal Census gathered information in a uniform manner, so research highlights and items to look for were easy to point out. However, other items like church, land, probate, and even military records varied depending on the exact type of record, location, and year in which it was recorded. As such, we've had to discuss these items in more general terms, leaving out specific discussions on most of the hundreds or even thousands of breeds of source document that one might stumble across in their research.

Hopefully the information presented provided the researcher the knowhow to follow up on source documents specific to their family tree. In some cases, especially if a certain state has digital content, more information on these collections can be found in the chapter on individual state resources.

The following chapter presents websites that will aid you in your search, as well as discusses what type of content different websites offer and whether said websites charge for their material. These are websites that host broadly reaching collections and indexes, either from across the nation or across the world. Websites and resources that focus on specific states are discussed in a later chapter.

General Internet Resources

When discussing genealogy, it seems that everything ties in with something else. We first discussed what types of questions to ask your relatives and how to look for certain information about your ancestors. Next, we discussed nationally available documents, what they contain, and how to make sense of them. Now we move on to the resources (e.g., libraries, repositories, and third-party online databases) that will help you actually get your hands on the document you want. Although much of this could have been combined with the previous chapters, hopefully this will be a more convenient way to present the information so you can decide which avenue you'd like to wander down first.

Remember that this is a list of resources I'm aware of or have used personally, and it should not be considered all-inclusive. There are literally thousands upon thousands of websites that focus on genealogy, so I've tried to hit some of the highlights. My exclusion of a website doesn't mean it's not worth using but might simply mean that I was unaware of it or hadn't used it myself. And don't forget that, as discussed previously, certain types of documents are more readily accessible online while others haven't been indexed or digitized yet. For example, in my experience many wills, deeds, and naturalization documents are more difficult to find online than many vital records.

One thing to keep in mind is that you can search the text for any website, whether listed below or not, even if there isn't a search function available on the site itself. Let's say you're on a website with loads of information, but no embedded search function. If you don't want to read or search through each webpage individually, you have an option to search the entire site at once. First, open Bing or Google and type in the search term(s) as you would normally. Next, and before actually starting the search (either by clicking the "search" button or pressing enter), leave a space at the end of your search term(s), then type "site:" (without the quotation marks). Finally, without leaving any spaces after "site:" type in the website that you'd like to search. As an example, if I wanted to search my personal website (www.ryan-elson.com) for the term "genealogy," my search, through a search engine like Bing or Google, should appear as follows:

genealogy site:http://www.ryan-elson.com

I think this is a valuable shortcut when searching a large website without its own search function.

Another item to remember is that websites undergo occasional redesign. So, even if a particular website's write-up, either in this chapter or a later one, indicates where to locate a collection, remember that those details might change based on a webpage redesign. For example, a write-up might indicate that a link is located on the left-hand side of a webpage. However, the website might have been redesigned and the link might be located somewhere completely different now. Don't worry because the collection is probably still there somewhere. Just browse around or use the search bar to locate it.

Now, without further ado, here is a list of valuable resources, roughly organized by category, followed by a lengthy discussion on each.

General, National, and Worldwide Resources
    National Archives and Records Administration
    Ancestry.com
    Archives.com
    MyHeritage.com
    Other Family Tree Options
    Family History Library (Utah)
    FamilySearch.org
    Cyndi's List
    HeritageQuestOnline.com
    USGenWeb.org

Vital Records
    Western States Marriage Search
    DeathIndexes.com

FindAGrave.com
Legacy.com
CDC Vital Records
VitalChek.com

Military
Fold3.com
Daughters, and Sons, of the American Revolution
NPS Civil War Soldiers and Sailors Database

Immigration
Castle Garden
Ellis Island Passenger Search

Books and Newspapers
Chronicling America Newspaper Search
GenealogyBank.com
Google Books
Internet Archive
WorldCat Library Search

Land Records
BLM General Land Office Records
Plotting Land Records with Earth Point and Google Earth

Miscellaneous
Freedman's Bureau
Town/County Look-Up
Reading Old Handwriting

National Archives and Records Administration (NARA)
http://www.archives.gov

This is the official website for the National Archives and Records Administration.   Many of the physical documents that are indexed and available online through other websites are actually held by NARA, so if you're able to visit, you'll find a wealth of information. The main holdings of the National Archives are located in Washington D.C., although branch offices also have miscellaneous records.   Census, military, land, and immigration records are some of the most important genealogical documents available through the Archives. A search of the website describes the records that are housed at each National Archives branch location. Numerous searches are online, but most of these are merely to determine which collections are available and not searches based on individual names. That being said, a few of the name indexes online are for land and naturalization records, while others are military in nature, such as casualty lists for the Vietnam and Korean Wars. Many of the online indexes for land and naturalization records are for select areas and shouldn't be considered comprehensive. As such, more information is available if you visit in person, by ordering microfilm, or by hiring a researcher; details for employing any of these options can be found online.

Many websites that have undertaken preservation projects in conjunction with the Archives can also be accessed from computers at any National Archives facility. Even subscription-sites like Fold3.com, Ancestry.com, and Heritage Quest can be used free of charge. Copies of records can be ordered by filling out the appropriate forms.

Ancestry.com

http://www.ancestry.com

This may be the most well known of the online genealogical resources, and there's a good reason for that. It has loads of material online, and the little leaves that pop up for your ancestors (genealogical hints) can make your life much easier. Plus, Ancestry.com spends a boatload on commercials. First, let's discuss what the site is.

Contrary to popular belief, you don't have to pay to use Ancestry.com, at least not in its most basic form, since free accounts allow users to create their very own family trees. You can even take advantage of Ancestry's search features to get some basic transcribed data. Of course, that basic data is only enough to let you know that you might have found a record worth seeing. In order to actually view the record you'll have to pay for access. Fourteen-day free trials are available, and there are different packages that offer access to United States records only or access to all of Ancestry's available records. Unless you know that your relatives came to the United States recently, my recommendation would be to start with a United-States-only package. You can always upgrade to an international subscription later. Or you might use the website for the family tree feature only and save your money for other vices. It's up to you. Let's tackle what's available on Ancestry.com and why you might consider getting a membership.

First of all, Ancestry.com allows you to connect with other users who may have the same relatives as you. If they've done a thorough job with their research, you might get a ton of information without doing anything except grabbing the information from their tree. Just remember that other users' data isn't checked for accuracy by some all-knowing moderator. There may be inconsistencies, inaccuracies, or missing information. It's up to you to determine how thorough the other family tree is and whether it's accurate or not. When in doubt, use this information as a starting point and prove to yourself, by looking over the source data, that everything holds together.

Secondly, there are billions and billions of records available online, and not just records, but indexed and searchable records. With no need to flip, page by page, through an old collection, you'll save a ton of time. Everything you can imagine is available: old city directories; state and federal censuses; military records of all kinds; various state and county histories. You name it and Ancestry.com probably has it or is in the process of trying to acquire it. With that said, be aware that, as with any genealogical website, some records are merely indexed and source documents aren't online, while others have been transcribed incorrectly. While states are working to digitize and index their older records, many of these documents still reside on microfilm, in state archives, or in an individual county clerk's office, so not all collections of interest are available online yet. This is especially true of old wills, probate, land, and tax records.

As time passes, Ancestry.com will put more and more documentation online. And as users correct transcription errors and attach documents to their ancestors, the hints and searches will get better and better.

My opinion is that Ancestry.com is a valuable resource, and I currently have a subscription. In hindsight, I could have easily started with a United-States-only subscription and saved myself a few bucks. When I got to the point that I needed access to international records, I could have upgraded. Oh well. If you don't already have an account, consider whether you need international access right away. Something else to consider when deciding whether to set up an account is which resources you need to search. Although there are billions of records available, most of my family lines now reach far enough back that I'm having less luck finding information through Ancestry.com than I was originally.

While this is the most user-friendly, helpful family tree and genealogical website I've found, since most of the records I'm currently focused on (wills, probate, and land records) aren't yet online, I may considering cancelling my subscription temporarily until they're digitized. According to the site, my family tree will still be available and all historical records will still be attached, although I won't be able to search Ancestry's online files or view historical records any longer. As long as I make sure to use the same user ID when I start my subscription again, I'll retain everything in the tree, including attached historical records.

Another available feature is the option to download your family tree as a GEDCOM file. This is a standard genealogical computer file which will provide you a backup copy of the tree and allow you to upload it to another website if you choose to, though the attached records and images won't copy over, so you'll probably have to redo some of the details.

Technically an Ancestry.com community and not part of the website itself, it's appropriate to discuss RootsWeb at this time. Located at **http://www.rootsweb.ancestry.com**, Rootswebs is a free resource that allows users to create websites, post messages, and search records. There are a lot of searchable online databases, and some RootsWeb-hosted sites also include miscellaneous indexes of their own. There is a lot of great information, but since much of this is user-contributed and not necessarily comprehensive, it's difficult to say what content you'll find for a particular town or county.

Archives.com
http://www.archives.com

Archives.com is another genealogy website with lots of databases and records online. This site will let you build a family tree, access records, and search for your ancestors. It's priced significantly lower than some similar websites, and at the beginning of 2013 it had over 2.5-billion records online. As a comparison, at that time Ancestry.com's website said it had over 11-billion records. Since both sites have the most popular records online, it might be worth using this site to save the extra money you would spend elsewhere, at least to start.

If you decide to give Archives.com a try, its functionality is very similar to other sites. While I don't personally feel that the hints or the search functions are as advanced as those at Ancestry.com, that may be because my family tree was already well developed when I started using the website. Searches will return census records, vital records, newspaper and yearbook collections, and more at a fraction of the cost. Additionally, one can request on-site county records research through the site, order vital records certificates, or request a report on a living individual, though each of these come at an additional cost.

A free seven-day trial period is available, so log on and start building your family tree. If you already have a developed family history, you can upload your GEDCOM file and see whether anything new jumps out at you during the trial period. If you're new to the field, the billions of available records coupled with the low entry price may make this an attractive option.

MyHeritage.com
http://www.myheritage.com

This is another website that allows users to build free family trees online, and for the beginning researcher, it's not a bad option. Once again, you can upload a GEDCOM file if you have one or you can simply start building a new tree by adding relatives. The free version of the site allows you to add 250 people to your tree, though when I uploaded a GEDCOM with more individuals in it I didn't seem to lose functionality or get locked out of the account. Some time later, however, I did receive an email which told me I was over my limit and I wouldn't be able to add anyone new.

Free accounts can search historical records, though only a small number of these results are actually viewable to non-paying customers. Users can upgrade (by paying the monthly or annual fee) to a larger account that not only allows for more people in their family trees but also provides the ability to search and view all available historical records.

Other Family Tree Options

Since there are loads more options for one to create a family tree online, there simply isn't time to discuss each one in detail. As such, I've lumped a few other websites and options together in this section.

MyTrees.com works just like the three previously mentioned websites, and it provides users a 31-day free trial period. WeRelate.org is a free collaborative genealogical website, sponsored by the Foundation for On-Line Genealogy, Inc, in partnership with the Allen County Public Library (discussed in the Indiana section of the following chapter). This site allows others to modify your work, though you can post on a "User Page" which is password-protected. Other websites, like TribalPages.com and MyFamily.com also allow users to create family trees. MyFamily.com's website indicates that the family-tree feature was created by teaming up with Ancestry.com, so although the website isn't free, one can be sure that the family-tree portion of it is of high quality.

Family History Library (Utah)

This chapter is supposed to focus on general Internet resources for all your genealogical needs, and while I'm aware that a brick-and-mortar library cannot itself be hosted on a web server, the Family History Library in Salt Lake City is simply too important not to mention here. After all, it may be the largest repository of genealogical information in the solar system. In fact, if you perform a few searches on other websites like Ancestry.com and pay attention to the source information attached to the records you locate, you'll find that some of them come from the Family History Library. This library was started in 1894 to assist members of the Church of Jesus Christ of Latter-day Saints with their genealogical research. However, you don't have to be a member to use the facility. The library is open to the public and better still, it's free. If you have an opportunity to visit, you really should. I've not been, but if I'm ever in Salt Lake City I'll definitely drop by. In addition to the library in Utah, there are also Family History Centers (FHCs) around the country and around the world. The Regional FHCs don't have as many books and reels of microfilm as the Salt Lake City library, but their holdings are still enormous. Most of these facilities are located in the western United States, though the London Family History Centre is located, not surprisingly, in London. And not London, Kentucky, in case you wondered, though based on the way centre was spelled you had probably already surmised that London, England was the city in question. There are also smaller affiliated libraries that can order microfilm for you. To find a physical location near you, visit FamilySearch.org, discussed below.

FamilySearch.org
http://www.familysearch.org

FamilySearch.org is the Family History Library's official website, and it is the largest genealogy organization in the world. Users can submit family tree information (which is searchable), but that isn't the main feature of this site. Rather, the main feature is the tons upon tons of digitized and indexed material that anyone can search, absolutely free. Many of these collections include images of the original source documents. The website also has hundreds of free online genealogy courses on a myriad of topics that are tailored to research all over the world. If you're interested in helping index collections that have already been photographed, you can do that too. FamilySearch.org hosts collections from all over the world and some resources include: birth, death, marriage, church records, military, probate, census, baptisms, divorces, immigration, naturalization; you name it and there's probably a related record. Whether you actually search by name or just browse to the location you're interested in, you'll likely find that the effort was worth your time.

In my experience, the search feature returns superior results over searches on similar websites. Since name misspellings and variations used to be common, as discussed in "Chapter 1 - Genealogy Basics, Tips, and Tricks," a better search feature can be the difference between locating your ancestors or not. For example, I have performed particular searches for records related to surnames like Elson and Cummins on subscription websites without locating any pertinent results. However, when I performed the exact same searches looking for the exact same records (which were available on both websites), FamilySearch's results included the desired documents, even though the surnames had been recorded as Elston and Cummons.

I use this site in conjunction with other membership sites and find that some of the collections on FamilySearch.org aren't available elsewhere, even through pay sites. Examples include a collection of Ohio marriage records and a collection of Slovakian Church and Synagogue Records, both of which appear to be available only on FamilySearch.org at the time of writing. The bottom line is that if you're looking for a huge amount of valuable, free information, this may be the best website out there.

Cyndi's List

http://www.cyndislist.com/

This website probably has the most links to genealogical Internet resources. Period. With over 325,000 links in categories ranging from vital records to biographies, the United States to Norway, blogs to biographies, and everything in between, this is a great website. Although I would like to think I've identified and written about some sites that aren't yet on Cyndi's List, the odds are that most of them are already there. While a book such as this one will never be able to discuss 300,000-plus resources, hopefully the websites discussed here provide a level of depth not available elsewhere. If you need additional resources on a particular area but don't know where to start, try Cyndi's List. Because, in addition to the general and state-level websites discussed here, Cyndi's List has links to websites that focus on specific regions, counties, towns, and locations across the globe, many of which are beyond the scope of this book.

HeritageQuestOnline.com

http://www.heritagequestonline.com

Access to this website is generally only available at participating libraries. However, some libraries allow their patrons to use it remotely. Try browsing to your state's library or archives homepage to see if a link for HeritageQuest is provided. If one is, you'll likely have to provide your library card number or some form of state ID, depending on which state you live in. However, some states only require a phone number and zip code to authorize access for their residents.

This is a good genealogical resource for census data, books, a periodical search index, Revolutionary War records, and even the Freedman's Bank Records, an important African-American collection. Keep in mind that some books and original census records have images online, but the periodical search index (PERSI) doesn't include original images.

USGenWeb.org

http://www.usgenweb.org

USGenWeb is a national project that has links to genealogical webpages for individual states, each of which we'll discuss in the next chapter. The site has multiple projects in the works, and while there is a lot of good information, since USGenWeb isn't a comprehensive transcription of all county, state, or national records, it lacks a certain level of uniformity (much like RootsWeb). The beneficial thing about not being limited solely to official records is that one may find transcriptions of family bibles or newspaper clippings, information which isn't normally easy to attain elsewhere online. The information provided for each state necessarily varies, though each state has county-specific webpages which can be helpful if you already know what county your relatives hailed from.

Western States Marriage Search

http://abish.byui.edu/specialCollections/westernStates/search.cfm

Although not a truly national or general resource, this is a searchable marriage index for a number of states in the western United States. These records are not linked to online images of source documentation but provide transcribed data instead.

DeathIndexes.com

http://www.deathindexes.com

With a name like DeathIndexes.com, it's easy to imagine what this website is about. What you might not realize is what an amazing resource this is. This is basically just a large collection of links, organized by state, which directs users to miscellaneous death-related websites. These may include state or county resources and can range from death records themselves to cemetery, probate, wills, obituaries, and even church records. A great website for finding death-based online resources.

FindAGrave.com

http://www.findagrave.com

FindAGrave.com is a very useful website that relies on the assistance of volunteers. At the time of writing, the site had more than 95-million online memorials, both in the United States and abroad. Cemeteries are listed online and are searchable. In addition, one can search for memorials by name, state, county, birth or death date, as well as maiden name (assuming it's been recorded). Finally, photo volunteers can sign up to take pictures of gravestones in nearby cemeteries, and any user can submit a photo request, which will hopefully be fulfilled by a photo volunteer. The website is free, but you have to sign up for a free user name in order to become a photo volunteer or submit memorials.

As mentioned, not all memorials have associated images, though they can be requested. When searching for your relatives, you may have to expand your search beyond the information you already know. The reason is that every memorial isn't transcribed with exact information as it's written on the gravestone. For example, a gravestone image might clearly list the birth and death dates of your relative, while the memorial entry only lists the death date. Also keep in mind the abbreviations we mentioned in "Chapter 1 - Genealogy Basics, Tips, and Tricks," when we discussed gravestones.

While there are competing websites--BillionGraves.com, Interment.net, and others--I personally prefer FindAGrave. However, for the sake of completeness, I will say that both FindAGrave.com and BillionGraves.com have Android Apps to interact with their content. While the BillionGraves app is free and allows for pictures, one must upgrade to the full version in order to view memorials on your phone. Find Grave is a free app for the FindAGrave website, and it allows users to view and/or create text-only memorials (i.e., it doesn't allow one to take and upload a picture). It doesn't appear to be put out by FindAGrave but seems like it might be a third-party app. Keep in mind that new versions of these apps may have been released since the time of writing, so content could have changed. Although it's a useful app, due to Find Grave's somewhat limited functionality (no options for searching nearby photo requests or uploading photos to a memorial), I even had a notion to write my own third-party app for interacting with FindAGrave content, though I haven't yet found the time to make that happen.

Legacy.com
http://www.legacy.com

This is a website which is useful for finding obituary and death information. While the first search option is for locating obituaries, in my experience most obituary results are for recent deaths. Even though you probably won't find an older obituary here, a more recent one could be available in its entirety. Another benefit is that a second search option is for the SSDI. Again, this won't provide death records from *that* long ago, but it's completely free and might be worth checking out.

CDC Vital Records
http://www.cdc.gov/nchs/w2w.htm

If you're looking for an official state record (birth, marriage, death, or divorce), this website put together by the CDC is a great place to start. It has fee information and details for how to acquire vital records in all fifty states. This isn't an online search for your relatives, so if you're not interested in an actual copy of a record, this probably isn't the best place to look.

Since there isn't one centralized national online repository for historical vital records, other options for locating your relatives online are covered in the chapter on state-specific resources.

VitalChek.com
http://www.vitalchek.com

If you need an official birth, death, marriage, or divorce record, this is another website that researchers can use in conjunction with the CDC website discussed above. Even though many states have separate vital-records departments, lots of them use VitalChek.com to handle all of their orders.   These are not generally the best documents to request for genealogical purposes as they can be costly. In addition, the law may prevent you from ordering certain documents at all.   For example, recent birth records are generally available only to the individual and possibly close family.

Fold3.com
http://www.fold3.com

Fold3.com (formerly Footnote.com) is a website that focuses mainly on military documents (as far back as the Revolutionary War) but has a few other collections as well. Searches provide very basic information for free, but in order to view most images of actual documents, you must subscribe to the website. That being said, some collections are accessible free-of-charge. At the time of writing many collections were completely available online while others were works in progress. Some websites, like FamilySearch.org, will return Fold3.com results when you perform a search, though to view the actual records you'll need a Fold3 membership. Numerous libraries have subscriptions to Fold3, so if you don't feel like paying for a membership, find out whether your local library has one. I don't have a membership myself, but when I've accessed Fold3's free content or accessed the website through a subscribing library, I've found that the information was most helpful. This is probably the best website for military source documentation.

Daughters, and Sons, of the American Revolution

Daughters of the American Revolution (DAR) and Sons of the American Revolution (SAR) are societies for those who can trace their lineage to someone who served in the Revolutionary War. Some subscription websites have copies of previously submitted applications online, and if you can find your ancestors in one of these applications, you may find a host of other related information. Just remember that the information may not be one-hundred-percent complete or accurate, even if the information was reliable enough to get the application approved. Both the DAR and SAR websites have online searches for those who served in the war.

NPS Civil War Soldiers and Sailors Database
http://www.nps.gov/civilwar/soldiers-and-sailors-database.htm

This is a collaborative effort between the National Park Service (NPS) and several partners. There are separate searches for soldiers and sailors, though the soldier search covers vastly more records; the sailor search only covers African-American sailors who served during the war. In either case, one can search for relatives by name, as well as performing more advanced searches with additional information. Both searches are transcribed, and sailors' details seem more complete, possibly including place of birth, age, height, date of enlistment, and perhaps even muster records. The soldier search provides less information, but it does provide a film numbers which can be used to order records from the National Archives. If nothing else, a name and regiment should be helpful in advancing your search. A number of other searches are available on the website, but the main ones that are searchable by name are a cemetery search for veterans which might include images of headstones, a prisoner search, and a Medal of Honor award winner search. Although this website doesn't provide images of original documents, it's still a valuable tool for learning about your relative's place in the Civil War.

Castle Garden

http://www.castlegarden.org

Castle Garden was the lesser known immigration center that preceded Ellis Island. Located just across the water from Ellis Island and south of the World Trade Center, this was the official United States immigration center from 1855 until Ellis Island opened. However, even though Ellis Island opened in 1892, Castle Garden has some records from after that time period. In fact, CastleGarden.org has records from 1820 to 1913. These records have been transcribed from original ship manifests, and although searches are free, you won't find images of original ship manifests. If you happen to find a relative on this website and their arrival date is from after the opening of Ellis Island, you may be able to find original documentation at the website below.

Ellis Island Passenger Search

http://www.ellisisland.org/

Much like the Castle Garden website, the Ellis Island passenger search is all about finding immigrants who came to America. These records don't go as far back as the Castle Garden records, however, as Ellis Island didn't even open its immigration station until 1892. Ellis Island records are available from 1892 through 1924. Without registering, one can search records for free, but you'll only find name, age, year of arrival, and residence. If you want to view the image of the original record, then you'll have to register with the website. Registration is also free, but the password requirements are very specific (ten characters exactly and it must begin and end with a number). So much for using your go-to password.

When looking at ship manifests, one might find information such as name, age, ethnicity, occupation, ship name, departure port, final destination, and perhaps most importantly, the name and address of a relative either in the United States or in an immigrant's homeland. Remember that some records don't include all of this information, so try not to be too disappointed if you don't find what you're looking for. You should also be aware that many ship manifests are more than one page, so after you find an interesting record make sure you browse forward to see if a second page with more information exists.

Chronicling America Newspaper Search
http://chroniclingamerica.loc.gov/

If you need to locate an old newspaper's archives online, the Chronicling America section of the Library of Congress' website is very helpful. There is a feature that allows one to view an index of newspapers published from 1690 up until the present for any given location. This is a valuable feature in itself as any of the listed newspapers might contain birth, marriage, or death announcements (obituaries) for your relatives. If a particular newspaper you're interested in isn't online, you can consult local libraries to see if they have microfilm for the newspaper in question. If you don't live near a library that has copies of these newspapers, you can usually pay a small fee for a librarian to perform a search on your behalf.

While the newspaper index is valuable, for genealogical research on the Internet, the searchable digital content is even more valuable. Chronicling America has a great many newspapers that are free to search and view online. So if you know when your relative passed away and the appropriate newspaper has already been digitized, you should be able to quickly locate the obituary, assuming there was one. If you don't know when a relative passed away, you can try a simple search for his or her name to see what results are returned. Just keep in mind that not all newspapers are available online and some that are available may be missing editions here and there.

GenealogyBank.com

http://www.genealogybank.com

This is a subscription website which focuses on newspaper archives related to family history. According to the website, most of its newspaper collections are not available on other websites. Free 30-day trials are available, and the annual fee is reasonably low for the amount of data available. If you're having trouble finding biographies for your relatives, local newspapers from the 1800s and early 1900s often had information on everyone in town, so this may be a good place to look. These newspaper write-ups were sometimes about day-to-day happenings, so you might learn that your ancestors went to dinner at a relative's house in the next county. Not a particularly helpful tidbit in this example, but at least you found a reference to your relatives.

Search results might turn up from a town you didn't even know your ancestors lived in, but on the other hand, if your relatives are from a town whose newspapers aren't yet available online, then this site might not be overly helpful.

Google Books

http://www.books.google.com

Google may not seem like the best place to go for genealogical research, but it is. Okay, maybe it's not the *best* place to go, but it is a valuable resource. From Google's homepage, go to the subsection entitled "Books." It may be accessible through a dropdown menu at the top of the homepage. Keep in mind that if the homepage is redesigned, you may have to dig further to get to the Books section. Alternately, just follow the link above. Google also has a large selection of newspaper archives which can be searched or browsed through Google's "News" webpage.

Google has tons of books, both in copyright and out, available on its website. And the best part is that a large number of these books are searchable and provide a small preview when you view search results. So feel free to enter the names of your relatives and see what you find. It really might be that easy. That being said, let's look at how Google Books works and what to do if you can't immediately locate your relatives.

After you perform a search, a "Search Tools" option should appear at the top of your screen (again, the location could change if Google redesigns the website). One of these options will be for the type of books to search. You'll receive the most search results by leaving the option set to return all books, but if you limit your search to "Free Google eBooks," then you'll be able to read them online in seconds. These books are free because they're old enough that they're out of copyright protection. While you need a Google account in order to access free eBooks, you merely have to click on the "EBOOK-FREE" button to add a book to your library. At that point, you simply have to read it. If you don't want to read the whole book, just use the search function and type in your ancestor's name.

Another option is not to search for your ancestor's name through the Google search bar, but instead to search for the county you're interested in. Many authors put together county histories, complete with biographical sketches, in the late 1800s and early 1900s; being out of copyright, many of these can be accessed online for free. Just type in the name of the county in question and browse through the results to see if anything interests you.

Suppose I were searching for my relatives in Tippecanoe County, Indiana. A Google Books search for "William Vanmeter" might not give me the results I desire, but a search for "Tippecanoe County, Indiana," returns a free eBook called *Biographical Record and Portrait Album of Tippecanoe County, Indiana: Containing Portraits of all the Presidents of the United States from Washington to Cleveland, with Accompanying Biographies of Each; a Condensed History of the State of Indiana; Portraits and Biographies of Some of the Prominent Men of the State; Engravings of Prominent Citizens in Tippecanoe County, with Personal Histories of Many of the Leading Families, and a Concise History of Tippecanoe County, and its Cities and Villages.* Whew!, that was a long title. And although the title has the words "condensed" and "concise" in it, the title itself is anything but. By searching for "Vanmeter" in this ponderously titled book, I find two references to William Vanmeter's children. Jackpot!

When searching for your ancestors' names, if you think there might be a biography for one of your relatives, consider searching for the last name without its starting letter. For example, if your relative's last name is Johnson, try searching not only for Johnson, but separately for "ohnson." The reason for this is that many older texts used drop caps, printing the first letter of a new paragraph or section in a much larger and more ornate font. If the biographical section on your ancestor starts with his or her name, the first letter may be in a different font, and the computer program (or dimwitted person) that indexed the book might have handled this incorrectly. In the case of my relatives, I have tried searching for my last name, Elson, many times. Often I get intriguing results, but upon closer inspection find that the surname of the biographical sketch's subject is actually Nelson. Since the "N" was in a different font, the indexed version of the information thought that the "N" and Elson were separate. Along similar lines, one may see this problem when a word is split at the end of a line. For example, I have run across the name Mickelson at the end of a line of text. When it is split with "Mick" on the first line and "elson" on the second line, an index might erroneously turn up "Elson" as a result, but not "Mickelson." This is true not only for Google, but for all indexed material I've come across.

Another problem is that some books simply have inaccurate transcriptions and the surname in question may turn up in search results when it's not there at all, and vice versa.

Some books you find will no doubt be under copyright protection, in which case you'll have to either purchase them or check them out from a library. If there is a free preview of a copyright-protected book, you might be able to glean enough information from the preview that you don't even have to locate a copy of the book itself. Other books that are no longer protected under copyright law might not be available as a free eBook through Google. In that case, you should check out the next resource.

Internet Archive
http://www.Archive.org

You've already visited Google Books and found a book you'd like to read. Unfortunately, it's not available online through Google's website. Your next stop should be Archive.org. This is the home of the Internet Archive, a non-profit organization founded to create an Internet library. The Wayback Machine, a service that archives webpages, is probably the Internet Archive's most recognizable tool, though the Internet Archive also contains audio, software, text, and video content. We're interested in the texts section specifically. Just type in the name of the book you're looking for to see if it's available online. You can also search for the name of your relative or their county of residence directly, as discussed in the previous section. Books can be read online, downloaded as a PDF file, and even viewed as a text document.

If you open a book on your computer, be aware that a search for your relative's name might not produce any results when the individual is, in fact, mentioned within its pages. If you search the text-only version of the book instead, you may receive slightly different results so consider checking multiple versions of each book. Be aware that these text transcriptions might not be one-hundred-percent accurate either.

Some of these books have indexes at the back, a good starting point if a search doesn't return any results. However, even for books with indices, time may be required to dig out all the details you're looking for. The reason is that your relatives may not be the subject of their own sketches but might only be mentioned in another subject's biography. For example, a unique entry for William Vanmeter might not exist, but one might find a reference to "Eliza Vanmeter, daughter of William Vanmeter" elsewhere in the book.

Some books not available on Google might be available here, and vice versa, so check and search both websites.

There are other online libraries and information repositories, but Google and the Internet Archive are my favorites for locating out-of-copyright books online. For more links to other online libraries, click the "About" tab on the Internet Archive website.

In addition to books, Archive.org makes available Federal Census records for free. Although they are not searchable by name like they are on some other websites, if you know where you're looking or simply need to scan through a census record, then this option is a no-cost way to look at census records from the privacy of your own home. The Internet Archive also hosts many older publications put out by state historical societies.

WorldCat Library Search
http://www.worldcat.org

Have you identified a book that you think might be helpful, but it's not available online through Google Books or the Internet Archive? Point your browser to WorldCat and you'll find out where to look. WorldCat is an online library search, so just enter the name of the book (or a keyword in the title) and your zip code and WorldCat will return a list of nearby libraries that have the book you want. It'll be up to you to actually visit the library, but knowing where to look is a huge timesaver.

BLM General Land Office Records
http://www.glorecords.blm.gov/search/default.aspx

Have you lost track of your ancestors somewhere along the line? Perhaps they moved prior to 1850 (the year censuses first recorded all free persons and not only heads of households), and you've been unsuccessful figuring out where they went. *Is this John Smith in Iowa the same John Smith I'm looking for?* Or perhaps you just want to flesh out your research to make it more complete. One resource to consider is the Bureau of Land Management's

(BLM) General Land Office records.

Although this BLM land-patent search only covers "Federal Land States," there are links to search most other states through related websites, some of which are discussed in the following chapter on state-specific resources.

If you find a document, it probably won't be the smoking gun you're looking for. This is true for a couple of reasons. The first is that it might be hard to identify a particular person as your ancestor even if the name is correct (is this your John Smith, or another one?). The second is that there's not much genealogical information in these documents. That doesn't mean the information won't be valuable though; as with everything else, at least you have a starting point.

We first need to address how to determine if the document you found pertains to your relative or merely someone else with the same name. This can be challenging as the documents don't often include helpful genealogical material. All of the documents that I've inspected include a description of the land and the purchaser's name. Land patents granted as a result of military service indicate which unit the soldier served with. Other information you might find is where the purchaser came from. In searching for "William Vanmeter," a relative of mine that I know lived in Butler County, Ohio, at one point, I find several records. Two of these records show that a William M Vanmeter of Butler County, Ohio, purchased land in Indiana at the proper time. Perhaps I can't say with one-hundred-percent certainty, at least not yet, that this is the correct William Vanmeter, but it certainly seems like it is. And now I've got locations from the land records to follow up with.

To help prove one way or the other whether a record relates to your ancestor, one option, and perhaps the most helpful, is to request the associated Land Entry Case File through the National Archives, discussed earlier in this chapter. The odds are that these records will be digitized eventually, but since that's mere speculation on my part you might be better served by ordering files on interest; they cost $50 at the time of writing.

As discussed in the previous chapter, you can also look for surrounding land owners through the BLM website. If you search for additional land owners from the same township and section, make sure you look for individuals with the same surname or from the same county as your relative. Alternately you can perform a more general search by surname.

If you perform a search for all land owners in a particular section, perhaps to see if your relative's neighbors are already known to you, be careful when handling the results. Search results for some township sections include land owners for each piece of land, others don't have information on every parcel in the section, and still other sections list more than one owner for the very same parcel. When you actually look at the original documentation for the overlapping land patents, you'll likely find that one was transcribed incorrectly. So you may have to dig a little bit to find all of your ancestor's neighbors.

Wills and additional land transactions will also help tie everything together. Perhaps you find the same parcel of land is later sold by your relative to his son-in-law. Or perhaps you find that the parcel of land was willed to a child or left to a spouse. If you had any doubts as to whether the purchaser you identified earlier was your relative, these connections should help assuage them. For more details on using these land records, consult the section on land records in the previous chapter.

Plotting Land Records with Earth Point and Google Earth
http://www.earth.google.com
http://www.earthpoint.us/TownshipsSearchByDescription.aspx

I promised that we would discuss how to plot federal land records when they were briefly discussed earlier in the book. Plotting an exact location will give you an idea of where your ancestor lived, and if you're so inclined you can even visit said piece of land. Plotting your ancestor's land holdings also makes it easier to visualize where owners of adjacent parcels were located.

The simplest way I've found to plot your ancestor's land holdings is first to download Google Earth. It's free software, though you do have to download and install it on your computer. Next, point your web browser to EarthPoint.us, a website with numerous tools for use in conjunction with Google Earth. When you get to the website, simply enter the state, township, range, and section from your ancestor's land patent. After you click the button "Fly To On Google Earth," a small file will start downloading on your computer. Once the download completes, simply open that file and Google Earth will show you the location of your relative's land.

Freedman's Bureau
http://freedmensbureau.com/

The Freedman's Bureau was established in 1865, and if your relatives were refugees or freedmen in the post-Civil-War era, the Bureau might have records you're interested in. Depending on the state of residence, one may find lists of residents, employees, marriages, and even murders.

Town/County Look-Up

http://resources.rootsweb.ancestry.com/cgi-bin/townco.cgi

Many records are located at the county level, perhaps at the county courthouse or the county clerk's office. So what do you do when you only know the town but not the actual county it's located in? Just use this simple tool. Type in the name of your town and you'll get the name of the county lickety-split. Partial names are okay, as long as the portion you enter is at the beginning of the town's name. For example, if you enter Santa as the town name and California as the state, your search results will include counties associated with the cities of Santa Cruz, Santa Rosa, Santa Barbara, and any other town or city that starts with Santa. On the other hand, if you only type in Cruz, you won't get any results. You can also use a search engine to identify the county that a city is associated with, but this website is a pretty convenient way of figuring out the county in question.

Keep in mind that the search results will only return current counties. So if you're looking for a town's original county from a specific year, you may have to do a little more digging. Many of the state-specific and county-specific websites that are part of the USGenWeb Project (discussed early) have detailed information on when and how counties formed. Genealogy Inc (www.genealogyinc.com) also has county formation maps which may help you visualize county border changes.

Some towns have also changed names or disappeared altogether, but an online search will often help you iron out these details.

Reading Old Handwriting

In the past, handwriting didn't always appear as it does today. For example, the letters "s" and "f" appeared to be very similar when written down. This problem is even worse when you're not a native speaker of the language. However, there are resources to assist you.

Let's say that your relatives came from French-Canada and you have already located a copy of their marriage record in a collection of church documents. The odds are that the only things indexed are their names and the date of marriage. However, many churches followed a pattern, first listing the marriage date, and later listing the bride and groom along with the names of their parents. If you can read this information, then you've put another piece of the puzzle together, and you can start looking for the parents' names in other documents from the same church.

I don't have one favorite site for deciphering old handwriting, so my advice is to use a search engine when necessary. Just search for the language (if you know it) and "old handwriting" or "paleography." You'll get more advice and help than you know what to do with. Many of these sites will include images of letters and words written in different ways, and some even have free online courses.

If you're not having much luck with these websites and you think you know what the document is about, you can always search for translations online. For example, most vital records include a date. So you can start by searching for how to write months, days, and years in the language of your document. "How to write months in French," might be an adequate search to return a list of months with English-to-French translations. This still doesn't mean that you'll be able to read the month in your ancestor's document, but it might be of assistance.

Even documents written in English can be difficult to read sometimes, so use a search engine to aid you. Once you find an accurate transcription of a document similar to your own, you'll have a much easier time transcribing your own records.

Finally, if you still can't make sense of the information you have, consider hiring an expert. You'll have to pay for the service, but it could be just what you need to get past your sticking point.

We've covered a lot of different resources in this chapter, and while some of them are based on visiting a particular location (the Family History Library, for example), most of these resources are available online. Additionally, while some of them are fee-based, many are absolutely free. Although these resources are very helpful and may provide exactly the information you're looking for, other state-specific information may not be readily available through these websites. To continue our search, we must dig deeper to locate websites and resources for specific states.

State-by-State Resources

Already having gone over genealogical details relevant to your search and where those details can be found, basic descriptions of some nationally available documents, and a list of general Internet resources (focusing mainly on websites with indexed or digitized material), this chapter focuses on websites and digital content specific to individual states.

In case you haven't heard, the Internet is a rather large place. As such, determining the next website you want to visit can be a difficult proposition. If you've already searched the resources discussed in the previous chapter to no avail, it may be time to start searching websites dedicated to the actual state your relatives hailed from.   Unfortunately, there simply isn't one comprehensive, indexed, online database which contains complete historical information on every resident of every state. If there were, you could easily research your relatives, would never hit a brick wall or sticking point, and I wouldn't have written the book which you are now reading. It is that lack of a centralized genealogical repository which makes it necessary to go over Internet resources in the following state-by-state manner.

While there are many more resources online than those covered in this chapter, the content hosted on the following websites should help shed light on your ancestry and provide a state-based starting point for your research.

As always, remember that if the below resources don't provide enough information for you, try to narrow down the location of your ancestor's residence to either a particular city or county, and then use the resources mentioned in the previous chapters or use a search engine to identify additional genealogically relevant collections.

Each state's write-up provides the date of admission to the United States, a list of neighboring states, and a brief statement about previous affiliations (i.e., was this state part of another state or territory?; have the borders changed?) before Internet resources are discussed.

With regard to each state's previous-affiliations description, information is largely limited to boundary changes that might affect your genealogical search. As such, the focus is on inhabited areas with a functioning government. While there were vastly more land claims than those described below (Spain, Great Britain, and France all had vast land holdings in the present-day United States, and many of the thirteen original colonies once claimed land west to the Mississippi River and beyond), this information is mostly outside the scope of this section since unincorporated and uninhabited areas were not likely to have much in the way of genealogical records. Even when a city was founded under a foreign government, records of genealogical relevance were generally handled locally and as such are normally found in state or county databases, not overseas. Additionally, states are not, as a rule, designated as Union or Confederate, unless it's pertinent to border changes or establishment.

Along the same vein, although each state was originally inhabited by Native Americans, unless a website hosts a genealogical index or collection, then this information doesn't aid in most online family history research either, and as such, it is not included. Some of the following websites do provide assistance with Native-American research even if the situation didn't warrant mention in that state's discussion on border changes.

Entire books have been written on the subject of state borders but since there isn't space to go into such detail, nor is that level of detail necessary for most genealogical research, minor border changes aren't generally described below. If you need that level of detail with regard to a state's borders, try visiting Genealogy Inc (www.genealogyinc.com). It has state-specific maps that detail border changes, even down to the county level. Looking online for old maps will help clarify any confusing border changes highlighted in this section.

Remember that some online collections described in this chapter are also available through previously discussed websites (e.g., Ancestry.com, Archives.com, and FamilySearch.org), while other collections might be available exclusively through the below-listed websites themselves. If the collection is available on multiple sites, sometimes one site will have original images online, while another will only have transcribed data. So if you find a collection you're interested in but it doesn't include images of the source documentation, browse around as those original images might be online elsewhere.

Finally, if you're unable to locate the information you were hoping for at any of the following state-specific websites, but you haven't thoroughly searched the more general websites discussed in the previous chapter (e.g., FamilySearch.org, Ancestry.com, Archives.com), make sure to go back and check them too. Sometimes those sites host valuable collections that aren't easily found elsewhere online, even through the institutions where they originated. One reason for this is that institutions such as State Archives, cities, and county historical societies don't always have the funding or capability to digitize their records. In situations like these, companies like Ancestry.com will sometimes undertake the digitization process themselves in exchange for the rights to host these collections online. Although some researchers might think that for-profit companies shouldn't be allowed to use public records in this way, partnerships like this allow public records to be digitized and preserved for posterity. Without these partnerships, certain records would languish in obscurity until such time as the host institution raised the money for digitization or until the building they were housed in burnt down.

Alabama

Date of Statehood: 14 Dec 1819
Neighboring States: Florida, Georgia, Mississippi, Tennessee
Previous Affiliations: Alabama Territory, Georgia, Mississippi Territory

Most of the southern half of present-day Alabama became part of the Mississippi Territory in 1798 after a treaty with Spain set the United States' southern boundary at 31-degrees north latitude. The northern portion of present-day Alabama was added to the Mississippi Territory after the United States Government acquired it from Georgia in the wake of the Yazoo land scandal. Finally, the southernmost portion of present-day Alabama was an area disputed by the United States and Spain. After a group of settlers in the Spanish territory of West Florida declared their independence, the United States annexed the eastern portion of West Florida into the Mississippi Territory in 1812. At this point, the Mississippi Territory contained present-day Mississippi and Alabama. Alabama formed its own territory in 1817 when Mississippi entered the Union as the 20th state.

Alabama Department of Public Health - Vital Records
http://adph.org/vitalrecords/Default.asp?id=1564
This is the official Alabama Department of Public Health webpage for vital records, and it has a list of microfilm indexes available for purchase. There is no associated online search, but microfilm rolls of marriage, divorce, and death records can all be ordered. The reason birth records are not available is that they are protected under Alabama state law until 125 years after the date of birth. Since the Alabama Center for Health Statistics didn't even start filing birth certificates until 1908, we haven't hit that magical 125-year mark yet and won't for some time. Certain relatives can order birth certificates, and a small birth index is available on FamilySearch.org. County clerks may have older documents than state offices.

Alabama Department of Archives and History (ADAH)
http://www.archives.alabama.gov/research.html
The ADAH provides some of its digital content to Ancestry.com, a website we discussed in an earlier chapter. A few ADAH collections with

online indexes include voter registration from 1867, Civil War Soldiers, and a WWI Goldstar database.

From the "Research" page, you have a few options.   Visitation information is provided (the facility is in Montgomery, Alabama), and if you're unable to visit in person, the website details how to request research on your behalf.   If you choose this option, keep in mind that vital records themselves are not located here but are handled by the Department of Public Health, as discussed above.

If you click "Search Our Collections" on the left-hand side of the page, you'll find holdings information and a number of indexes.   Remember that not all indexes are searchable by name.   For example, the "Local Government/County Records on Microfilm" link allows you to search holdings by county, but not to search within those databases by name, while the previously mentioned WWI Goldstar and 1867 Voter Registration databases are searchable by name.   If you select "Digital Collections," you'll be redirected to a selection of scanned documents.   The "Alabama Textual Materials Collection" includes various diaries, letters, and book excerpts, while another collection contains copies of *The Alabama Historical Quarterly*.

If you instead hover over "Other Sources" on the left-hand side of the page, you'll see an option for "Alabama Internet Resources."   If you follow that link, a long list of additional resources will pop up.   Near the bottom of the webpage are two sections of genealogical links, one that focuses solely on Alabama and another that focuses on more general resources.   Some of the links provided are for websites already discussed elsewhere in this book.

Alabama Genealogical Society (AGS)

http://algensoc.org/main/searchable.html

The AGS first started printing the *AGS Magazine* in 1967, and although a surname index isn't available, the website provides an article index for issues up until 2005.   If your ancestors were early settlers in the state, try searching the name index to the Society's First-Families-of-Alabama certificate program. Another online index is to 1937's *Sketches of Alabama Towns and Counties*.

While these are all good resources, my favorite feature of the site is the "Loose Records Project Web Index."   This is an ongoing project, but it is, essentially, an index of all loose county records for the state of Alabama; these may include marriages, divorces, estate cases, guardianship files, and more. Although this is merely a transcribed index and source images are not available online, once a record is found it will contain microfilm reel numbers for both the Family History Library (in Utah) and for the ADAH.

ALGenWeb
http://www.algw.org/

This is the Alabama website associated with the USGenWeb project (see the write-up on USGenWeb.org in the previous section). It contains a lot of great information about the state, especially links to county-based resources. One thing to keep in mind is that, as with most USGenWeb sites, there are actually two separate county-level sections associated with the website. Although county-specific webpages can contain all manner of genealogical information, additional county-level information is sometimes found through the USGenWeb Archives Project. Make sure to check both locations to ensure you don't miss anything.

Birmingham Public Library Databases
http://bpldb.bplonline.org/db/index

Several databases are available through the Birmingham Public Library, but you won't find images of source documents online. Some of the information indexed includes church registers, coal mine fatalities, a WPA biography project, and local obituary and cemetery records. This website has several indexes that provide information from around the state, as well as several that are strictly local.

Alaska

Date of Statehood: 3 Jan 1959

Neighboring States: Country of Canada

Previous Affiliations: Alaska Territory, Russian America, Department of Alaska, District of Alaska

Before the United States purchased Alaska in 1867, the area was a Russian-owned one with borders defined by the Treaty of St. Petersburg in 1825. The Department of Alaska was established and existed until 1884, when the District of Alaska came into being. In 1912, the Alaska Territory was established prior to statehood in 1959. A territorial dispute between the United States and Canada over how the southern portion of the border was defined was resolved through arbitration in 1903.

State of Alaska - Bureau of Vital Statistics

http://www.hss.state.ak.us/dph/bvs/

The Bureau of Vital Statistics is the place to go if you need a copy of a birth, marriage, or death certificate. Keep in mind, however, that under Alaska state law, birth records don't become part of the public record until 100 years after the event, while death, marriage, and divorce records are sealed for 50 years, all of which are fairly standard waiting periods in most states. Even if you're a close relative who can legally purchase a vital-record certificate or the date of your ancestor's birth/marriage/death occurred long enough ago to be part of the public record already, this doesn't mean you're necessarily going to be able to find the record you're looking for. Since state offices don't have vital records from before the 1890s and many of these events weren't reported to the state until the 1930s, if your ancestor's paperwork for a birth/marriage/death wasn't registered with the Bureau, you may be out of luck. The odds are you'll have more luck with the next resource.

Alaska State Archives

http://archives.alaska.gov/for_researchers/for_researchers.html

The Alaska State Archives has quite a lot of information available, but only a portion of it is searchable online. Probate and naturalization records are available as PDF files which you can search through your web browser or software like Adobe Acrobat Reader.   These documents give some basic name, date, and location information, as well as a case number or collection name and page number.   Using that information, one can locate the original documents in the State Archives themselves.

Under the "Genealogy Resources at the Archives" section of the website, links to the aforementioned probate and naturalization indexes are provided. Although the webpage also lists vital-statistics and WWI-veteran-records holdings, those collections aren't online at this time.

Other webpages contain genealogical links to external websites and detail how to submit research requests in case you don't live in Juneau (home of the State Archives).

Alaska State Library
http://library.state.ak.us/forpublic.html

By browsing around the State Library's website, you'll no doubt find some information that piques your interest.   One helpful item is the "Online Historical Collections" webpage, which can be reached via a link on the right-hand side of the page or by first clicking the "Alaska Historical Collections" link and going from there.   Once you bring it up, you'll find a guide to microfilm holdings for Alaskan newspapers as well as indexes for names found in old newspapers, obituaries, and biographies.

If you browse to the "Genealogy: Finding your goldrush relative" webpage, you'll find another cluster of genealogical links.   Some of these are links to resources already mentioned here, while others are for local historical societies.

While there are a large number of digital collections online, it goes without saying that a vast amount of source documentation isn't yet digitally available. If you're unable to visit the library in Juneau, you can request research assistance; the library also accepts image requests for items that aren't already in the digital archives, though this may require payment.

AKGenWeb
http://www.rootsweb.ancestry.com/~akgenweb/

This is the Alaska website associated with the USGenWeb project.   It provides links to biographies, online directories, church records, and more. Newspaper indexes, census data, and obituaries are also available.   The website contains a search bar, so you can quickly determine whether your ancestors are anywhere on the site.

Arizona

Date of Statehood: 14 Feb 1912

Neighboring States: California, Nevada, New Mexico, Utah, Colorado (kitty-corner), Country of Mexico

Previous Affiliations: Spain, Mexico, New Mexico Territory, Arizona Territory

The majority of present-day Arizona was acquired through the Treaty of Guadalupe-Hidalgo in 1848. That land became part of the New Mexico Territory when it was established two years later in 1850. The Gadsden Purchase in 1853 added the southernmost portion of Arizona (the area below the Gila River) to the New Mexico Territory. In 1863, the Arizona Territory was established by the United States, just after an Arizona Territory with different borders was established by the Confederacy. The United States version of the territory included present-day Arizona, as well as southern Nevada, while the Confederate version split the New Mexico territory in half lengthwise instead of vertically; as such, the Confederate version of the Arizona Territory included the southern halves of both present-day Arizona and New Mexico. The Arizona Territory, which later became the state of Arizona, took its present form after the state of Nevada annexed its southern tip in 1866.

Arizona Department of Health Services - Birth and Death Indexes

http://genealogy.az.gov/

State law in Arizona stipulates that birth records must remain sealed for 75 years, while death records must remain sealed for 50. Although this may sound like a long time, it's actually not; consider Alabama, which doesn't make birth certificates a matter of public record until 125 years after the fact.

This is an excellent vital-records website. Not only does it provide searchable birth records from 1855 onwards and death records from 1861 onwards, but each search result comes with an online image as well. Keep in mind that older records, which there are fewer of to begin with since the Office of Vital Records didn't officially record either event until 1909, may have been copied at some point in the past and may not be original. Many older records that I found were copied onto more recent birth- or death-certificates in the early part of the 20th century. The information is still valuable, but it might not be a scanned copy of the original record itself.

Another great thing about the website is how much of each record was transcribed. You'll find that in addition to the subject's name and a date of birth or death, other information may include: father's name and birthplace; mother's name and birthplace; mother's maiden name (if available). Since all of this was transcribed and there's only one name field (well, two--first and last), you'll receive the broadest, most comprehensive results possible.

For example, let's say you have a female ancestor named Cora Johnson, but you don't know whether she had any children or to whom she was married. Well, if you search only for "Johnson," you'll receive results not only for the subject of each vital record but based on the parents' names as well. So if you search for "Johnson," one of your results might be a death record for a Joe Jackson, whose mother's name was Cora Johnson; you found this result because her maiden name was Johnson. Be cautious though, because if you're trying to find information based on a parent's name, then too much information might limit your results. I've found that when searching for "Cora Johnson" instead of "Johnson" by itself, then the Joe Jackson record no longer turns up in my search results. What's going on here? It turns out that the way the parental information was transcribed means that I need to leave the first-name field blank and enter both the first and last name in the last-name field. This will give the desired, more limited result versus if we had merely entered a last name (Johnson) or a first name (Cora) and last name (Johnson) separately, the latter of which would filter out the very result you desire. If you choose to search for a parent's name by typing both the first and last names in the last-name field, make sure you enter them in the proper order. In this situation, name order matters, and "Johnson Cora" won't return any results.

Mesa Regional Family History Center (Mesa Regional FHC)
http://www.mesarfhc.org/

This website includes not only Arizona information but also provides external links to access vital records from each of the other forty-nine states. There aren't many Arizona-specific resources besides those mentioned earlier, but you can search for Arizona obituaries by name. This is a branch of the Family History Library in Utah, and its holdings (both in print and on microfilm) are searchable online. Some historical books (not necessarily about Arizona) are also available digitally on the website. As a regional branch of the Family History Library, the main online search tool associated with the Mesa Regional FHC is FamilySearch.org.

Arizona State Library and Archives
http://www.azlibrary.gov/archives/

The Arizona State Library has loads of information available, from microfilmed newspapers to private manuscript collections, city directories, biographical indexes, and more. While an index to most of these holdings is available online, the majority of this information has not been transcribed so that one can search by relatives' names. There are a few exceptions, however, and the "Biographical Database" may be the most helpful online tool. This is a database of names complied from obituaries, newspaper articles, books, and more. Search results will return the name of the individual found, along with source and title information so that the original documents can be consulted.

Clicking the link for "Genealogical Resources" brings up another list of helpful resources that are available. Some of these include assessment rolls (i.e., tax rolls), voter registration lists, prison records, land records, wills, and probate records. Most of this information isn't available online or even necessarily indexed, but lists of holdings seem to be complete.

Other links include the Arizona Memory Project, which has numerous family history collections, some of which pertain to specific families or counties. Others are more unique, like those pertaining to Arizona State University science pioneers, minutes from early-20th-century meetings, and mining fatality reports, the latter of which might include the names of workers injured or killed in mining accidents.

Specific research requests can be submitted online, and library staff will perform a minimal amount of research free of charge. Additional assistance requires a research fee.

Arizona State Genealogy Collection
http://www.lib.az.us/is/genealogy/index.aspx

This resource is similar in nature to the above. However, it is housed at the Law and Research Library and focuses more on books, microfilm, and computer resources from all 50 states (and some foreign countries), not only from Arizona. There's not much in the way of online indexes, but the library has on-site access to HeritageQuest and the Ancestry.com Library Edition.

Arizona Pioneers' Home Resident Index

http://www.sharlot.org/archives/gene/aph/index.html

The Arizona Pioneers' Home is a state-run retirement home for those who meet certain requirements. It was established in 1911 and the searchable index includes names, counties, and a page number that can be used to locate the actual record associated with a resident's indexed entry.

AZGenWeb

http://azgenweb.org/

The Arizona page of the USGenWeb Project has lots of helpful genealogy links, including some to the previously mentioned resources. In addition, there links to separate webpages for each Arizona county, as well as many different genealogical societies across the state.

Arkansas

Date of Statehood: 15 Jun 1836

Neighboring States: Louisiana, Mississippi, Missouri, Oklahoma, Tennessee, Texas

Previous Affiliations: Louisiana Territory, Missouri Territory, Territory of Arkansas (Arkansaw)

The land in present day Arkansas was first acquired by the United States when it was purchased from France as part of the Louisiana Purchase. At that point, it was part of the Louisiana Territory. When Louisiana became a state in 1812, present-day Arkansas became part of the Missouri Territory. In 1819, the Arkansaw Territory was established, though it contained both present-day Arkansas and much of present-day Oklahoma, not to mention an archaic, though more intuitive, spelling of the state's name. The territory's size decreased until its final extent became the state of Arkansas in 1836.

Arkansas Department of Health - Vital Records

http://www.healthy.arkansas.gov/programsServices/certificatesVitalRecords/

Vital records and certificates are available through the Department of Health, located in Little Rock. Keep in mind that this website doesn't have an online index but is simply the official channel through which to purchase vital records. Marriage records are available from 1917 onwards, but older records are located at the county level.

Arkansas History Commission (State Archives)

http://www.ark-ives.com/

The Arkansas History Commission is the official name of the State Archives. In addition to the main location in Little Rock, there are two other regional archives--Southwest Arkansas Regional Archives (SARA) and Northeast Arkansas Regional Archives (NEARA). Although the three locations house different information, all three use the same online search tool, CARAT. CARAT is, in addition to a unit of gemstone weight, the acronym for "Catalog of Arkansas Resources and Archival Treasures." From the CARAT homepage, one can search numerous collections. These include:

land records; Confederate pensions, home (assisted-living) records and 1911 questionnaires and reunion registrations; two separate negative/photographic collections; World War I discharge records; a Biodex--basically a vertical file index that is searchable by name. Some of these online collections are still works in progress.

County searches can also be performed, but these don't list individual names. Instead, one must search by county for a particular type of record, perhaps probate, marriage, or birth, and then look for that collection elsewhere, either at the Archives, in the Family History Library, or even through websites like FamilySearch.org or Ancestry.com. Keep in mind that some documents may not be available online and are only accessible through county records. None of the searches I performed through the CARAT website brought back original images.

If you find a Biodex, land, photograph, or other record that you would like a copy of, you have a couple of options. First, you can try to search other websites to see whether the collection is online and searchable elsewhere. Second, you can make a trip to the appropriate repository to look up the information yourself. And third, you can request the file be copied for you. Although the staff doesn't perform research, free or otherwise, they will make photocopies. The order forms are buried, so from the homepage click "Plan Your Visit," and then "How to Research." Clicking the Order-Forms link will bring up a number of different order forms, so just fill out the appropriate one and you're all set.

Other records (census, military, etc.) are available in person, but they are not searchable online. To find out whether a particular title is available, click on the Arkansas-Records-Catalog (Ark-Cat) link and a search page will pop up. Search results will present a brief summary of what each book or collection includes.

ARGenWeb
http://www.argenweb.net/

As with most state websites that are part of the USGenWeb Project, the Arkansas site has links to separate county webpages with specific research information. While the site has a lot of information (including a list of volunteers willing to do lookups for you), in my mind, the most valuable link is the Genealogy-Research-in-Arkansas one. Click on the Arkansas-Research link on the homepage, and the first option should be "Genealogy Research in Arkansas." This will bring up another webpage full of links, some of which are quite helpful. While most don't have online indexes for locating your ancestors, there is a lot of information about where records can be found, by whom they were transcribed, and whether collections are complete. Lists of genealogical societies, libraries, and archives (some of which we've discussed already) are also provided.

Another link is to the RootsWeb page for Arkansas. As mentioned briefly in the previous chapter, RootsWeb is a project largely composed of user-contributed information and websites. As such, some links provide valuable information while others only cover information we've already discussed. There is definitely a lot of good information, though you may have to dig to find your relatives.

Arkansas Genealogical Society (AGS)

http://www.agsgenealogy.org/

The AGS has a few unique resources for the Arkansas researcher. First of all, the AGS makes all of its quarterly publications available and searchable online. As these publications may include family histories, indexes, queries, and more, they can be quite helpful. AGS also provides online PDF files of member-submitted Ancestry Charts and Family Group Sheets, as well as an index to Arkansas Ancestry Certificates, certificates granted to early settlers of the state.

California

Date of Statehood: 9 Sep 1850
Neighboring States: Arizona, Nevada, Oregon, Country of Mexico
Previous Affiliations: Spain, Mexico

The entirety of the current state of California was ceded by Mexico to the United States as part of the 1848 Treaty of Guadalupe Hidalgo. As part of the Compromise-of-1850 package of bills, California gained statehood with its current borders without ever being a territory.

California Department of Public Health - Vital Records

http://www.cdph.ca.gov/certlic/birthdeathmar/Pages/default.aspx

Vital records for the state are maintained by the Department of Public Health, though there is no searchable online index. If you don't need an index and just want to order a certificate, birth and death records are available from 1905 onwards. Marriage records are better obtained at the county level, as are birth and death records from prior to 1905.

California Digital Newspaper Collection

http://cdnc.ucr.edu/

This collection contains California newspapers that are out of copyright protection (at the time of writing, this included newspapers from before 1923). According to the website, newspapers that have been digitized as part of the National Digital Newspaper Program are also available on the Chronicling-America website that was discussed in the previous chapter.

California Genealogical Society (CGS)

http://californiaancestors.org/

This library is located in Oakland, and daily-use fees are $5 if you're not a Society member. While a name index is searchable online, you'll only find basic information since source documents haven't been digitized. However, locating your ancestor through the index may help you decide if you would like to order the pertinent file or pay a staff member to do research on your behalf.

A couple of online databases are available to the general public, but others are only accessible if you're a member of the Society. Somewhat surprisingly, the CGS Manuscript database, one of the few items available to the general public, isn't limited to surnames with early ties to California. In fact, some finding aids only discuss family names and their histories on the east coast or in the Midwest, not mentioning California at all.

A list of documents available at the library can also be found online.

Family History Libraries and Centers

The Family History Library (FHL) in Salt Lake City has numerous affiliated libraries located in California. The largest of these are located in Los Angeles, Oakland, Sacramento, San Diego, and Orange County. As with other facilities affiliated with the FHL, the main website is FamilySearch.org, though each library/center may also have its own site. Holdings for these facilities vary but include thousands of books and rolls of microfilm.

CAGenWeb
http://cagenweb.com/

The California website for the USGenWeb Project has an online map collection and links to individual county webpages. If users don't want to browse by county, then they can use the website's search feature to locate their relatives.

The website appears to have been redesigned recently and while the appearance is clean, I had some trouble locating many of the valuable links that were more easily accessible before the redesign. By digging through the options on the "Search" page, one will locate the California Pioneer Project, a compilation of early California settlers (those who were born in or migrated to the state before 1880).

Other transcribed items, whether accessible through county-level webpages or the California portion of the USGenWeb Archives, include pioneers, biographical records, directories, wills and probate, and even church records. Many of these items are only for a limited time period in a limited number of counties, so they shouldn't be considered definitive collections.

Foreign-Born Voters of California in 1872
http://www.jwfgenresearch.com/GR1872Home.htm

Put together by Jim W. Faulkinbury, this section of his website has an index to all foreign-born voters in the state of California in 1872. If you're looking for San-Francisco-specific information, the website also has a few collections that were compiled from local newspaper records.

California State Library
http://www.library.ca.gov/research/#cal

The California State Library has numerous collections and genealogical resources. Some highlights include U.S. Federal Censuses, an indexed 1852 state census, voter registers, marriage and death indexes, directories, newspaper indexes, biographical files, and the California Information File. While some of these resources are searchable online by location and keyword, it appears that none can be searched online by name. For that, you'll need to visit the library in Sacramento and perform the research yourself. Alternately, the library can provide a list of private researchers, though library staff members are unable to do research themselves.

California State Archives
http://www.sos.ca.gov/archives/collections/family-history-resources.htm

The California State Archives' website includes holdings' information for county records and other collections of interest to family history researchers. In general, the "Family History Resources" webpage indicates whether each collection is indexed or not, though most of these indexes aren't online.

For purposes of locating your ancestors through the website, try the index to Spanish and Mexican land grants or the California Youth Authority index. The latter includes names from three schools, all of which appear to have been set up for juvenile offender reform.

Early California Population Project
http://www.huntington.org/Information/ECPPlogin.htm

This is a database, developed by the Huntington Library, which contains information from mission registers for the years 1769 to 1850. Available information includes baptismal, marriage, and burial records. Access is free, but it does require that you enter your name and email address. In my personal opinion, the search page is a little bit cumbersome. However, for information you're not likely to find elsewhere, this is a great resource. There are also some helpful write-ups on how to use the search features and the database itself.

Colorado

Date of Statehood: 1 Aug 1876

Neighboring States: Kansas, Nebraska, New Mexico, Oklahoma, Utah, Wyoming, Arizona (kitty-corner)

Previous Affiliations: Louisiana Territory, Missouri Territory, Kansas Territory, Nebraska Territory, New Mexico Territory, Utah Territory, Mexico, Texas (country and state)

The western portion of present-day Colorado was under Spanish and then Mexican control until the United States acquired it in 1848 via the Treaty of Guadalupe Hidalgo. A portion of this area was also governed by the Republic of Texas from 1836 to 1845 and then the state of Texas afterwards. In exchange for debt relief, Texas gave up its land holdings in present-day Colorado and elsewhere as part of the Compromise of 1850. The Utah and New Mexico Territories were also established at that time, and portions of each would later become part of the Colorado Territory. The eastern portion of present-day Colorado was purchased from France as part of the Louisiana Purchase (there were other minor border changes, but they're not really important to our discussion). This became the Louisiana Territory and later the Missouri Territory. After Missouri became a state, the rest of the area wasn't immediately reorganized; as such, it was considered an unorganized territory. In 1854, the Kansas and Nebraska Territories were established, and portions of each would go on to become part of the Colorado Territory when it was established in 1861. The bottom line is that present-day Colorado evolved from numerous directions until all of its separate parts were finally brought together to form what we know today as the state of Colorado.

Colorado State Archives

http://www.colorado.gov/dpa/doit/archives/

If you're looking for Colorado-specific genealogy information, this website should be your first stop. Loads of collections have been indexed and each is searchable online, including miscellaneous county collections from before the state began requiring vital-records information itself. More databases are being indexed all the time, but in addition to old county-level records, one may find probate case records, school censuses, eighth-grade promotions, wills, teacher certificates issued, tax lists, and a penitentiary index. Remember that some of these databases are limited to a select number of counties and some counties only have minimal records available. If the record you want isn't online, that doesn't mean it doesn't exist. Consider contacting the State Archives to find out.

The simplest way to search the website is to click on the "Historical Records Database" link. This will bring up a webpage with a list of all indexed collections. Search results won't include full transcripts of documents nor images of said documents, but you may find enough information to confirm that the record pertains to your ancestor (i.e., you might find a familiar name in a marriage, divorce, or court record). If you locate an interesting record, you can add it to your inquiry by clicking the button at the top of the results page. When you add records to your inquiry, all you're really doing is compiling those records into a list that you can view by following the "view your selected records" link. You aren't actually able to order those records online, but the website provides information on how request them. An alternate search option is to follow the "On-Line Indexes" link and search or browse specific collections individually.

One note about the search feature is that it only returns 200 results. If all you have is a common last name and a broad date range, this can be an issue because you're likely to end up with far more than 200 results. Since results are returned alphabetically you'll never see any records that pertain to individuals whose first names start with a letter from the end of the alphabet. If you're having trouble getting around the 200-result maximum, try limiting the date range or limiting the number of collections you're searching. You may have to repeat this process multiple times, but hopefully it will allow you to see every result.

Other links from the Archives' homepage include a Digital Archives website which has original images of numerous documents (not likely any you want) and a Family History website which is much more helpful. The links on this webpage contain information about vital records, penitentiary and corrections records, the Civilian Conservation Corps (CCC), an old city directory, and more. It appears that some of this information, like the corrections records, shows up in the search results for the Historical Records Database, described above. Other collections, like the city directory and the CCC index, don't seem to show up in the search results, so you'll need to search them separately. Finally, the vital-records links take you to the Colorado-Department-of-Public-Health-and-Environment's website so you can order certified copies of records.

This write-up has gotten rather long, but the last thing to mention is that you can visit the Archives yourself and do your own research. At the time of writing, the public research room was open Monday through Friday, with the exception of Wednesday.

Denver Public Library

http://denverlibrary.org/research-topics/125
http://digital.denverlibrary.org/cdm/genealogy/

The Denver Library's genealogical offerings have been rated in the top ten for public libraries across America. Although some online searches are restricted to library card holders, other searches are accessible to the general public.

The first helpful item is a link to the Catholic Archdiocese of Denver. Here, one can search an archive of the *Denver Catholic Register*, although only by keyword, not by surname specifically. The second, more helpful item is an obituary index. To access it, simply click on the link for the "Denver Obituary Index." This will bring up a list of years that have been indexed for the *Denver Post* and the *Rocky Mountain News*; each year is linked to a PDF file that contains names and obituary dates for the deceased.

Strangely, obituary indexes for additional years are available through the library's Digital Collections page. Just click on the second link above, and you'll be greeted with a list genealogical collections--the obituary section will lead you to the previously mentioned extra indexes. There are also indexes for collections related to pioneers, insurance files, the military, burials, tax assessments, marriages, and more. I didn't find a surname search specifically, but the search-bar returns fairly good results.

The "Genealogy and Obituaries" section of the library's website (the first link above) is most helpful if you're a library card holder, so my recommendation is to search it quickly so you can focus your time on the digital genealogical collections accessible through the second link.

Colorado Historic Newspapers Collection

http://coloradohistoricnewspapers.org/

This collection has digital copies of many Colorado newspapers from the years 1859 to 1923 (at the time of writing). Digitization is ongoing so check the website to determine which newspapers are already online. If a newspaper of interest hasn't been digitized yet, the website provides contact information for the Colorado Historical Society, an institution that can help locate a print or microfilm copy.

According to the FAQ, some newspaper articles might have been split into multiple articles accidentally due to the computer software used. In these cases, the user should view the full page of the newspaper as opposed to just the article itself.

Colorado Genealogical Society (CGS)

http://www.cogensoc.us

The CGS website provides an extensive list of online resources and research locations for those doing genealogical research in Colorado. While we've discussed some of these resources at length already, there are many more that we're unable to discuss due to space constraints. In addition to the list of resources, my favorite part of the website is the surname index for *The Colorado Genealogist*, the Society's quarterly journal.

COGenWeb

http://cogenweb.com

A great resource for locating county-specific webpages, this site also has loads of miscellaneous information available. Since some of this information was user-submitted, it's not all-encompassing and you'll have to dig around to find out if your ancestors are online. Military, obituary, and cemetery information is available, as well as a listing of historic towns and cities located in the Colorado-Places Special Project. This is my favorite section of the website, as it provides a directory to cities and towns in Colorado, along with the county those cities and towns are (or were) located in.

Connecticut

Date of Statehood: 9 Jan 1788
Neighboring States: Massachusetts, New York, Rhode Island
Previous Affiliations: New Haven Colony, Saybrook Colony, Dominion of
    New England, Connecticut Colony

As with many of the original colonies, there was a period of boundary fluidity for the Connecticut Colony. That is to say, the borders of the colony weren't terribly well established and changed somewhat regularly. The Connecticut Colony merged with the Saybrook Colony first and then the New Haven Colony, both in the mid-1600s. Although Connecticut claimed areas encompassing most of Rhode Island, Long Island, and even westward through parts of Pennsylvania, Ohio, Michigan, and beyond, most of these claims were resolved before the Constitution was signed. Likewise, several other colonies claimed areas in present-day Connecticut, but these, too, were mostly resolved before the signing of the Constitution.

There are, however, a couple of notable exceptions. Connecticut didn't give up its claim to northeastern Ohio until 1800, the last claim the state held so far west. The other exception has to do with the Southwick Jog, a small notch in the top of the state's border. Due to an incorrect survey of the Connecticut/Massachusetts border, the states had trouble agreeing on which state the land belonged to. Eventually an agreement was reached, and the area was divided between the two states in 1804.

Connecticut State Library and State Archives
http://www.cslib.org/handg.htm

As opposed to many states where the two are separate, the Connecticut State Library website also doubles as the State Archives' website. We'll briefly discuss the "History and Genealogy" section of the State Library's website (the link I've included above) first, links to digital collections second, and the State Archives third.

From the State Library's "History and Genealogy" section (the link above), one will find collection-specific information as well as how to contact local researchers if you're unable to visit the library yourself. There are also write-ups on genealogical indexes, although most of the indexes themselves aren't searchable or viewable through the library's website yet. Available onsite indexes include: the Barbour Collection, a compilation of early vital records; newspaper notices; church records; census information; bible records; probate records. Although these collections aren't directly searchable on the library's website, some of this data has been microfilmed and can be searched through sites like Ancestry.com and FamilySearch.org. Alternately, library staff will search the indexes for a fee.

Another valuable tool the library provides is the Digital Collections section of the website. Since the digital collections don't all pertain to genealogy, only a select number of them will aid your search. From the Digital Collections homepage, the best category to browse is "Personal and Family Vital Records." If you're looking for a particular name, just type it in the search bar and see what comes up. In my experience, the search returns accurate results without having to visually scan each document yourself.

Finally, the State Archives (**http://www.cslib.org/archives/**) has a number of additional resources. My favorite feature of this website is the online database collection. These databases are searchable by name, and at the time of writing, available databases included: records pertaining to Connecticut veterans of the Civil War, the Spanish-American War, and WWI; prison records; court records pertaining to minorities. Since the State Archives has started making these databases available online, it seems likely that more will come online in the future. While these indexes provide valuable information, they do not include images of original documents.

If you plan to visit, you should know that the State Archives are located at the State Library in Hartford, Connecticut.

CTGenWeb
http://www.ctgenweb.org/

The Connecticut GenWeb website provides links to separate webpages for each county in the state. Many external genealogical links are provided, as well as contact information for volunteers who will look up your ancestors in collections they own or have access to.

Connecticut Society of Genealogists (CSG)
http://www.csginc.org/

The CSG puts out a quarterly publication entitled *The Connecticut Nutmegger*. While the quarterly has been indexed and a surname search is available, one must sign up as a member in order to access digital copies of *The Nutmegger*.

Alternately, copies may be available at local libraries. Try searching the WorldCat website, discussed in the previous chapter, to find out. Society members have access to additional online material.

Dunham-Wilcox-Trott-Kirk
http://dunhamwilcox.net/

This website is named after the owner's grandparents, and it contains a wealth of information about Connecticut, several other New England states, and the owner's home state, Michigan. Lots of information, from collections like the Barbour Collection (vital records), church records, deeds, and more, has been transcribed and organized by county. Other transcribed data comes from out-of-copyright publications. With over five-million visitors, those who can trace their ancestry to Connecticut (and the surrounding area) are certainly taking advantage of this website.

Delaware

Date of Statehood: 7 Dec 1787
Neighboring States: Maryland, New Jersey, Pennsylvania
Previous Affiliations: Virginia Colony, Maryland Colony, Province of
    Pennsylvania

When the Maryland Colony was formed in 1632, it contained all of present-day Delaware. After the Province of Pennsylvania was formed, William Penn petitioned for land west of the Delaware River. Although this area was given to Pennsylvania and the two colonies continued to dispute ownership, boundaries were more clearly defined by the Mason-Dixon Line in the 1760s. At the time of the Revolutionary War, Delaware established a separate state government from Pennsylvania and went on to become the first state in the United States.

Delaware Public Archives
http://archives.delaware.gov/
There are a couple of ways to look for genealogical information on the Delaware State Archives' website. The first, and easiest, way is with the name search located on the bottom of the Archives' homepage. Just type in your ancestor's name and see what you can find. Numerous collections, such as death registers, naturalizations, probate records, orphans court records, and bastardy bonds (yes, that's the correct term and spelling) are included in the search. If you find a record you're interested in, you can enter your email address and someone will contact you with a price quote for a copy of the original record. Otherwise, you can make note of the information and visit the Archives yourself.

Another helpful tool is the Digital Archives section. While not all of the digital records pertain to family history, several collections do. The "Documents" section is broken down into categories, several of which-- coroner's reports, naturalizations, orphan case files--have links to individual files. Each of these contains images of original documents which may provide more information. Only a few cases are accessible in the coroner's-reports section, but each one is multiple pages long and contains depositions pertinent to the case.

The Civil War section of the Digital Archives also has some very helpful information. First, find your ancestor in the soldier lookup. The files are alphabetized, but you'll have to scroll through each indexed image until you find your ancestor. His index card should indicate what company or regiment he was in. Next, in order to access your ancestor's compiled service records, select his unit from the dropdown menu. Names of soldiers in each unit are once again presented in alphabetical order.

In the "Public/Finding Aids" section of the website, there are webpages which provide lists of historical societies, record repositories, churches, libraries, universities, museums, and pretty much any other entity which may hold historical records.

A Delaware library card will grant users free access to collections that Ancestry.com "has digitized for the Delaware Public Archives."

Delaware Genealogical Society (DGS)
http://www.delgensoc.org/

The DGS website has quite a bit of information. Not only are there surname databases for the *Delaware Genealogical Society Journal* and queries submitted to DGS, but there are also numerous other indexed publications available for purchase. Some of these publications are on CD while others are available in print. Available publications include 1782 tax and census lists, orphan records, probate records, marriage and death notices from newspapers, and even a research guide for the state. The research guide received high praise in a 2005 *National Genealogical Society Quarterly* review, so it might be a good tool for Delaware-related research. There are also external links to other national and state-specific resources, as well as an entire page of websites that focuses on families who lived in Delaware before 1860. Be aware that some of the links were not functional at the time of writing.

DEGenWeb
http://theusgenweb.org/de/

Although there are only three counties in Delaware, the Delaware GenWeb website still has links for separate webpages dedicated to each individual county. In addition, it has lists of libraries and genealogical societies in the state, as well as external links to other genealogical websites.

Catholic Cemeteries Database

http://www.cdow.org/csdatabase.html

Although FindAGrave.com is endeavoring to list gravestones from cemeteries across the country (and world) already, this website is searchable by name for three different cemeteries. It might seem like a waste of time to search this website, but when I tried to cross-check the names I found with those on FindAGrave, I learned that some names listed in the Catholic Cemetery database were not on FindAGrave at all, at least at the time of writing. On the off-chance that your relatives could be buried in any of these cemeteries, do yourself a favor and run a quick search.

Delaware Historical Society

http://www.hsd.org/gengd.htm

The Society's research library is open to the public during the week, with the exception of Wednesdays. Hours vary so make sure to check timing before you visit. Although the material held by the library is not fully indexed online, a genealogical surname file does exist at the library. A step-by-step research guide is available on the website and provides information on Delaware-specific resources to consult. If you're unable to visit the library yourself, the staff will do preliminary research for a fee, but the time of the search is not meant to exceed one hour.

Florida

Date of Statehood: 3 Mar 1845
Neighboring States: Alabama, Georgia
Previous Affiliations: Britain, Spain, Florida Territory

Under British and Spanish rule, the Florida panhandle extended farther west than it does today. When the Spanish-controlled West Florida Territory declared its independence, this area was annexed by the United States three months later; portions of it were added to the Orleans Territory and the Mississippi Territory, while Spain retained present-day Florida. Although the area was still in dispute, the Adams-Onís Treaty of 1819 settled matters, granting ownership of Florida to the United States while giving Spain more land in Texas and New Mexico, land that the United States had previously claimed was part of the Louisiana Purchase. The Florida Territory was created shortly after the Adams- Onís Treaty was ratified.

Florida Memory

http://floridamemory.com/

The Florida Memory website was created to provide access to archived material in both the State Library and the State Archives. Documents are searchable by name and images of the originals are returned. Some of the available collections include WWI service cards, Spanish land grants, and Confederate pension applications. A searchable photography collection is also online.

State Archives of Florida

http://dlis.dos.state.fl.us/index_researchers.cfm

The website for the State Archives allows users to search its holdings online. Just click on the "Archives Online Catalog" to get started. Try locating your relatives in the online index or simply browse the collections to see if they might be of assistance; the website will return Series/Collection numbers for each item in the search results. Use that information to access the records by either visiting the Archives yourself or having a researcher make copies on your behalf. See the website for details on research assistance and copying fees. Some archival material is available through the above mentioned "Florida Memory" website.

State Library of Florida
http://dlis.dos.state.fl.us/Library/

While the library has lots of genealogical links, a few are more helpful than others (in my opinion). The first is the "Electronic Databases" link. Although many of these electronic databases require a library card, others, like "Florida on Florida," do not.§

The second is the "Collections" link on the left-hand side of the webpage, a subtopic of which will lead the genealogist to the Reference Department. Here, one will find a list of newspaper holdings on microfilm, a link to the Florida Collection, and several genealogical resources and indexes.

FLGenWeb
https://sites.google.com/a/flgenweb.net/official/

This website provides links to individual county webpages, as well as information on Native Americans and a surname spreadsheet. Special Projects include marriage, cemetery, and obituary collections.

Florida State Genealogical Society
http://www.flsgs.org/index.php

For me, the most interesting feature of this website is the Pioneer Index. This is an index of individuals who were living in Florida prior to statehood. Since any descendent who has already been awarded a pioneer certificate must have had appropriate supporting documentation, if you find your ancestors here, you can bet there's at least one traceable line to the present. A member surname search is also online. Other in-progress projects relate to cemetery and county-level records. Although the *Florida Genealogist* publication is available for purchase on CD, it doesn't appear to be searchable online at this time.

---

§ The name "Florida on Florida" reminds me of the HGTV television show *Holmes on Homes* and the Rodney Carrington song "Fred's Riding Fred," a hilarious listen if you're so inclined.

Georgia

Date of Statehood: 2 Jan 1788

Neighboring States: Alabama, Florida, North Carolina, South Carolina, Tennessee

Previous Affiliations: Georgia Colony, Province of Carolina, Province of South Carolina

Georgia was the last of the thirteen original colonies, having received its charter in 1732. The colony was formed from some of the land that was originally part of the Province of Carolina (and then the Province of South Carolina). Although Georgia's charter specified that its boundaries extended westward, as many of the original colonies' charters did, the Georgia Colony's area didn't initially extend as far south as it does today. Eventually, the colony claimed land to the south to the border of Spanish Florida and to the west to the Mississippi River. A small sliver of land at the state's northern border was claimed by South Carolina until 1787, and the western border was set in its current location after the Yazoo land scandal in the early 1800s. Occasional lawsuits regarding the Georgia/South Carolina border have also been heard over the years.

Georgia Archives

http://www.sos.ga.gov/archives/InformationForGeneralPublic/default.htm

From the Georgia Archives' website, one can search digital or paper records online. If searching for digital records, one will use what the state calls Georgia's Virtual Vault. The Virtual Vault's search tool at the top of the webpage includes all of the site's digital collections (e.g., deed books, church records, colonial wills, Confederate documents, county records, death certificates, a plat index, marriage records). Some of these resources, like the County Records Microfilm Index, are merely scanned card catalogs that show the holdings of the Archives; the records themselves are not actually searchable or viewable online. Other records, like the wills and deed book collections, are scanned and viewable online. Keep in mind that although wills are indexed by the name of the deceased, they have not been fully transcribed. Other collections, like Chatham County Deed Books, haven't been indexed yet, so the search tool might not return a pertinent record even if it has already been digitized. You will probably have to read through these unindexed collections on your own to determine whether the information pertains to your relatives.

When searching paper records, several links return users to the Virtual Vault while others provide finding aids for any items identified in the Archives' holdings. The Archives also provides information on hiring professional researchers, as the Archives' staff is unable to perform research themselves.

GAGenWeb
http://www.rootsweb.ancestry.com/~gagenweb/

Although loads of resources are discussed and made available on the GAGenWeb website, the best information (in my opinion) appears to be the data presented on the county-specific webpages. Other special projects on the website include cemetery, census, and military projects.

Georgia Genealogical Society
http://www.gagensociety.org/

The Georgia Genealogical Society puts out a quarterly publication creatively named *Georgia Genealogical Society Quarterly (GGSQ)*. If you're a member of the Society, you can search the first twenty years of the *GGSQ* by name, and PDF files for those years are also online. Members also have access to naturalization records, some land records from the 1770s, and copies from "some later years" of the *GGSQ*. A member surname exchange and links to other genealogical societies are also online, and these are free even to non-members. Non-members can also browse the table of contents from volumes nine through forty-one of the *GGSQ*.

Georgia Pioneers
http://www.georgiapioneers.com/

The Georgia Pioneers website has a lot of valuable information for Georgia genealogical research. Loads of material is available to members, though not much free content is available to non-members. The site is subscription-based, so you might want to look over which records are available to members before you pay for your subscription. That being said, the website was developed by Jeannette Holland Austin, a professional genealogist and prolific author on the subject, so I have to believe that the content is worth your time and money. Not having any relatives from Georgia, I haven't had a need to research through her website; as such, I cannot speak from personal experience.

Hawaii

Date of Statehood: 21 Aug 1959
Neighboring States: Does the Pacific Ocean count??
Previous Affiliations: Kingdom of Hawaii, Republic of Hawaii, Territory of
Hawaii

The United States annexed the Republic of Hawaii and created the Territory of Hawaii in 1898. It remained that way until statehood.

Hawaii State Archives

http://ags.hawaii.gov/archives/

The Hawaii State Archives might not be where you want to spend your Hawaiian vacation, and that's okay. Because Hawaii has some good online indexes and databases, you may not have to visit in person at all.

The site's Genealogy webpage is probably the best place to start. It provides links to indexes and databases that cover vital records, ship manifests, naturalizations, and more. These resources are discussed in the following two sections.

Several forms are also available so that one can order copies of original documents if unable to find said documents online and unable to visit the Archives in person.

Hawaiian Genealogy Indexes

http://ulukau.org/gsdl2.7/cgi-bin/algene

This website has digitized, searchable images of the Hawaii State Archives' vital-records indexes. Although online images are of the indexes themselves and not the original records, indexes are arranged by island and include death, marriage, divorce, and citizenship records. Depending on the type of record, you may find a date and a source reference (i.e., book and page number) to follow up with. If you aren't able to visit yourself, you may want to order a record using the forms mentioned above in the Hawaii-State-Archives section.

Hawaii State Archives Digital Collections

http://archives1.dags.hawaii.gov/gsdl/cgi-bin/library

The digital collections of the State Archives include images from many Hawaiian genealogical resources. Some of these collections include ship manifests, WWI records, land and name records, and more. There is even a vital-records collection which provides copies of source documents, as opposed to the previously mentioned website which only provides images of indexes. Keep in mind that some of these records may be in Hawaiian, not English.

Finally, it's important to remember that digitization is still a work in progress and not all records housed by the Archives are available online. The search bar doesn't cover every digital collection either, so make sure you remember to separately check those collections not covered by the search tool itself.

HIGenWeb

http://www.higenweb.org/

As Hawaii's website for the USGenWeb project, HIGenWeb provides county-based information, as well as links to many other Hawaiian and national genealogical resources.

University of Hawaii at Mānoa Library - Genealogy

http://guides.library.manoa.hawaii.edu/genealogyhawaii

There are a lot of valuable resources on this website. Although much of the information merely discusses library holdings, an anti-annexation petition and several newspaper indexes are among the online collections that might mention your ancestors by name. Some of the online indexes are accessible through the following resource.

University of Hawaii at Mānoa Library - Hawaiian and Pacific Collections

http://library.manoa.hawaii.edu/departments/hp/

Associated with the above resource, this website hosts additional collections that pertain specifically to Hawaii and the Pacific Islands. Not every item is genealogically relevant, but there are quite a few newspaper indexes, as well as an oral interview index.

Hawaiian Roots

http://www.hawaiian-roots.com/

This non-profit Hawaiian genealogical website has lots of good information about everything from land records and ship manifests to newspaper obituaries and censuses. This is a well-thought-out website that provides a wealth of information on how to get your Hawaiian family history research started on the right foot.

BYU Hawaii - Archives and Special Collections

http://library.byuh.edu/library/archives

The Church of Latter-day Saints has done it again, providing lots of valuable information about Hawaiian genealogy. There are photographic collections, yearbooks from BYU-Hawaii, collections of interviews and diaries, and a collection of more than 100,000 records of sugar plantation workers from the early part of the 20th century.

Idaho

Date of Statehood: 3 Jul 1890

Neighboring States: Montana, Nevada, Oregon, Utah, Washington, Wyoming, Country of Canada

Previous Affiliations: Oregon Territory, Washington Territory, Idaho Territory

The Idaho Territory was formed in 1863 and was, at that time, substantially larger than the state is today; it encompassed Montana as well as most of Wyoming. Portions of the Idaho Territory were split off to form the Montana Territory and later the Wyoming Territory until the present boundaries of the state were attained in 1868.

Idaho State Historical Society (ISHS)

http://history.idaho.gov/

Established as a state agency in 1907, the ISHS is in charge of several historic resources including the Idaho State Archives. To access a list of the Society's holdings and online resources, simply point your mouse to the "Connect with Collections" tab at the top-center of the webpage. While hovering there, you'll see a drop-down menu, from which you should select "Archive Collections." From this webpage, one will learn what newspapers and county-level records are available in the Archives. The Archives also has numerous yearbooks, a collection of death certificates, photographs, maps, and more. Research requests can be submitted online, for which fees may apply. However, not everything is available online.

To see if your ancestors turn up in any of the online indexes, simply click on the "Searchable Indexes" link on the left-hand side of the webpage. There are indexes for Civil War soldiers, naturalizations, inmates, pension records, a general biographical index, and even an attempt at reconstructing who lived in Idaho around 1890, the year of the largely destroyed Federal Census. These indexes are all transcribed and each one opens as a separate PDF file. Unfortunately, this means that the original images associated with the indexed entries are not available directly. That's where our next resource comes in.

Idaho Digital Archives

http://idahohistory.cdmhost.com/cdm

The Idaho Digital Archives are associated with the ISHS, mentioned above, and as such can be reached from that website also. Since digitization is an ongoing process, most of the indexes mentioned in the previous section are not yet available online. However, there are several collections of photographs, oral histories, and information related to the CCC, the mining industry, and even Civil War soldiers. At the moment, this doesn't appear to be the most genealogically relevant site (it's lacking in digitized vital records), but you may get lucky and locate your relatives anyhow. If your ancestors were named in a photograph's or document's description, you might locate them by simply typing their name in the search bar at the top of the page.

Libraries Linking Idaho: LiLI

http://lili.org/

This is the Idaho Commission for Libraries' online portal for Idaho residents. HeritageQuest is a genealogical database available through the website (for Idaho residents only), but in glancing through the LiLI.org offerings, it doesn't appear that non-residents are missing out on much else.

BYU Idaho - Special Collections & Family History

http://abish.byui.edu/specialcollections/famhist

BYU has a well-built website with several searchable online indexes, including the Western States Marriage Index (discussed in the previous chapter), two separate death indexes, and an index of Japanese immigrants. Some death records include names of parents or even newspaper obituary information, while others simply provide names and dates. The Japanese immigrant index is searchable by name, but if you find your ancestors, don't forget to click on the associated links below their names. If the initial record you located was for the original immigrant, the associated links may detail family members, residences, occupations, and more.

There are several helpful learning guides and numerous links to resources that focus on other western states. We've already discussed most of the Idaho links presented (elsewhere in the chapter), but one additional item is an obituary index for the *Idaho Statesman*. The index, which goes back to the 1960s, is actually available through the Boise Public Library (**http://www.boisepubliclibrary.org**). If you have a Boise library card, you aren't limited to the index, since you can also search and access the newspaper's archives online.

Family History Centers

The Family History Library (FHL) in Salt Lake City has numerous affiliated centers located in Idaho. The largest of these are located in Idaho Falls and Pocatello. As with other facilities affiliated with the FHL, the main website is FamilySearch.org, though each center may also have its own website. Holdings for these facilities vary but include thousands of books and rolls of microfilm.

Idaho Genealogical Society (IGS)
http://www.idahogenealogy.org/

Although few databases are online, the Idaho Genealogical Society's website is still one you should consider visiting. There are links to county resources, old maps that detail enumeration irregularities (for example, the Idaho Territory's portion of Yellowstone National Park was enumerated with Wyoming from 1880 to 1920), IGS publications are available for purchase, and one can even apply for several certificates if your ancestors were among Idaho's earliest settlers. An online surname index to *Footprints through Idaho*, a publication related to early settlers, is available online.

IDGenWeb
http://www.idgenweb.org/

The Idaho version of the USGenWeb project contains the usual links to county-specific webpages and resources. Some of IDGenWeb's other links relate to the websites discussed above, and external resources for various ethnic groups in Idaho are also presented. While a separate IDGenWeb project is related to Native Americans in the state and some interesting information is presented there, a cursory search didn't provide much of genealogical interest.

Illinois

Date of Statehood: 3 Dec 1818

Neighboring States: Indiana, Iowa, Kentucky, Missouri, Wisconsin

Previous Affiliations: Northwest Territory, Indiana Territory, Illinois
Territory

After the Revolutionary War ended and the United States acquired the rest
of the British landholdings to the Mississippi River, the Northwest Ordinance
was passed to create the Northwest Territory in 1787. This territory included
the area west of the state of Pennsylvania, north of the Ohio River, and east
of the Mississippi River; as such, it included the entirety of the present-day
states of Michigan, Illinois, Indiana, and Wisconsin, as well as portions of
Minnesota and Ohio. The Illinois Territory was established in 1809 from the
Indiana Territory, and it included the current state as well as present-day
Wisconsin and portions of Minnesota and Michigan.

Illinois State Archives Databases

http://www.cyberdriveillinois.com/departments/archives/databases/
home.html

The Illinois State Archives' website hosts a ton of indexed databases,
including those pertaining to marriage and death records, veterans,
emancipation, land records, and probate and wills in various counties.
Although some of these searches don't provide a whole lot of information
besides a name and case number, that information can then be used to track
down the original files through county or state records that aren't fully
transcribed online. And depending on the collection, you might even be able
to find some of the records elsewhere online. For example, the statewide
death index for 1916 to 1950 only includes name, date and place of death,
sex, possibly age, and the death certificate number. However, the
corresponding documents are more fully transcribed and available on
websites like Ancestry.com; this more fully transcribed version of the
collection includes information about the deceased's parents.

If nothing else, this website will let you know if a record for your ancestor
exists, and you can look for the original in the correct location. For a fee, the
Illinois State Archives staff will assist you on your research.

While some original records listed on the Archives' website are housed at the Illinois State Archives, other records are part of the Illinois Regional Archives Depositories (IRAD) and are housed elsewhere. Once you find your relative, take note of where that record is located. It would be a shame to show up at the State Archives looking for a record, only to learn you're in the wrong place. If you need assistance and are unable to visit one of the IRAD locations yourself, free research assistance is provided, though photocopy charges may be applicable.

Finally, not all of the Archives' holdings have been indexed and made searchable online. In order to find out what other holdings each IRAD facility has, click on the "Local Government Records in the IRAD System" link. Here, you can search either by county, subject, or repository.

If one of the IRAD locations doesn't have the county vital records (for example, death records) that you need, your next option is to consult the county clerk where the death actually occurred. This may also require a fee.

ILGenWeb Project
http://ilgenweb.net/

As with other USGenWeb sites, ILGenWeb provides links to individual county webpages. Unlike some other websites, there are also transcriptions for 1883 Civil War pensioners from many counties. User-submitted information and links to other genealogical societies are also online.

Illinois State Library
http://cyberdriveillinois.com/departments/library/

Although the State Archives has more information online, the State Library's website is still worth visiting. The Illinois Veterans' History Project is searchable by name, and most of the data appears to be from WWI onward. For the project, veterans and their families could submit information and remembrances, and much of this information is available in the Illinois Digital Archives, our next topic.

The Digital Archives link is located partway down the homepage for the State Library. A multitude of records are accessible through the website, including the previously mentioned Veterans' History Project. There isn't space to list the entire holdings here, but some items of interest are local historical records, photographs, and letters.

The library is open Monday through Friday for public use, but the staff doesn't handle research requests. If you're unable to visit yourself, many resources are on microfilm and can be shared through interlibrary loans. Some records available at the library include federal and state censuses, as well as numerous military records.

Illinois Historic Preservation Agency (IHPA) - Newspaper Index
http://www.illinoishistory.gov/lib/default.htm

Some of the resources available through the IHPA are also available through the Abraham Lincoln Presidential Library, a division of the IHPA (see below), so don't be surprised when you bounce between the two websites. The first item of note is an index to the *Illinois State Journal* (and its predecessors) from 1831 to 1860. The index is presented in two massive PDF files, so if you've got a slow Internet connection, you may have to wait for it to load. As the content is in alphabetical order and is also searchable, these files are great resources to use when looking for references to your relatives.

The other two databases, a surname search and a newspaper obituary search, can be accessed through links on the right-hand side of the webpage. While these searches are far from comprehensive, they do provide a valuable source of information. If you find a relative of yours, you'll also receive information about the source document so you can follow up yourself (or have a researcher make a copy the information for you). Obituaries provide a newspaper name and date, while the surname search provides the book and page number of the biographical sketch. Some of the books referred to by the surname search have been digitized and are available online through websites like Google or the Internet Archive, as discussed in the previous chapter.

Abraham Lincoln Presidential Library
http://www2.illinois.gov/alplm/library/Pages/default.aspx

The Abraham Lincoln Presidential Library is a division of the above-mentioned Illinois Historic Preservation Agency. As such, one can also access the resources discussed above through this website. An entire section of the website focuses on genealogy, though not all material held by the library is indexed and searchable online.

Indiana

Date of Statehood: 11 Dec 1816
Neighboring States: Illinois, Kentucky, Michigan, Ohio
Previous Affiliations: Northwest Territory, Indiana Territory, Michigan Territory

After the Revolutionary War ended and the United States acquired the rest of the British landholdings to the Mississippi River, the Northwest Ordinance was passed to create the Northwest Territory in 1787. This territory included the area west of the new state of Pennsylvania, north of the Ohio River, and east of the Mississippi; as such, it included the entirety of the present-day states of Michigan, Illinois, Indiana, and Wisconsin, as well as portions of Minnesota and Ohio. Although the Northwest Ordinance had defined Indiana's future eastern border, the act establishing the Indiana Territory in 1800 defined a slightly different one.

When Ohio became a state in 1803, the Indiana Territory gained a portion of present-day eastern Michigan and the Indiana/Ohio border came into line with the Northwest Ordinance's original definition for it. When Indiana became a state, it was formed from the current Indiana Territory and a small section of the Michigan Territory, which was formed in 1805.

Indiana State Library Databases

http://www.in.gov/library/databases.htm
http://www.in.gov/library/3266.htm
http://www.in.gov/library/genealogy.htm

The Indiana State Library website has a lot of online databases (hence the multiple links above), although several subscription databases are only available via computer access while at the library in person. The searchable databases include various marriage, death, and military collections, as well as several biography and newspaper indexes. There are also external links to other genealogical websites and county-by-county holdings information. Marriage indexes for pre-1850 and the years 1993 through 2004 are online. A marriage index for 1957 to 1997 is also available in person at the library.

This site has a lot of information, and if you dig deep enough, you might be able to navigate your way to some of the following resources, starting with the Indiana State Digital Archives.

Indiana State Digital Archives

http://www.indianadigitalarchives.org/

The Digital Archives is a growing collection of all things Indiana. Searchable by name, one may find death, military, institutional, land, and naturalization records, as well as a number of county-based records, including but not limited to wills, African-American registers, and bar admissions.

Indiana State Archives

http://www.in.gov/icpr/2358.htm

Although there is some overlap with the digital archives and the information provided by the library, the Indiana Commission on Public Records handles the State Archives' website itself.

While the State Archives has a vast amount of helpful information, vital records are not included. Where to locate vital records is explained at length on the website, so a brief summary will serve our purposes here. Early birth records are available at the county level, although more recent records (1907 and later) can be obtained through the State Department of Health. Death records should be searched for at the county level or through old newspaper archives, while those after 1900 are also available through the Department of Health. Partial indexes for each were put together by the WPA and cover approximately 1882 to 1920. Remember that these are partial indexes, so just because you don't find your ancestor doesn't mean you should stop looking. Divorce records were first kept in 1852 and are available at the county level. Some marriage records from 1850 to 1920 were also indexed by the WPA, and marriage records from 1993 to 2004 and pre-1850 are available through the State Library's website, as discussed above.

Holdings information and additional online indexes are also accessible through the website.

Indiana Pre-1882 Death Records - Allen County Public Library

http://www.genealogycenter.info/search_pre1882deaths.php

This is a partial database available through the Allen County Public Library's Genealogy Center. Since death records were not required by the state at this time, information has been gathered from other sources, such as Civil War pension files, obituaries, biographical sketches, and more. A small collection of family bibles and a list of surnames being researched by Genealogy Center visitors are also online. Other online indexed databases include War-of-1812 pensioners, orphans, students of Central Normal College, African-American settlers, and a number of collections that pertain to certain counties.

INGenWeb
http://www.ingenweb.org/

This is the Indiana offering to go along with the USGenWeb Project. There is a site-wide search engine, and some of the information located in the archives includes county-by-county biographies, vital-records information, censuses, directories, and more. Some of this information was user-submitted.

My favorite feature of the site is not, however, the archives section. My favorite feature is the county-specific webpages, which often contain more detailed and helpful information than the USGenWeb-Archives webpages dedicated to each county.

Iowa

Date of Statehood: 28 Dec 1846

Neighboring States: Illinois, Minnesota, Missouri, Nebraska, South Dakota, Wisconsin

Previous Affiliations: Louisiana Territory, Missouri Territory, Unorganized Territory, Michigan Territory, Wisconsin Territory, Iowa Territory

The land that makes up present-day Iowa was acquired entirely through the Louisiana Purchase and subsequently became part of the Louisiana Territory. After Louisiana became a state, Iowa became part of the newly created Missouri Territory. When Missouri became a state, Iowa was no longer part of an incorporated area at all. This situation lasted until the early 1830s when Iowa, along with portions of the Dakotas and Minnesota were added to the Michigan Territory. Later in the decade, that land became part of the Wisconsin Territory before finally splitting off as part of the Iowa Territory in 1838. Although Iowa became a state in 1846, its boundaries were smaller than those of the Iowa Territory and the remainder of the territory continued to exist until the Minnesota Territory was formed in 1849. Iowa is somewhat unique among states west of the Mississippi River, as each territory it was part of fully encompassed it. Never were portions of the present-day state separated into multiple territories.

Iowa Genealogical Society (IGS)

http://www.iowagenealogy.org/

The IGS website has a lot of great information concerning Iowa-specific resources and the IGS' genealogical holdings. That being said, you're not liable to find much concrete information about individuals online. Your best bet is to look through the list of Iowa Pioneer certificates that have been granted by the Society. These certificates are indexed online and you'll find names of settlers and their spouses, as well as birth and death dates and locations. If you find a collection in the holdings for which you'd like additional information, the Society will perform research for a fee. Some of the Society's holdings include censuses, city directories, military records, and vital records. The county guides provide a wealth of information on where to find information for specific counties, including vital records, probate, newspapers, land records, and more.

State Library of Iowa

http://www.statelibraryofiowa.org/services/services/genealogy

Surprisingly enough, the State Library of Iowa doesn't have any genealogical material. If you need to prove it to yourself, you'll see that the library's genealogy page is merely a list of other websites and organizations. Could I have left this item out of the book? Yes. Do you need to follow the link? Probably not. But it's here if you want to check it out.

State Historical Society of Iowa

http://www.iowahistory.org/libraries/index.html

This is the home of the Iowa State Archives. Lists of newspaper and county-record holdings are online, though they have not been digitized for the website at the time of writing. Census records are available, and the State Archives has partnered with FamilySearch to provide indexes for the 1885 and 1895 state censuses (the links take users to FamilySearch.org); this can be especially helpful in light of the missing 1890 Federal Census data. While vital records are among the Historical Society's holdings, the only collection that is indexed online appears to be a portion of the pre-1935 death records.

Most of the website's digitized collections aren't especially helpful for the genealogist. However, there are collections of WWII press clippings, an African-American women-student collection from the University of Iowa, and a small collection of children's diaries, among other items that appear to be mostly political and historical, thus offering minimal help in tracing your ancestors.

IAGenWeb

http://iagenweb.org/

In addition to the obligatory county-level websites that are always linked to USGenWeb projects, IAGenWeb (Iowa's contribution) has several other important offerings. These include places for users to share their own family information, Civil War soldiers (names and regiments, in addition to a small number of biographies, diaries, and obituaries), gravestone projects, WWI soldiers, orphan train riders, and articles from early Iowa newspapers. Many of these collections are small, but if your ancestor happens to be mentioned, you'll be thankful you took the time to look.

Kansas

Date of Statehood: 29 Jan 1861
Neighboring States: Colorado, Missouri, Nebraska, Oklahoma
Previous Affiliations: Spain, Mexico, Louisiana Territory, Missouri Territory,
    Republic of Texas, Unorganized Territory, Kansas Territory

Most of Kansas started out as part of the Louisiana Territory and then the Missouri Territory. After Missouri became a state, the area was no longer part of an organized territory at all. The southwest corner of the state was part of Spain, Mexico, and then the Republic (and later state) of Texas after the area was ceded to Spain in 1819. In 1854, the Kansas Territory was created and the eastern portion of that territory became the state of Kansas in 1861.

Kansas Historical Society (KHS)

http://kshs.org/portal_genealogy

The Kansas Historical Society is the official home of the State Archives. The KHS website hosts several indexes that are searchable by surname. The first is the Kansas Names Index which searches the 1895 Kansas state census, biographical sketches, death notices, marriage records, pioneer women, lists of physicians and midwives, and several more collections. The second is the Kansas Military Index which includes collections from the Civil War, the Spanish-American War, WWI, WWII, and even casualties from more recent conflicts (Korea, Vietnam, Iraq, and Afghanistan). Neither index returns images of original documents, but both give source information when available. A separate index for cavalry enlistments in the 1860s can be accessed from the Kansas Military Index page.

The Society also has extensive microfilm holdings of newspapers and county-level documents. While some of these newspapers have been digitized on the Chronicling America website and some county-level documents are searchable through websites like FamilySearch.org, not everything is available online. If you're unable to visit Topeka and search for yourself, staff will perform research for a fee.

The Kansas Collection

http://www.kancoll.org

If you find your relatives in the Kansas Names Index discussed above, you may want to point your browser to The Kansas Collection. That's because The Kansas Collection hosts an indexed and transcribed copy of *History of the State of Kansas* on its website. As such, you might find your relative's actual biography online.

Loads of *Kansas Historical Quarterly* issues are transcribed online, as well as numerous other books, articles, and diaries. Some of these books can also be located on websites like Google and the Internet Archive, discussed in the previous chapter.

Kansas Memory

http://www.kansasmemory.org

This website was put together by the KHS (discussed above) in order to share some of its vast collection. While I didn't find an extensive genealogical collection online, it might still be worth searching for your ancestors. The most directly related categories are probably in the "Home and Family" and "Military" sections, though your relatives could pop up elsewhere.

KSGenWeb

http://www.skyways.org/genweb/

According to Blue Skyways, a service of the State Library, KSGenWeb is "THE place to start for Kansas genealogists…" There are the usual links to individual counties, as well as transcriptions for a multitude of military records, books, and even a voter index from the 1850s. The Kansas GenWeb project is searchable through Blue Skyways, our next topic.

Blue Skyways – State Library resource

http://skyways.lib.ks.us/heritage.html

Blue Skyways is a "shared information service" provided by the State Library of Kansas. While clicking on the Genealogy link will direct you to the above-mentioned KSGenWeb website, there is also a "Heritage" webpage that has links to other digitized collections. Some of these have already been discussed, but others, including the Kansas Heritage Group, Kansas History, and the special collections of Wichita State University, may be useful for locating rare manuscripts, letters, or other correspondence from your relatives.

Kentucky

Date of Statehood: 1 Jun 1792

Neighboring States: Illinois, Indiana, Missouri, Ohio, Tennessee, Virginia, West Virginia

Previous Affiliations: Virginia, Virginia Colony

Although other countries claimed Kentucky at various times, the Colony of Virginia provided the main early government for this area. When Virginia became a state in 1788, present-day Kentucky was located within its borders. It became its own state four years later without ever being part of a separate territory.

Kentucky Department for Libraries and Archives

http://kdla.ky.gov/researchers/Pages/visitingthearchives.aspx

Although the Kentucky State Archives has a lot of valuable genealogical information--vital records, census, military, wills and deeds--I was unable to find an online index or comprehensive list of holdings online. As such, it's probably going to be difficult to use this website to accomplish much research from your computer. However, lists of professional researchers, as well as records request forms are available on the website. When you bring up the "Records Request Forms" webpage, it has a few links to some of the Archives' holdings; available birth, death, and miscellaneous court records are listed by county, though no indexes are online.

A more helpful, at least in terms of immediate access from your computer, section of the website is the e-Archives (Electronic Records Archives). Here, one can search for Confederate pension applications and bring up digital images of the original records. These applications asked for county, state, and year of birth, particularly helpful information for the researcher.

The Archives has a small collection of microfilmed newspapers but mainly handles government documents. Non-government documents may be located more easily through the next resource.

Kentucky Historical Society (KHS)

http://history.ky.gov/

Formed in 1836, the KHS is now an agency of the state government. The

KHS Martin F. Schmidt Research Library has loads of information in print, on microfilm, and even online. Some collection highlights including church and bible records, land records and soldier indexes, city directories, tax records, court records, and even vital records. If you're unable to visit the library yourself, the Society will do research for a fee. The Collections Catalog page will help you search a full list of holdings.

While many of these documents and collections aren't online, others are made available through the Digital Collections section of the website. A search feature can be used to access oral history interviews, photographs, and even manuscripts, including family bibles, diaries, deeds, and more. Other items of interest are a cemetery database and an external link to the Kentuckiana Digital Library, a website that includes a selection of newspapers and yearbooks.

Kentucky Genealogical Society (KGS)
http://www.kygs.org/

The collection of the KGS is housed at the KHS library (see above). Some of the Society's archives include county-level newspaper clippings, deed indexes, and marriage records, along with user-submitted information of all sorts. The contents of each issue of *Bluegrass Roots*, the quarterly publication of the KGS, are listed by subject and copies can be ordered for $5 per issue. Although a cumulative index for issues from 1973 through 1984 was previously for sale (it was compiled by Brian Harney and Chuckie Hensley-- the write-up for Brian's website is below), it no longer appears to be available for purchase. External links to other county and statewide websites are also provided.

Brian Harney's Web Pages - Kentucky Genealogical Index
http://www.brianharney.net/

The Kentucky Genealogical Index is a project of Brian's that includes more than 3.1-million entries, mostly on Kentucky. Brian's website indicates that this publication isn't available on the Internet yet, but he may move in that direction at some point in the future. Other resources online are miscellaneous yearbooks from the 1920s up through the 1980s. According to the KGS website (see above), Brian is not doing any custom searches with his index, but if that information is outdated or changes, this could be a good resource when/if it becomes available in the future.

KYGenWeb

http://www.kygenweb.net/

This is the state and website that prompted the whole USGenWeb Project. There are research links for biographies, vital records, county websites, cemeteries, soldiers, user-submitted information, and even hangings in the state. It may take some time to look through everything, but the search feature should help speed things along.

Kentucky Vital Records Project

http://kyvitals.com/

Death records comprise the majority of the content available on this website, although the FAQ page indicates that users may have also contributed birth and marriage records. Even though you probably won't find many (or any) birth or marriage records, this website is still worth checking out for the scanned images of original death certificates. Most records appear to be from about 1911 to 1921 and include parents' names and the mother's maiden name.

Kentucky Vital Records Index

http://ukcc.uky.edu/vitalrec/

Marriage and divorce indexes run from 1973 through 1993, and death indexes are online from 1911 through 1992. As these indexes were part of a 1994 research project, they are not being updated. Additionally, there is a limit of only 50 results, so if you're trying to search for a common last name, you may have to narrow your search criteria in some way.

Louisiana

Date of Statehood: 30 Apr 1812
Neighboring States: Arkansas, Mississippi, Texas
Previous Affiliations: France, Spain, Louisiana Purchase, Territory of Orleans

When the United States completed the Louisiana Purchase, the borders of the purchase were not well defined. As such, when the Territory of Orleans was established in 1804, it wasn't well defined either. In fact, even after Louisiana achieved statehood, its western border was still disputed with Spain; this wouldn't be resolved until seven years later when the border was defined by the Adams-Onís Treaty of 1819. On the other side of the state, the area east of the Mississippi River was also a point of contention. After a group of settlers in the Spanish territory of West Florida declared their independence, the United States annexed the western portion of this area into the Territory of Orleans in 1810. Again, the Adams-Onís Treaty provided the final word on the border, and in it Spain ceded the rights to all territory east of the Mississippi.

Louisiana State Archives
http://sos.la.gov/tabid/88/default.aspx
The State Archives Research Library is a great place to start your Louisiana genealogical research. Although the library has far more content on-site than what is available online, numerous databases are now searchable through the State Archives' website.

The first is an index for six months' worth of passenger arrivals in 1851. This may not sound like much, but the collection is part of an effort to fill a gap of unindexed information. Microfilmed indexes are available for New Orleans passenger lists from 1820 through 1952, with the exception of 1851 and 1852. This index helps fill that gap. Other available online indexes include Confederate pension applications and select birth, marriage, and death records. Some of the State Archives' holdings may also be available through websites like FamilySearch.org. Keep in mind that online data provides basic indexed information but not images of original documents. Library staff will search records for a fee.

New Orleans Public Library - Louisiana Division

http://neworleanspubliclibrary.org/~nopl/spec/speclist.htm

Although most of the databases and indexes available through the library are only pertinent to the city of New Orleans, owing to its size and population relative to the rest of the state, I believe they're still worth mentioning here. Some of the available online indexes include a Biography/Obituary Index, marriage records, and vertical files. Additional indexes and records including birth announcements, naturalization records, and city directories are available at the library.

Even the indexed databases won't allow you to view source documents online, but they will give you the information you need to follow up on your own. The library staff will also make copies of most indexed information for two or three dollars per reference. If you can't visit the library yourself, check out the website for a complete list of available records and fees associated with ordering them.

LAGenWeb

http://www.lagenweb.net/

This website has links to individual webpages for each county in the state. But just make sure you don't call them counties. In Louisiana, they're called parishes. As usual, there are other genealogical links also, but we've already discussed a number of them so won't rehash that information here.

Louisiana State Library

http://www.state.lib.la.us/library-collections/genealogy

A lengthy guide to the State Library's genealogy collection, most of which is on microfilm, is available online in a PDF file. While helpful, the guide doesn't provide any surname indexes. Staff doesn't perform genealogical research either but will provide assistance to those who can visit in person. According to the aforementioned guide, staff will answer brief inquiries and fee information for making copies is also provided.

Louisiana Digital Library

http://louisdl.louislibraries.org/

The Digital Library has some information that could be very valuable. Unfortunately, even though the content is organized by subject and into collections, I didn't find the website's layout to be very intuitive. As such, your best bet is probably to use the search bar and not spend too much time looking for a specific collection that pertains to your ancestors.

On the plus side, there are some interesting source documents like court records, which could be difficult to locate elsewhere online. Not all collections are genealogical in nature, so you'll just have to look around and see what you can find.

Maine

Date of Statehood: 15 Mar 1820

Neighboring States: New Hampshire, Country of Canada

Previous Affiliations: Province of Maine, Province of New York, Massachusetts, Country of Canada, New Holland, Dominion of New England

Although the French and English each made settlement attempts in the early part of the 1600s, the Province of Maine was first named as such in 1622. Soon thereafter, that land was split in two separate provinces, and by the mid-1600s the northern province of the two came to be part of Massachusetts. Even though the Dutch briefly conquered Acadia in 1674, the Province of New York governed a portion of present-day Maine as Cornwall County, and the Dominion of New England took charge in the late 1680s, Maine ended up being governed by the newly established Province of Massachusetts Bay after it was established in the 1690s. This occurred in spite of continuing colonial border disputes and the fact that Maine and Massachusetts were physically separated by the New Hampshire Colony.

Present-day Maine continued to be affiliated with Massachusetts until well after the Revolutionary War was over. In fact, Massachusetts had already been a state for more than 30 years by the time Maine eventually entered the Union. The northern portion of the state was a disputed area between Maine and Canada; that issue was resolved by the Webster-Ashburton Treaty of 1842, resulting in Maine's present-day borders.

Maine Historical Society (MHS)

http://www.mainehistory.org/gen_overview.shtml

The MHS has a vast amount of genealogical material, and the Society's holdings can be searched through its online catalog. Members can use the library for free, and anyone can request that the Society perform fee-based family history research.

Some online collections, including those in the Maine Memory Network (discussed below) and an index to *Maine History*, are available to the general public. Other online resources, such as naturalization and voter records, as well as fully searchable editions of *Maine History*, are only available to MHS members. A genealogy forum allows researchers to collaborate on their research.

A separate website, run by the MHS, is dedicated to Henry Wadsworth Longfellow and has a detailed family tree for him. So if you find out that Henry Wadsworth Longfellow is your fourth cousin five times removed, as he is for me, you might be able to double check some of your information.

Maine Memory Network
http://mainememory.net/

Just like the Henry Wadsworth Longfellow website, the Maine Memory Network is part of the MHS. An online resource that contains digital copies of thousands of historical documents, this site is fully searchable. While the focus isn't specifically on genealogy, several Civil War collections and a collection of 1924 Portland tax records are available online.

Maine State Archives
http://www.maine.gov/sos/arc/

The first link on the left-hand side of the website is for "Archives Interactive." This option allows users to search various databases for his/her ancestors. Also on the left-hand side of the webpage are links to searchable marriage and death indexes. The marriage records begin in 1892 while the death records only go back to 1960.

Next is the "Databases for Downloading" webpage. This page has downloadable Microsoft Access databases for War-of-1812 veterans, Mexican War soldiers, Maine's Civil War Navy, and Revolutionary War pension and land grant applications, among others. If you don't own Microsoft Access, a free download of Open Office should allow you to view the databases. While the technical details are beyond the scope of this book, an online search should provide the necessary information to view the collections without Microsoft Access. If you're still unable to open the files, download them on a computer that already has the proper software installed or ask your kids for help.

Farther down the left-hand side of the webpage is a link for "Researchers." A list of professional researchers (for hire) is provided, as well as information on where to find particular types of records. The main place you'll find online genealogical information is under the "Military" link, where several Civil War collections and a Revolutionary War Land Grants and Pension Applications Index are located.

Maine State Library

http://www.state.me.us/msl/services/genealogy/index.shtml

Unfortunately, I wasn't able to locate any Maine-specific indexes or databases on the State Library's website. On the plus side, there is a lot of valuable information on where to find the information you require. The site discusses the Library's subscriptions to services such as Ancestry Library Edition and HeritageQuest. The library is also affiliated with FamilySearch.org and can, for a fee, order microfilm. Although state vital records are generally sealed until they are old enough to meet state requirements, one can skirt this rule by obtaining a Maine CDC-issued genealogical research card (certain requirements must be met).

Finally, the website has an obituary search. Unfortunately, this is not an online index, but it is an option to receive obituary research help if you're unable to visit the library yourself. If you choose to obtain obituary research assistance, simply fill out the online form and pay the $5-per-obituary charge; no fee is collected if an obituary is not located. The State Library requires the date of death, so check the death index on the State Archives' website if you don't already have that information.

MEGenWeb

http://www.rootsweb.ancestry.com/~megenweb/

As you might expect, this is the Maine website for the USGenWeb Project. It links to county-specific webpages, each with varying types and quantities of information. One section of the website is dedicated to books and diaries, and several of those resources are indexed.

One of MEGenWeb's unique features is a county-court-records searchable index. It only covers certain years for three separate counties at present, but if your relatives lived in those counties, this may be a valuable tool. Links to miscellaneous genealogical societies and other resources, some discussed in this book, are also provided.

Maine Genealogical Society (MGS)

http://www.maineroots.org/

Although the MGS didn't have much in the way of genealogical collections online at the time of writing, there are a number of good reasons to visit the website. First is the links page, with resources specific to Maine, New England, and the entire United States. Members can also post queries about their family history.

In addition to *The Maine Genealogist*, a quarterly publication, the MGS has published nearly 70 works dealing with genealogy in Maine. From the webpage dedicated to the *Maine Families in 1790* series, one can search an online index of heads of household. An Every-Name Index is also available for purchase, and although I've not had an opportunity to consult the series yet, it seems to be the definitive collection for Maine research in 1790.

Finally, each chapter of the MGS has its own website. Although available information varies by chapter website, death and marriage notices, as well as deed indexes, may be online.

Maryland

Date of Statehood: 28 Apr 1788
Neighboring States: Delaware, Pennsylvania, Virginia, West Virginia
Previous Affiliations: Virginia Colony, Maryland Colony

When the Maryland Colony was first established, it was formed out of the Virginia Colony and extended east to the Delaware River and north to the 40th parallel; this was just north of Philadelphia. Approximately 50 years later, the Province of Pennsylvania was established to the north. Although its southern boundary was set at 40-degrees north latitude (the same as Maryland's northern border), it was assumed that the 40th parallel would intersect the Twelve-Mile Circle, a twelve-mile radius from present-day New Castle, Delaware, and it was under this assumption that the charter was written. Unfortunately, the 40th parallel was actually north of Pennsylvania's newly established capital city, Philadelphia. Eventually, Maryland lost both present-day Delaware and the northernmost portion of the colony to Pennsylvania. A small chunk of land was also ceded to the Federal Government so that Washington D.C. could be established.

Maryland State Archives

http://www.msa.md.gov/msa/homepage/html/family.html

The State Archives has quite a few write-ups on how to go about your Maryland research. Information on how to order specific records is online, and the best genealogical content is located through one of the following sections of the website: Guide to Government Records; Special Collections; Library (the Archives' Library); the Archives of Maryland (Archives of Maryland Online).

From the "Guide to Government Records" webpage, click on the "Reference and Research" tab. This will bring up a list of records and indexes held by the Archives. Not all collections or indexes are available online, but those that are include: a census index for records from 1776, 1778, 1870, and 1880; an early settlers index; national guard records; a 1783 tax assessment; the 1890 Federal Census veterans index. While some original documents are available online, I found it difficult to quickly determine which collections had associated images.

One particularly interesting, but difficult to locate, collection is the

Huntington Collection. Although cumbersome to locate and use, at least in my opinion, this can be a valuable resource for colonial-era wills. Since this section of the website only appears to be searchable by series number, not by name, it's important to know that the Huntington Collection is designated as series TE1. So in order to bring up the collection itself, simply type "TE1" in the Series ID search box. Users can help transcribe records, though most I found were not yet transcribed at the time of writing. Even so, the last few files in the collection (starting around TE1-253) are indexes, and as such are probably the best place to start.

Special Collections focuses on non-governmental documents, like newspapers, letters, and diaries. By clicking "Special Collections Online" on the left-hand side of the webpage, one can access indexes for: minutes from Maryland's Court of Vice Admiralty, 1754 to 1775; women legislators; medical practitioners. The "Biographical Research" link provides more resources, though they are accessed indirectly through the previously mentioned "Guide to Government Records." Some of these indexes include teachers, African Americans, soldiers and sailors, and even 17th-century residents of St. Mary's County. Not every collection identified through this webpage is online, so you may have to follow up on your own.

The Library link can be used to search by title or author, or uniquely, by family name for genealogy. Your search results will return the pertinent book's call number and author.

The Archives of Maryland Online (AOMOL) has links to land records, probate records, and military records. While there are other collections on AOMOL, most are not related to genealogy directly. There are quite a few links for land records and some of these are accessed through the "Guide to Government Records" mentioned earlier. Other land records are on the AOMOL website itself, while a free username is required to access a third set of records on the MDLandRec.Net website. One interesting thing to note is that "Kent County Court Bonds, Indentures, and Land Records," listed under "Land Records," has two separate documents to choose from; the first of these includes a number of vital records. If you follow the "Probate Records" link, it provides access to various collections, some of which are on the AOMOL website itself, while others are hosted on external websites. There is also an index to probate records from the colonial period.

Maryland State Archives - Vital Records Indexing Project
http://mdvitalrec.net/cfm/index.cfm

A vital-records website run by the State Archives is our next topic. Unfortunately, and in spite of the name, the website contains only a death index and doesn't have vital records for birth, marriage, or divorce.

The online death records are broken up into separate categories. For the city of Baltimore, a limited number of years (1875 to 1880, 1943 to 1949) are searchable by surname online. Other counties, and the rest of Baltimore's records, have alphabetized indexes that aren't directly searchable by your ancestor's name. If you find a record you're interested in, a certified copy can be purchased through the website.

MDGenWeb
http://www.mdgenweb.org/

Along with county-specific website links, MDGenWeb also provides lists of genealogical societies and my favorite feature, transcribed tax lists from the late 17th-century.

Maryland Genealogical Society (MGS)
http://www.mdgensoc.org/

The MGS has a surname exchange and lists of queries from 2000 to the present are available to the general public, while church and cemetery databases can only be accessed by members. The Society puts out a publication known as *The Journal,* previously *The Bulletin,* and back issues can be ordered online. Although the tables of contents are online, these publications aren't indexed by surname. The MGS will provide research assistance for a fee.

Maryland Historical Society (MdHS)
http://www.mdhs.org/

Although I didn't find much in the way of helpful online genealogical collections, the MdHS library appears to be a great resource for on-site research. There are vast amounts of records of all sorts; from the "Library" webpage, click on "Research Resources," then visit the "Subject Guides" section and click on "Genealogy" to bring up the guide and the library's list of genealogical holdings. Some of the indexes include a Genealogical Index, the

Dielman-Hayward Card File, and the Norris Harris Church Register Index.

Massachusetts

Date of Statehood: 6 Feb 1788

Neighboring States: Connecticut, New Hampshire, New York, Rhode Island, Vermont

Previous Affiliations: Massachusetts Bay Colony, Plymouth Colony, Province of New York, Connecticut, Dominion of New England

The Massachusetts Bay Colony and the Plymouth Colony were the two principal entities that merged when the Province of Massachusetts Bay was formed in 1691. Although boundary disputes between all the New England colonies were commonplace, most of these disputes were resolved by the time the United States gained its independence. One notable exception is the Southwick Jog, a notch in the border with Connecticut. This didn't get resolved until 1804 when the area of the notch was divided and a portion was given to Massachusetts after having been part of the state of Connecticut for more than 15 years. Present-day Maine was also part of Massachusetts until it became the 23rd state in 1820. Numerous border disputes with Rhode Island occurred and weren't fully resolved until the mid-1800s.

New England Historic Genealogical Society (NEHGS)
http://americanancestors.org/

According to the Society, the NEHGS (not a very pleasing acronym, is it?) website has more than 3,000 searchable online collections with data on more than 300-million people. You can search names for free, but you'll need a membership to view any results that are returned. Some collections include lists of early settlers, vital records, wills, church and bible records, and loads more. Search results also list whether your ancestors were included in quarterly publications put out by various genealogical societies located throughout New England. Several collections are available online with a free username, but many others require a subscription.

If your ancestors lived in New England (and many immigrants did, at least initially), this may be a website worth visiting. Although I've placed it under the Massachusetts section here, content is related to the whole of New England so don't skip over this resource just because your ancestors aren't from Massachusetts itself.

Some genealogical libraries, societies, and State Archives have subscriptions to the website, so check with your local genealogical association to find out if it has a subscription.

Massachusetts Archives Division

http://www.sec.state.ma.us/arc/arcgen/genidx.htm

The Massachusetts Archives has a lot of valuable information on where to find everything from probate records and name changes to vital records and adoptions, as well as a myriad of other documents of genealogical importance. A list of the Archives' collections is online, and a few collections are indexed and searchable. These can be found, as you might expect, by clicking the link on the left-hand side of the page that says "Searchable Collections."

Indexed collections include vital records from 1841 to 1910, an ongoing project to transcribe passenger manifests from the second half of the 19th century, and an eighteen-volume collection of miscellaneous documents from the 17th and 18th centuries. These collections, though valuable, do not offer scanned images of original documents through the website, and it appears that the Massachusetts Archives doesn't have many digital collections at this point in time.

Massachusetts State Library

http://www.mass.gov/anf/research-and-tech/research-state-and-
        local-history/genealogical-resources.html

There are numerous resources at the Library, some of which are even available online.   Some genealogical links merely indicate State Library holdings, such as annual town reports, probate records, and city directories. Though many of these are undoubtedly valuable, these have to be accessed in person, not via the Internet.   However, a Massachusetts-vital-records link is provided (these books of vital records are actually hosted online at the Internet Archive, discussed in the previous chapter).   Downloadable military books and the Zimmer Index, an index to Boston-area newspapers from the late-19th and early-20th centuries, are also online.

The Digital Collections webpage has several Revolutionary and Civil War PDF files on soldiers from the state, and the Real Estate Atlas Project contains a ton of old maps, some of which contain owners' names written on each parcel.

Massachusetts Vital Records Project

http://www.ma-vitalrecords.org/

If you merely want to do a quick search of Massachusetts' vital records, this is a great website to start with. Over 1.5-million records have been transcribed and each record has a link to the page of a public domain book that lists the original record. You'll have to go elsewhere if you want to see a copy of the source documents, but this is a very easy-to-use website that will give you a push in the right direction.

MAGenWeb

http://magenweb.org/

As you are no doubt aware, the MAGenWeb Project has county-level websites with miscellaneous genealogical information. You're likely also aware that Massachusetts participates in a number of USGenWeb projects. However, you may not be aware that the site's "Resources" webpage also provides valuable links to off-site collections. Some of these are links to resources we've already discussed: the New England Historic Genealogical Society, the Massachusetts Vital Records Project, the State Archives, and various FamilySearch collections. Other information includes town clerk contact information (for vital records), email lists and message boards, information on where to locate probate records and deeds, transcriptions of 1790 census data, and external links to websites with city directories and various other Massachusetts-specific records.

Michigan

Date of Statehood: 26 Jan 1837
Neighboring States: Indiana, Ohio, Wisconsin, Country of Canada
Previous Affiliations: Northwest Territory, Indiana Territory, Illinois
   Territory, Wisconsin Territory, Michigan Territory

After the Revolutionary War ended and the United States acquired the rest of the British landholdings to the Mississippi River, the Northwest Ordinance was passed to create the Northwest Territory in 1787. This territory included the area west of the new state of Pennsylvania, north of the Ohio River, and east of the Mississippi; as such, it included the entirety of the present-day states of Michigan, Illinois, Indiana, and Wisconsin, as well as portions of Minnesota and Ohio. The Michigan Territory was established from the Indiana Territory in 1805 and over the years would grow to include areas as far west as the Dakotas. When Michigan began preparing for statehood, the Wisconsin Territory was formed, an area which originally included much of Michigan's Upper Peninsula. As it prepared for statehood, Michigan finally acquired the rest of the Upper Peninsula in exchange for ending a border dispute with Ohio over the Toledo area.

Michigan Department of Community Health - Genealogical Death Indexing System

http://www.mdch.state.mi.us/pha/osr/gendisx/search2.htm

This search currently encompasses death records from 1867 to 1897. Online records are not original images, but, rather, have been transcribed. Date, location, and cause of death are transcribed, as are age and birthplace. While parents' names and place of residence are also provided, in my experience the mother's maiden name is rarely given.

Seeking Michigan

http://seekingmichigan.org

Seeking Michigan is an "online platform for the Michigan Historical Center,"--discussed below--according to the website.

All of Seeking Michigan's collections are searchable online and return actual images of original documentation, as opposed to just transcripts. Numerous historical collections are available as well as several Civil War collections. My favorite collection, however, is another collection of death records. Whereas the above website provides death records from 1867 to 1897, Seeking Michigan provides records from 1897 to 1920. Between the two, you should be covered for most of Michigan's recorded deaths from 1867 to 1920.

Michigan Department of Natural Resources - Michigan Historical Center

http://www.michigan.gov/dnr/0,4570,7-153-54463_54475_18660---,00.html

Apparently, the Michigan Historical Center is organized under the Department of Natural Resources, and the Archives of Michigan part of the Historical Center. At least that's how it appears to me. As such, it took me some time to find this resource, but I think you'll agree that it's a good one.

Numerous online indexes are available, including Spanish-American War medal recipients, WWII Honor List, WWI Clubroom register, Civil War principals and substitutes, and naturalization records. Although none of these indexes actually link to digitized source documents, staff will do research and make photocopies for a fee.

Library of Michigan

http://www.michigan.gov/libraryofmichigan/0,2351,7-160-18635---,00.html

Although the Archives of Michigan (see above) and Library of Michigan are located in the same building, when planning your visit, keep in mind that their hours are different. Since the Archives and Library work closely together, some indexes (like the naturalization one mentioned above) have already been discussed. There is a searchable index for the 1870 census and copies of the *Michigan Genealogist* newsletter are online, but my favorite index that we haven't already mentioned is the "Sons of the American Revolution" collection, which is accessed by clicking "Library Collections" on the left-hand side of the webpage, then on the "Rare Books" link. Searchable by applicants' and ancestors' names, this index may help fill in the gaps in your family tree. Unfortunately, the index isn't linked to online images of original documents, but it does provide volume and ID numbers, with which you can follow up.

Subject guides to the Genealogy Collection are available on the website, as is a list of the Library's newspaper holdings.

MIGenWeb

http://www.migenweb.net/

County webpage links, for me, are the main draw of this website. That being said, there are also user-submitted Family Group Sheets and Michigan-specific webpages for Native-American, Irish, and Polish research.

Michigan Family History Network

http://www.mifamilyhistory.org/

There are quite a few records available on this website. Some are transcribed from original ledgers, while others are taken from books or submitted by users. Church records, a school census search, rural directories, and a mining accident report are among records that don't appear to be readily available elsewhere online. Additionally, the 1883 list of Michigan Civil War pensioners and an 1840 list of military pensioners are both transcribed.

Western Michigan Genealogical Society (WMGS)

http://data.wmgs.org/

Not only does this website have a page full of links to additional websites, it also has lists of biographical sketches and numerous online databases. Over two-million records are searchable online in collections that include Western Michigan newspapers, the WMGS quarterly publication *Michigana*, veterans' records, marriages, deaths, and even the Kent County school census. Searches are free, as is some information like member-submitted family trees and manuscripts. Copies of other records can be purchased for $5 each. Members of the Society will do research on your behalf for a fee. That research is limited to the records held by the Genealogical Collection at the Grand Rapids Public Library.

Minnesota

Date of Statehood: 11 May 1858

Neighboring States: Iowa, North Dakota, South Dakota, Wisconsin, Country of Canada

Previous Affiliations: Northwest Territory, Indiana Territory, Illinois Territory, Michigan Territory, Louisiana Territory, Missouri Territory, Unorganized Territory, Wisconsin Territory, Iowa Territory, Minnesota Territory

Being home to the source of, and split by, the Mississippi River, portions of Minnesota were part of a great many territories. The eastern portion of the state was acquired as a result of the Revolutionary War. It was originally incorporated as part of the Northwest Territory, though it was placed in numerous other territories as they were established. These included the Indiana, Illinois, Michigan, and Wisconsin Territories, the latter two territories coming to include the western portion of the present-day state as well.

The western portion of the state was acquired via the Louisiana Purchase and a British cession in 1818. This land was, in large part, part of the Louisiana Territory, the Missouri Territory, an unorganized territory, and then part of the Michigan and Wisconsin Territories when the eastern and western halves of present-day Minnesota were joined. The halves were split once more and the western portion of the state became part of the Iowa Territory in 1838. Eventually, after Iowa and Wisconsin became states, the Minnesota Territory was formed, the eastern portion of which would eventually become the state of Minnesota.

Minnesota Discovery Center

http://mndiscoverycenter.com/research-center/genealogy

The Minnesota Discovery Center is an excellent resource for genealogical research, as well as a fun place to spend the day with the family. And while that might seem impossible, it isn't. That's because the Discovery Center is not only a designated repository for government records, but also boasts a museum, park, trolley, and miniature golf course. The on-site Iron Range Research Center has an impressive collection of materials and the website provides local genealogical links as well as an online name search. You won't find scans of original documentation online, but you can easily order copies of anything you locate.

Minnesota Historical Society (State Archives)
http://www.mnhs.org/genealogy/

The Minnesota Historical Society is the custodian for the State Archives, and in addition to its sizeable holdings in Saint Paul, there are several searchable collections online. Some of these online resources include birth, death, veterans' graves, and census indexes, as well as helpful information on how to go about doing your own personal research. The right-hand side of the webpage has links that pertain to research services, newspapers, court records, and Native-American records. If you click on the "Search Collections" link, you can enter your ancestor's name in the search bar. Some results include images, while others provide basic information without a digital copy of the actual item in question. Items you may find through the search tool include World War I files, oral histories, and photographs. Loads of other resources are listed on the website, though many of them refer to library holdings that aren't available online.

Immigration History Research Center (IHRC)
http://www.ihrc.umn.edu/research/

The Immigration History Research Center is maintained as part of the University of Minnesota's College of Liberal Arts. Although I didn't find any comprehensive online collections of naturalization records, there's enough content that you'll definitely want to visit this website if your ancestors immigrated to Minnesota. Try searching for your ancestors directly, and you may find that items such as personal correspondence, newspaper clippings, and photographs are available. If you don't have any luck, try searching by ethnic group and following up if any collections sound promising.

Newspapers by ethnic group are listed online, one can search the IHRC's holdings, and digital collections can be searched by name or browsed by ethnic group.

Dalby Database
http://www.dalbydata.com/

With indexed directories, censuses, vital records, obituaries, church records, and more, this is an extremely helpful website if your ancestors are from Rice County, Minnesota. There are various records from surrounding counties (and I even ran across a couple of entries from Iowa), but the information will likely be most beneficial to those with ancestors from Rice County itself.

Although this isn't a website that's pertinent to everyone with roots in Minnesota, it was named a best website by *Family Tree Magazine* in 2005 and seemed worth mentioning.

Minnesota Genealogical Society (MGS)

http://mngs.org/

Although the MGS doesn't host many records collections online, there is still a great deal of information on the website. Lists of research facilities, county resources, and links to other genealogical websites are provided. A list of available Catholic Church records is online but the records aren't indexed, so you'll need to know which church your relatives attended before you can easily proceed.

The MGS also puts out a quarterly publication called the *Minnesota Genealogist*. Though the journal has been in circulation since 1969, only copies from 2003 to 2006 appear to be indexed by surname at this point. A subject index is provided for 1969 through 1994.

A lot more information is available at the library itself, and if you don't live in the area, you can pay to have research performed on your behalf.

MNGenWeb

http://www.rootsweb.ancestry.com/~mngenweb/

Links to some of the resources discussed above are provided, as well as links to various projects under the USGenWeb/MNGenWeb umbrella. Member-submitted information is online, and other off-site resources are discussed. Finally, links to county-level webpages and resources are provided.

Mississippi

Date of Statehood: 10 Dec 1817
Neighboring States: Alabama, Arkansas, Louisiana, Tennessee
Previous Affiliations: Georgia, Mississippi Territory

Most of the southern half of Mississippi became part of the Mississippi Territory in 1798 after a treaty with Spain set the United States' southern boundary at 31-degrees north latitude. The northern portion of present-day Mississippi was added to the Mississippi Territory after the United States Government acquired it from Georgia after the Yazoo land scandal. Finally, the southern portion of present-day Mississippi was an area disputed by the United States and Spain. After a group of settlers in the Spanish territory of West Florida declared their independence, the United States annexed the eastern portion of West Florida into the Mississippi Territory in 1812. At that point, the Mississippi Territory contained present-day Mississippi and Alabama. The Mississippi Territory ceased to exist in 1817 after Mississippi entered the Union as the 20th state and the other half of the territory became the Alabama Territory.

Mississippi State Archives

http://mdah.state.ms.us/arrec/gen_research.php

The Mississippi State Archives has a comprehensive online catalog that will allow the researcher to determine what holdings are available at the Archives building in Jackson, Mississippi. Unfortunately, most of that content is not actually available through the Archives' website. A few indexes can be accessed by clicking on the "Online Catalog" link. Here, users will find a biographical index, cemetery indexes, and a Freedman's Bureau index. Researchers will perform one hour of work free of charge for state residents, though out-of-staters must pay for research assistance.

The Digital Archives hosts numerous collections online, though not all of them are of genealogical importance. Several of the more notable resources located here are collections pertaining to the Sovereignty Commission, Confederate pension applications, educable children records, and World War I service members. Numerous photographic collections are also available.

Mississippi Digital Library

http://collections.msdiglib.org/cdm/

Unfortunately, the Mississippi Digital Library doesn't host as many genealogically important collections as the Digital Archives mentioned above. Although many of the online items found here pertain to the Civil Rights era, there are only a few county and regional resources that may be useful to the genealogist. These selected collections have local and family history information as well as numerous photographs. As these collections don't cover the entire state, whether you're able to locate your ancestors depends on where they're from.

MSGenWeb

http://www.msgw.org/

In addition to the ever-present county-level information presented as part of the USGenWeb Project, MSGenWeb has several other valuable resources. County-level historical and genealogical societies are listed, and there are a number of special projects undertaken and/or made available through MSGenWeb. These include ex-slave interviews done by the WPA in the 1930s, county courthouse information, military casualties, marriages, family websites, and several smaller collections like tax lists and pre-1818 research, a category that encompasses everything having to do with the southwest corner of Mississippi in the pre-statehood era.

Mississippi Genealogy and History Network

http://www.msghn.org/

Although this is an independent website, in some ways it resembles the previously mentioned Mississippi portion of the USGenWeb Project. The reason I say that is because there are individual county-level webpages as well as a state-level index to Mississippi cemeteries (in progress at the time of writing).

One thing I like about this website over most USGenWeb sites is the uniformity of the information presented. Most county webpages are formatted exactly the same way as each other, and the information is presented in a clear and readable manner. This isn't true of every county-level page, but it's more consistent than many similar websites I've encountered.

Missouri

Date of Statehood: 10 Aug 1821

Neighboring States: Arkansas, Illinois, Iowa, Kansas, Kentucky, Nebraska, Oklahoma, Tennessee

Previous Affiliations: Louisiana Territory, Missouri Territory, Unorganized Territory

The land that makes up present-day Missouri was acquired through the Louisiana Purchase and, for a time, was part of the Louisiana Territory. It was then part of the Missouri Territory before becoming a state in 1821. The northwest corner of Missouri was not originally part of the state but was rather an area that was deeded to Native-American tribes; it was an unorganized part of the country in terms of United States Government. The Platte Purchase was completed in 1836, and the land became part of the state of Missouri the following year.

Missouri State Archives

http://www.sos.mo.gov/archives/resources/resources.asp

The Missouri State Archives, like many others, has a comprehensive list of its census, county, land, military, and other holdings online. Where this website shines is with regard to its digital collections. Simply scroll down to the "Online Resources" section and pick one of the collections to search. Some of the collections include images of original documents while others provide transcribed details. Offerings include birth and death records, military, naturalization, land, court records, and others. Of particular note is the pre-1910 birth-and-death database. Although images aren't provided online, birth records contain the names of both parents, including the mother's maiden name. Better still is the fact that an online search will retrieve records for the child's name as well as the parents' names. So if you want to search by the names of the parents, or even the mother's maiden name, you can.

External links to other genealogical resources are also provided.

Missouri State Genealogical Association (MoSGA)
http://www.mosga.org

MoSGA has lots of research links, though the majority of them are not actually for the state of Missouri. As such, if you've hit a stumbling block, you might consider checking out the website for records from other states. A quarterly journal is sent to active association members, and an article index is available online, though a surname index is not. One can use the website to connect with other researchers, and an index to recipients of Missouri First Family certificates is also online.

Missouri History Museum
http://genealogy.mohistory.org/

If your ancestors are from the St. Louis area, this website has a search feature that may help you locate them. A small percentage of the individuals in the index are from other areas of the state, but the search is most useful for the St. Louis region itself.

State Historical Society of Missouri
http://shs.umsystem.edu/research/index.shtml

The State Historical Society of Missouri has quite a bit of good content online. Digital collections include newspapers, Civil War documents, historical society newsletters, plat maps, and other manuscripts of all sorts. Guides to Missouri Genealogy are online and one can easily search the Society's holdings. What I like about the website's catalog search is that each collection has a detailed description online, so you'll have a good idea of what the collection contains even if it's not actually online. Research can also be requested through the website.

MOGenWeb
http://www.rootsweb.ancestry.com/~mogenweb/mo.htm

Contact information for libraries and societies across the state is provided along with some early marriage records, military rosters, county-level webpages, and several other MOGenWeb Special Projects.

Montana

Date of Statehood: 8 Nov 1889

Neighboring States: Idaho, North Dakota, South Dakota, Wyoming, Country of Canada

Previous Affiliations: Oregon Territory, Washington Territory, Idaho Territory, Montana Territory, Louisiana Territory, Missouri Territory, Unorganized Territory, Nebraska Territory, Dakota Territory

The portion of Montana west of the continental divide evolved with the state of Idaho, as part of the Oregon Territory, the Washington Territory, and then the Idaho Territory. The eastern portion of the state was acquired through the Louisiana Purchase, and was first part of the Louisiana Territory, and then the Missouri Territory, before it was part of an unorganized territory. Eventually, the area east of the continental divide became part of the Nebraska Territory and then part of the Dakota Territory before the Idaho Territory was formed in 1863. The year after the Idaho Territory was formed, it split and the Montana Territory was formed with the state's present-day borders.

Montana Historical Society (MHS)

http://mhs.mt.gov/research/default.asp

Unfortunately, when searching the Montana Historical Society's website, I didn't find many online collections that would help the genealogist. The Society does have a lot of valuable information, though most of it's not available online. Some of the "Online Resources" links are to other websites and resources already discussed in this section or to resources discussed in previous chapters.

The best part of the website, in my opinion, is the ability to search the Society's holdings, as well as the information on all of the collections in possession of the MHS. Some of these include individual and family manuscripts, state and local government records, and oral histories. The Society states that its newspaper collection includes 95-percent of all newspapers ever published in the state, so the odds are good that you'll be able to locate an ancestor's birth, death, or marriage announcement if it showed up in a local newspaper. Some of the state's newspapers are already available online through the Chronicling America project discussed earlier in the book. Sanborn Fire Insurance Maps, censuses, and all manner of other Montana-centric material are also available through the MHS.

If you're not able to visit the Montana Historical Society yourself, a staff member can assist with your research for a fee.

Montana State Genealogical Society (MSGS)
http://montanamsgs.org/

In addition to links to other genealogical societies, the MSGS has several state death indexes online. These transcribed records generally have basic information such as name, age, and date and place of death, though some records also have short notes. You'll have to request a copy of the original document to see if additional data is contained. The 1930 census has also been transcribed and two other collections, Norske i Montana marriages and Norske i Montana naturalizations, are supposed to be forthcoming. The latter two collections are based on Richard Fretheim's book, *Norske i Montana*, a compilation of records that relates to Norwegian settlers in Montana.

The Society also awards certificates for descendants of early settlers, and indexes of previously awarded certificates are online and searchable.

Montana Memory Project
http://www.mtmemory.org/

As with most of the other state memory projects we've encountered, the Montana Memory Project isn't focused solely on genealogy. That being said, there are a lot of collections that are worth perusing. These include various newspapers, pictures, yearbooks, prison records, obituary collections, Native-American documents, and more. Okay, who am I kidding? Though not every item is genealogically relevant and there are no collections of vital records, per se, the Montana Memory Project has digitized a lot of information that the genealogist will find interesting. So if you have ancestors from Montana, you should spend some time searching this website.

Northwest Digital Archives (NWDA)
http://nwda.orbiscascade.org/

The NWDA is an archives repository for not only Montana, but also Idaho, Oregon, Alaska, and Washington. I've placed it under the Montana section for no better reason than the fact that it had to be discussed somewhere.

Various colleges, universities, and historical societies from each participating state have contributed to the project. Most information is in the form of finding aids (i.e., detailed write-ups for each collection, sometimes including names), though some items contain links to digitized collections. Manuscript collections pertaining to individuals from all walks of life are among the items that might be online. Other items, like the guide to Montana State Prison records, sometimes have lists of names in the finding aids themselves.

MTGenWeb

http://www.mtgenweb.com/

In addition to the typical county-webpage links and military troop rosters found through many of the state-level USGenWeb sites, MTGenWeb has an Archives link which provides some unique information. Transcriptions of newspaper articles pertaining to Montana vital records are online, National Guard rosters from 1940 are provided, and several old (out-of-copyright) publications on Montana's history have been indexed and are now searchable by name.

Nebraska

Date of Statehood: 1 Mar 1867

Neighboring States: Colorado, Iowa, Kansas, Missouri, South Dakota, Wyoming

Previous Affiliations: Louisiana Territory, Missouri Territory, Unorganized Territory, Nebraska Territory, Dakota Territory

Part of the Louisiana Purchase, Nebraska was first part of the Louisiana Territory and then the Missouri Territory before Missouri became a state. At that point, the area wasn't part of any organized territory until 1854 when the Nebraska Territory was formed. Although this territory included portions of present-day Colorado, Wyoming, Montana, and the Dakotas (in addition to Nebraska), these areas were split off to form other territories prior to Nebraska becoming a state in 1867. A small portion of present-day northeastern Nebraska had been given to the Dakota Territory upon its creation but was returned to the state of Nebraska in 1882.

Nebraska State Historical Society (NSHS)

http://nebraskahistory.org

The NSHS has been around since shortly after Nebraska became a state, and as such, the Society has a great deal of information. Not only are the Society's holdings substantial, but there are numerous online indexes as well. There are finding aids for genealogical research in the state, for state- and county-level documents, and even for the Society's Manuscript Collections, which encompass any and all non-governmental records that the Society is in possession of. The Manuscript Collections include church, business, organizational, political, and even family records. Your best bet for locating your relatives online is in the Family/Individual Records section. You'll find write-ups on the various collections, but remember that these are simply finding aids and the collections themselves aren't actually online.

The write-ups for government documents, especially county-level documents, are quite thorough, and most counties have pages upon pages of background and holdings information.

Some indexes that are searchable by name (by hovering over "Search Collections," then scrolling down to "Additional Research Databases") include atlas/plat books, cemetery records, Civil War veterans, the 1890 and

1911 *Gazateer*, WWI draft cards, 1860 to 1954 tract books, and Nebraska public records (**http://nebpubdocs.unl.edu/**). The public records search, which is located off-site, is the only one of these resources that provides scanned images of original documents. And while many of the digitized records appear to be state- and government-type publications, it's still worth doing a quick search for your relatives, as there are also miscellaneous documents like lists of licensed veterinarians and newspaper editors.

Photographic collections can be searched and there are extensive lists of the Society's newspaper holdings, city/county/telephone directories, probate records, church records, and more. One can also search *Nebraska History*, a Society publication that's been in print for more than 100 years.

While some other websites have more digitized content than this one, you'd be hard-pressed to find a more comprehensive collection of finding aids, holdings, and indexes related to any given state.

Nebraska Memories
http://memories.ne.gov/index.php

If you're looking for digital material, this website, administered by the Nebraska Library Commission, has an assortment of good content. Much of the content appears to be photographic in nature, but some documents are also online. Unfortunately, it doesn't seem that most of this information will be of value to the researcher. That being said, more content will no doubt come online in the future, and you may even luck out and find something that pertains to your ancestors now.

Nebraska State Genealogical Society (NESGS)
http://www.nesgs.org/

Though links to county-level resources and genealogical societies are provided, these aren't the best resources that this website has to offer. Family Recognition certificates, awarded for early settlers of the state, are all listed online, and the NESGS has a searchable Tombstone Photo Project. Several other indexing projects, in collaboration with Ancestry.com, are underway, but none of these appear to be available through the NESGS website at this time.

NEGenWeb

http://www.rootsweb.ancestry.com/~negenweb/

The county-level resources from the NESGS (discussed above) actually point to the county webpages associated with the NEGenWeb Project. Though numerous NEGenWeb special projects are online, my favorite section of this website is the Online Library. Here, one may find various books on Nebraska's towns and counties, most of which include biographies of important residents. Most of the books are out-of-copyright, though some may have been made available with permission.

Nevada

Date of Statehood: 31 Oct 1864

Neighboring States: Arizona, California, Idaho, Oregon, Utah

Previous Affiliations: Spain, Mexico, Utah Territory, Nevada Territory, New Mexico Territory, Arizona Territory

The United States acquired the land that makes up present-day Nevada from Mexico in 1848 via the Treaty of Guadalupe Hidalgo. When the Utah and New Mexico Territories were established in 1850, most of Nevada was located in the Utah Territory, though the southernmost portion was located in the New Mexico Territory. The Nevada Territory was established out of the Utah Territory in 1861 and became a state in 1864. Borders expanded several times throughout the decade to include more of the Utah Territory to the east and part of the Arizona Territory, formerly the New Mexico Territory, to the south.

Nevada State Library and Archives

http://nsla.nevadaculture.org/index.php?option=com_content&id=58 7&Itemid=513

Since many genealogical entities link back and forth between each other, sometimes without particularly clear boundaries, deciding how best to present their material can be difficult. Such is the case with the Nevada State Library and Archives. Though the website also provides links to some of the databases and indexes discussed below, we'll try to limit this section to only those items that the State Library and Archives hosts directly.

First, let's discuss vital records. The State Archives only has limited vital-records holdings since, early on, counties were in charge of most of those records. While some births, marriages, and deaths from before 1900 were recorded, that occurred at the county level and as such those items are not online through the Archives' website. However, information on where to find county records is online, and there is even a link to a Carson City website that contains birth, death, and citizenship indexes. It appears that when a complete date was unavailable, these Carson City records indicate 1 Jan 1700. If you open any given record with a 1700 date, you may find additional (and more accurate) date information. Also on the State-Library-and-Archives' website are links to several additional death-record and obituary searches, a list of county recorders, and links to marriage searches for specific counties.

Civil War rosters and indexes to Korean and Vietnam casualties are provided, as well as a name index for Carson City newspapers that encompasses several years in the 1860s, '70s, and '80s. An index of prison inmates is also online.

The remainder of the information on the website pertains mostly to the holdings of the Archives and external websites, some of which have been discussed elsewhere in this book.

Nevada State Historic Preservation Office

http://nvshpo.org/

The main item of interest here is a database of searchable census records for the state. Years covered are 1860 (before Nevada became a state) to 1920, neglecting the missing 1890 census. Original images aren't available, but this is an easy (and free) way to search for your Nevada ancestors.

Nevada Digital Archives

http://nevadadigitalarchives.org

The Digital Archives can fill in some of the gaps where original records are not readily available elsewhere online. Territory censuses from the early 1860s have been indexed and digitized. Most of these records don't include much besides name, age, and sex, but they may still be useful to locate families or determine the town your ancestors lived in. The SSDI for Nevada is searchable, though this collection is also available elsewhere. Finally, there is an assortment of miscellaneous records which includes items like land patents and court cases.

NVGenWeb

http://www.nvgenweb.org/

Part of the USGenWeb Project, this website has links to county-level webpages and their associated resources. Additional features of interest include transcribed tax lists from 1863, marriage and death records from *Overland Monthly* and *Out West Magazine* from 1872, and the usual links to miscellaneous genealogical societies.

New Hampshire

Date of Statehood: 21 Jun 1788
Neighboring States: Maine, Massachusetts, Vermont, Country of Canada
Previous Affiliations: Massachusetts Bay Colony, Dominion of New England,
    Province of New Hampshire

Although the northern tip of the Province of New Hampshire was dually claimed by Quebec and New Hampshire and the present-day state of Vermont was dually claimed by New York and New Hampshire, the state's boundaries fell into line in the mid-1700s. Even though New Hampshire had already sold land to settlers in present-day Vermont (an area called the New Hampshire Grants), King George III declared that this area was part of the New York Colony in 1764. As might be expected, this led to numerous disputes and eventually Vermont's settlers declared themselves independent of both colonies, leaving New Hampshire's western border as it is today.

New Hampshire Deeds

http://www.nhdeeds.com

This is the website you should start with if you're in search of New Hampshire deeds. Simply find the county you want and get started. Most county webpages are formatted in the same way and allow for online searches, while a couple of county websites have different formats and either require a free username or do not post records online at all.

New Hampshire State Archives

http://www.sos.nh.gov/archives/genealogy.html

The information on the State Archives' website is simply an outline of some available collections that might be useful in your research. An alphabetical guide to the Archives is online and a few links to off-site resources are provided, but there are no vital-record indexes or digitized records.

The best options for locating your ancestors on the State Archives' website are accessed through the "Archival Holdings" link on the left-hand side of the webpage. Here, one will find a petitions index, a small collection of land survey records, and a link to a collection entitled "New Hampshire

State Papers." (Alternately, the New Hampshire State Papers can be accessed by clicking on the "Publications and Collections" link on the left-hand side of the webpage.)

When searching the New Hampshire State Papers, you should first locate your relatives in the Index file (it's a PDF). Then all you have to do is open the listed volume and turn to the page mentioned in the index. There are forty volumes of information so it's difficult to say exactly what you might find, but military service and court records are some of the items available.

New Hampshire State Library

http://www.nh.gov/nhsl/services/public/genealogy.html

Though a guide to the State Library's holdings and a town record index are both present, you won't find any helpful online indexes or collections that allow you to locate your ancestors directly. A newspaper index is searchable, but this resource only indexes papers back to the 1980s so isn't particularly useful for genealogy purposes.

It appears that the Library has a lot of worthwhile content (2,400 published family histories and a name index to early town records, to highlight but two items of interest), but only if you can visit in person.

Find NH History

http://findnhhistory.org

FindNHHistory.org is a database comprised of miscellaneous New Hampshire resources. Various libraries and historical societies participate in the project, and one can search available records by region or type of content. Vital records and cemetery indexes for different counties and towns are just some of the collections of interest to the genealogist.

Each collection has a detailed description, though the collections themselves are not always available online. Some collections have links to their associated host websites, but you may have to contact the proper managing organization for access to others.

Overall, this is a great website for searching loads of organizations with one quick stroke.

New Hampshire Society of Genealogists (NHSOG)

http://www.nhsog.org/

Many links to national- and state-level resources are provided, but the for-sale publications put together by the NHSOG appear to be the most valuable unique offerings. Two vital-records compilations are available for purchase along with a book entitled *New Hampshire Families in 1790*. The latter publication has an online index, so you can make sure that your ancestors are included in the book before you decide whether to purchase it or not.

New Hampshire History Bookshelf

http://www.library.unh.edu/diglib/bookshelf/

This is actually a joint project between the State Archives and the University of New Hampshire Library. There are webpages for state and provincial papers, as well as for soldiers in the Civil War. The State-and-Provincial-Papers-of-New-Hampshire webpage has links to volumes that contain probate records, military records, and more. These all appear to be older publications which are hosted on the Internet Archive, discussed earlier in the book. The register of soldiers may take a while to download since the PDF file is approximately 200 MB in size.

If you follow the link to the UNH Digital Collections Initiative, there are numerous digital documents like Civil War histories, newspapers, and even a few old genealogical publications.

NHGenWeb

http://www.usroots.com/usgwnhus/

"Live Free or Die" is an ominous-sounding motto for a state, so perhaps it should come as no surprise that New Hampshire is vaguely shaped like a giant cleaver. Regardless of shape (which has nothing to do with anything--I just wanted to mention it as it relates to the state motto), the state packs in a total of ten counties, all of which have their own webpages associated with the NHGenWeb Project.

In addition to county-level webpages, some of the more interesting NHGenWeb items are a webpage for family-specific websites and lookups, a Civil War index, and a probate index for the town of Hampton. The latter two items are actually links to external websites--Sons of Union Veterans of the Civil War [http://www.suvcw.org/id.htm] and the Lane Memorial Library in Hampton.

Be aware that some of the website's links don't provide direct access to the named collections but instead bring up email addresses so that you may send email inquiries to the owners of the named resources.

New Jersey

Date of Statehood: 18 Dec 1787

Neighboring States: Delaware, New York, Pennsylvania

Previous Affiliations: New Netherland, New Sweden, Province of West Jersey, Province of East Jersey, Province of New Jersey, Province of New York, Dominion of New England

For a time in the 1600s, portions of present-day New Jersey were actually Dutch and Swedish settlements. Although skirmishes with the Dutch continued for another ten years, a grant for a large area of New England, which included New Jersey, was made to the Duke of York in 1664. Later that year the Duke sold a portion of the area to a pair of Englishmen who created New Jersey. Spelled out in that document, the western border of New Jersey was meant to extend slightly farther north so that the province included a portion of present-day New York. Separate colonies of East and West Jersey existed until they were joined in 1702, though the border with New York was still disputed. That border dispute was finally settled shortly before the Revolutionary War.

New Jersey State Archives

http://www.nj.gov/state/archives/index.html

There are a lot of searchable databases available online through the New Jersey State Archives. Simply select "Search the Collections" on the left-hand side of the webpage and you can either browse the catalog by subject area (including genealogical holdings), by searchable databases, or by imaged (i.e., digital) collections.

New Jersey really has its act together with regard to indexing public records. One can search the following collections: marriage records from the late 17th, entire 18th, and mid-19th centuries; death records from the late 19th century; early land records from New Jersey's colonial days; citizens who applied for compensation from Revolutionary War damages; court records; name changes; military records; early state censuses. Some collections, like National Guard photos and WWI casualties, have images online while most others have basic transcribed information pertaining to the record. For those items, copies of the actual records can be purchased through the website.

Another option from the "Search the Collections" webpage is to browse the "Imaged Collections." Some of these collections consist of military pictures and service records for various wars, often searchable by name, as well as miscellaneous county collections such as vital, military, and slave records, and even shopkeepers' licenses.

Lastly, the "Collection Management" link on the left-hand side of the page brings up holdings information for the Archives.

New Jersey State Library

http://slic.njstatelib.org/slic_home/library_collections/genealogy_an d_local_history

Though the State Library has a good deal of online information about its collections, in most regards it doesn't hold a candle to the State Archives, discussed above. Genealogical collections, such as family histories and city directories, are discussed, but most of them aren't indexed and available online. Some that are available online can be reached by clicking the "Genealogy Electronic Resources" link.

Although certain licensed databases are only available online to state employees and authorized users from Thomas Edison State College, some other collections, most of which are discussed in this section or in another chapter, are also online.

One additional place to search for information is by clicking the "New Jersey Information" link on the left-hand side of the webpage. From here one can view lists of old New Jersey newspapers, available digital collections, and searchable publications. Most of the digital collections of genealogical importance actually link to the list of searchable publications mentioned a moment ago. Searchable publications include those pertaining to corporations, the Civil War, Revolutionary War, and a few others that appear to be less helpful to the researcher.

Princeton University - Department of Rare Books and Special Collections

http://www.princeton.edu/~rbsc/department/maps/

Available through the Department of Rare Books and Special Collections (RBSC) at Princeton University is a collection of Sanborn Fire Insurance maps from the late 1800s through the mid-1900s. The link to access the Sanborn map collection is located partway through the online write-up about the Department's Historic Maps Collection. A lengthy list, arranged by county, town, and year, provides hyperlinks to actual maps. Though none of the maps I consulted had owners' names listed, these detailed maps can be useful for pinpointing your ancestors' exact residence, especially if street names have changed and you're having trouble tracking down where they lived.

Click on the "Catalogs, Databases, and Finding Aids" link at the top-center of the webpage to bring up additional links, through which the user can search several other Princeton collections. Most of the results are merely finding aids that you'll have to follow up on. It doesn't appear that most researchers will find anything useful here, but as there are numerous family collections and diaries, you just might get lucky.

Princeton Library Online Databases
http://www.princeton.edu/~mudd/databases/

Overlapping slightly with the previously discussed resource is a list of online databases available through the Princeton Library. Many of the indexes are Princeton related, but one can search alumni as well as the archives of the *Daily Princetonian* and the *Nassau Literary Magazine*. Numerous other collections are available, and the online catalog allows users to search the library's holdings, even if the material they're interested in doesn't pertain to the university itself.

Genealogical Society of New Jersey (GSNJ)
http://www.gsnj.org/

A couple of interesting items on the GSNJ website are the *Genealogical Magazine of New Jersey* and the Collections Guide. An online article-and-author index is available for the magazine, though a name index is not. Although some older volumes are available for purchase and the magazine's description states that a name index is included in each year-end issue, unfortunately these name indexes cannot be searched online at this time.

The Collections Guide discusses Society holdings, and most helpfully, it also has a partial online index of family and bible records.

New Jersey Historical Society (NJHS)
http://www.jerseyhistory.org

If I were you, I would start my NJHS-website search by actually typing my family name in the search bar. Alternately, I would select "Explore our Collections" from the homepage, and then select the "Archives: Documents, Manuscripts, & Photographs" link below. Finally, select the "Browse the Archives" link on the right-hand side of the webpage. There are tons of finding aids for various collections, and although a "Genealogy Collections" link is provided, don't forget to look at some of the other collections too. Military records, estate papers, African-American collections, a biography index, and a list of family name files are some of the places you might find your relatives. The Family Names' webpage is only a list of family names for which the Society has folders, but if your ancestor's surname appears in the list, it might be worth following up. You won't know what's there until you ask.

NJGenWeb
http://www.rootsweb.ancestry.com/~njgenweb/

As might be expected, the New Jersey portion of the USGenWeb Project has its own unique assortment of collections and resources online. Browse the links on the Research page or just move directly to the county-level webpages and their associated information.

New Mexico

Date of Statehood: 6 Jan 1912

Neighboring States: Arizona, Colorado, Oklahoma, Texas, Utah (kitty-corner), Country of Mexico

Previous Affiliations: Spain, Mexico, Louisiana Territory, Missouri Territory, Republic of Texas, New Mexico Territory

The northeastern portion of New Mexico was originally acquired as part of the Louisiana Purchase; however, it was given to Spain in exchange for Florida as part of the Adams-Onís Treaty of 1819. Mexico became the new owner of New Mexico after winning its independence from Spain. From 1836 to 1845, the Republic of Texas, and from 1845 to 1850, the state of Texas, contained the eastern portion of present-day New Mexico. Mexico didn't acknowledge Texas' independence, so we can alternately say that this portion of present-day New Mexico became a United States' possession when Mexico ceded it to the USA via the 1848 Treaty of Guadalupe Hidalgo. The western portion of the state, along with vast amounts of the American West, was ceded to the United States in that same treaty. As a result of the Compromise of 1850, Texas gave up its land in present-day New Mexico and the New Mexico Territory was established. The Gadsden Purchase in 1853 added the southernmost portion of New Mexico to the territory. Over the years, portions of the New Mexico Territory were split off and added to the Colorado Territory and used to establish the Arizona Territory leaving, in 1863, the New Mexico Territory with its borders as we know them today.

Palace of the Governors Obituary Database

http://www.palaceofthegovernors.org/obitfiles/index.php?view=search

This obituary database, administered by the Fray Angélico Chávez History Library, covers several New Mexico newspapers beginning in the latter part of the 19th century and continuing up until 2005. Earlier entries cover a broader region, while entries from the middle of the 20th century onward are mostly for the Santa Fe area. As such, this database should not be considered comprehensive. If you find your relatives, the search results will include a date and newspaper reference. Some entries have a short line of text describing the particulars of the obituary (e.g., "Hanged in Lincoln" or "Died of typhoid"). You'll need to follow up and locate a copy of the newspaper elsewhere in order to read the full obituary.

New Mexico Archives and Historical Services Division (State Archives)

http://www.nmcpr.state.nm.us/archives/archives_hm.htm

Although the holdings of the State Archives are impressive--county records, church records, family histories, letters, diaries, wills--you'll have to content yourself by searching the online catalog without expecting access to much digital material. If you find any references to individuals with your ancestor's surname, be aware that most of the online items only contain brief descriptive information. As such, you'll have to visit the Archives or request copies of the original documents to learn more.

Rocky Mountain Online Archive (RMOA)

http://rmoa.unm.edu/

In addition to New Mexico, this online archive covers the states of Colorado and Wyoming. The Online-Archive-of-New-Mexico's website states that all of the information found there can now be found at the RMOA website also, which is why we're discussing that resource and not only the New-Mexico-specific website.

Just like with the above-mentioned State Archives website, most of the information found here is of the finding-aid variety, so you probably won't gain access to any images of primary sources. That being said, the finding aids for each collection are quite detailed, so they may be helpful in determining if a given collection pertains to your relatives.

New Mexico's Digital Collections

http://econtent.unm.edu/

At present, there are no digital collections of vital records available through New Mexico's Digital Collections website. There are, however, a number of photographic collections, digitized newspapers from the early part of the 20th century, and some of the items in the Center for Southwest Research (CSWR) Manuscripts section are even related to family history.

New Mexico State Library

http://www.nmstatelibrary.org/research-and-collections/collections

A lot of information about the State Library's holdings can be found online, but aside from that, not much is of interest to the genealogist. The best bet for locating your ancestors is probably through the library's digital collections, though since most of the items in the NM-State-Documents category appear to be fairly recent, even this might be a stretch.

Early volumes of *El Palacio* magazine are the only other items of interest in the library's digital collections.

Hispanic Genealogical Research Center of New Mexico

http://www.hgrc-nm.org/

If I had relatives from New Mexico, I would visit this website. Not only are there links to various other online resources and a subject index to *Herencia*, the Center's quarterly journal, but the Great New Mexico Pedigree Database is also online. This is a compilation that combines information from various published sources and information from computer genealogy (GEDCOM) files. There are over 170,000 names in the database, so spending a few minutes to search it might be worth your while.

University of New Mexico LoboVault - Marriage Records

http://repository.unm.edu/handle/1928/14546

This is an eleven-volume work that presents marriage information from the Archdiocese of Santa Fe for the years 1678 through 1869. Though each volume opens as a separate PDF file, I was able to easily search the text through my web browser which made quick work of what would otherwise have been a long and arduous task.

New Mexico Genealogical Society (NMGS)

http://www.nmgs.org

Various indexes of interest can be found on the NMGS website. Under the "Journal" tab and the "Articles" subheading there are various reprinted articles from the *New Mexico Genealogist* and a few other publications. Some of these articles deal with county-level marriage lists, deaths, tax lists, and passport and military records. The first forty years of the *New Mexico Genealogist*, complete with name index, can be purchased on CD. Other vital-records and reference publications are also available for purchase, and while these appear to contain name indexes, I was unable to locate the indexes online.

NMGenWeb
http://www.nmgenweb.us/

Along with the county-level webpages that all USGenWeb participating websites contain, the two items that I found most interesting were a name index to the *Historical Encyclopedia of New Mexico* and a state death index, the latter of which is accessible through the link to the New Mexico section of the USGenWeb-Archives website. As usual, additional content varies by county.

New York

Date of Statehood: 26 Jul 1788

Neighboring States: Connecticut, Massachusetts, New Jersey, Pennsylvania, Vermont, Country of Canada

Previous Affiliations: Province of New Jersey, Province of New York, Dominion of New England

Although the Duke of York was granted a large portion of New England in 1664, this area wasn't entirely under his control for long. Land for New Jersey was sold and portions of present-day Maine and Massachusetts, including islands like Martha's Vineyard, were also reassigned so that New York had shrunk considerably by the end of the century. New York had boundary disputes with every surrounding state and Canada, though most of these were settled by the Revolutionary War. Entire books have been written on how the state's boundary disputes were handled, so consider consulting these (and each original colony's charters) for additional details.

New York State Archives

http://www.archives.nysed.gov

Like many others, the New York State Archives has an online catalog and a lot of information on how to locate all types of records including probate, naturalization, and more. Also like other State Archives, not all of the write-ups and finding aids lead to online name indexes.

Selecting the "Research" link on the left side of the webpage brings up the most useful information for the genealogist. "Research Tips" has a lot of information on particular types of records, while "Research Topics" has a whole section on genealogy. Although some valuable information is presented and a vital-records index is available onsite, the index isn't searchable online. There is, however, a link to a searchable State Archives Name Index. Here one can search Civil War records, military land patents from the late 18th century, and a few other collections, even including inmates from the Attica Correctional Facility.

New York State Library

http://www.nysl.nysed.gov/

Several databases and indexes are available through the New York State Library, but most remote access is only available to New York residents and/or library card holders. Of course, if you're not a resident, you could always hire a researcher who is.

Available to the general public, another section of the website is entitled "Digital Collections." This section has statistical information on state censuses, not the actual digitized copies of records that a genealogist would be most interested in, and various military manuscripts. More documents are available in person than online, but if your relatives are from New York, it wouldn't hurt to see if anything pertaining to your relatives has been digitized.

Italian Genealogical Group (IGG)

http://www.italiangen.org

The Genealogy Federation of Long Island coordinated the indexing of New York City (NYC) vital records, though that organization doesn't host the online databases. Along with the below listed resource (the German Genealogy Group), the Italian Genealogical Group actually hosts many of these NYC databases from the 1800s and 1900s. There are indexed birth, marriage, and death records, along with naturalizations and an IGG surname database. If your relatives lived in New York City in the last 150 years, even if they're not Italian, take some time to search the indexes.

German Genealogy Group (GGG)

http://www.germangenealogygroup.com/

As a second host for many NYC databases, the GGG has some of the same searchable indexes that the previously discussed IGG has. However, the GGG has additional databases online including several that pertain to churches, cemeteries, deeds, the DAR, yearbooks, and a GGG surname index. The bottom line is that, even with overlapping collections, you shouldn't limit your search to either the Italian Genealogical Group or the German Genealogy Group. Make sure you check both resources.

New York Genealogical & Biographical Society (NYG&B)
http://www.newyorkfamilyhistory.org/

The New York Genealogical & Biographical Society has an eLibrary, which contains a growing number of digitized collections as well as an Early American Newspaper database. Those online resources require NYG&B membership, but there are a number of items available for free.

Research guides and external links are online, though my favorite feature of the website is probably the Worden's Index. This is an index to *The Record*, a NYG&B publication which was first published in 1870. Although anyone can search the index, only NYG&B members have online access to the publication itself.

The Society has also teamed up with the New York Public Library (NYPL--**http://www.nypl.org**) to combine their genealogical collections. The most interesting online NYPL content I found was a searchable 1940-directory website called Direct Me NYC 1940. The website makes use of directories to help locate individuals who lived in one of the five boroughs at that time. With an address in hand, the researcher can then use that information to find the enumeration district for the 1940 census itself. A few other NYPL items of interest are related to Civil War soldiers, Jewish newspapers, and an index to "Miscellaneous Personal Name Files."

NYGenWeb
http://www.rootsweb.ancestry.com/~nygenweb/

I believe that the county information available through the NYGenWeb Project is probably of the most use to the genealogist. That being said, several military collections are online, there is a tombstone transcription project, and links to other genealogical resources are also provided.

North Carolina

Date of Statehood: 21 Nov 1789

Neighboring States: Georgia, South Carolina, Tennessee, Virginia

Previous Affiliations: Virginia Colony, Province of Carolina, Province of North Carolina, South Carolina

When the Province of Carolina received its charter in 1663, it was formed out of a portion of the Virginia Colony and extended west to the Pacific Ocean and south to 31-degrees north latitude (along the present-day Florida/Alabama border). In 1665, the borders were extended to the north and south, with the northern border moving to the current North Carolina/Virginia border and the southern border moving south towards present-day Daytona Beach, Florida. In the late 1600s, the Province encountered irreconcilable differences, and it eventually became two distinct colonies, namely North and South Carolina. After the Revolutionary War, the western portion of North Carolina became the state of Tennessee.

Recently, the border between North and South Carolina was revisited and found to be slightly inaccurate. Not inaccurate enough to affect most residents, but problematic to the point where some South Carolina residents will find that they no longer live in the state even though they haven't moved. Final surveys to determine the boundary line are supposed to be completed in the spring of 2013.

State Archives of North Carolina

http://www.archives.ncdcr.gov/

Quite a bit of information is available through the State Archives' website. The problem is that the information isn't presented in a very intuitive manner, at least not for me. For that reason, I'll discuss this resource in several parts.

First, one can select "Record Types" from the left-hand side of the webpage. This will bring up several types of records including a section called County Records. In the County-Records section, click on the link entitled "Container Lists of Selected County Records." These lists cover all sorts of documents including wills, estates, marriages, civil actions, and more. It should be noted that none of these categories are complete records for the state, but instead a select number of counties are represented. Some categories have files from thirty or more counties, while other categories only have records from one or two. If you're looking for your ancestor's name and you don't want to search each county file separately, just use the "Search" link on the left-hand side of the webpage. I've found that the search feature includes the aforementioned county records.

The second place you'll want to search is the MARS Catalog. Although the search bar mentioned in the previous paragraph handles the Archives, Digital Collections, and several other associated websites, it doesn't search the MARS (Manuscript and Archives Reference System) online catalog. Through the catalog, you might locate land records, wills, pension files, court cases, and the like.

Although links to finding aids, the Outer Banks History Center, and the Western Regional Archives are also presented, the last item to be discussed here is the Online-Projects link on the left-hand side of the page. Through this webpage, one can access digital versions of old North Carolina newspapers, Sanborn maps, and more. Other collections of interest, like North Carolina Family Records Online, are part of the North Carolina Digital Collections. One can search family records by name, and things like bible records, newspaper marriage and death notices, and military records might be found. A separate Civil War collection is also part of the Digital Collections.

Finally, by searching the Digital Collections for "register of deeds" one will find links to off-site resources where users can search county-level records.

North Carolina State Library
http://statelibrary.ncdcr.gov/

Since there is a lot of overlap between the State Archives (discussed above) and the State Library, we don't need to discuss everything in detail. In fact, although you'll find a lot of good information by hovering over the "Resources" tab and selecting "Genealogy," we discussed a good portion of those databases and collections already. There are some how-to articles and although other databases can be accessed online, most of them require a North Carolina library card. As such, most of those databases aren't available online unless you're a resident of the state.

North Carolina Association Registers of Deeds
http://www.ncard.us/

Although many of the Register-of-Deeds county websites can be accessed through the Digital Collections, as mentioned in the State Archives section above, this website contains a more straightforward approach to locating each county's website. Website design varies by county, but once you land at the desired county's website, simply look for the search feature to see whether you can locate your relatives.

North Carolina Genealogical Society (NCGS)
http://www.ncgenealogy.org/

The NCGS has links to a lot of different state resources. However, the most valuable information online may be the North Carolina Loose Estates Records, an ongoing project to index said estates; the collection is actually online at FamilySearch.org.

The *North Carolina Genealogical Society Journal*, published since 1975, also has an online article index. Although a name index isn't online at this time, members can read the journal online, and anyone can purchase a searchable CD.

NCGenWeb
http://www.ncgenweb.us/

County-level websites are once again presented through the NCGenWeb Project, and numerous African-American resources, some county-level, are also available. Users have contributed records of all sorts, but one of my favorite collections is a yearbook index that consists mostly of college seniors from the early 20th century. This index pulls from those yearbooks available on the NCGenWeb Digital Bookshelf, but it doesn't include every individual from every yearbook.

Quite a few other publications, such as directories, newspapers, and even church histories are also linked through the Digital Bookshelf. Military information, executions, vital records, and more are either available on the website or through links to external websites, some of which have been discussed above or in previous chapters.

North Dakota

Date of Statehood: 2 Nov 1889
Neighboring States: Minnesota, Montana, South Dakota, Country of Canada
Previous Affiliations: Louisiana Territory, Missouri Territory, Unorganized
    Territory, Michigan Territory, Wisconsin Territory, Iowa Territory,
    Minnesota Territory, Nebraska Territory, Dakota Territory

Being split by the Missouri River, North Dakota's history evolved from several directions. Present-day North Dakota was partly acquired through the Louisiana Purchase and partly through a treaty with the British in 1818. As such, the state was first located in the Louisiana Territory, followed by the Missouri Territory, before not being a part of any organized territory. In the early 1830s, the portion of the state east of the Missouri River became part of the Michigan Territory and would eventually be re-designated as a part of the Wisconsin, Iowa, and Minnesota Territories before Minnesota finally became a state in 1858. After not belonging to any organized territory, the western half of the state became part of the Nebraska Territory in 1854 before the Dakota Territory was formed in 1861. Though the territory grew and shrank over the years, its final extent was split in two when it entered the Union as North Dakota and South Dakota in 1889.

State Historical Society of North Dakota - State Archives

http://history.nd.gov/archives/

Though archival holdings are listed online and a section entitled "Genealogy" has additional information on certain types of records, the State Archives doesn't have many searchable indexes on its website. In fact, although there are numerous links to the indexes discussed in the following sections, the only index unique to the site appears to be an oral history index of interviews completed in the 1970s.

North Dakota Department of Health - Public Death Index

https://secure.apps.state.nd.us/doh/certificates/deathCertSearch.htm

Although somewhat restrictive--you'll get an error if over 500 results are returned and you can't search more than a ten-year span at once--this public death index could be an easy way to locate your relatives. Records as recent as 2011 are returned, and the database appears to begin in the early 1890s (a record from 1892 was the oldest I found). If you find an ancestor of yours, you can order a copy of the record online.

North Dakota State University (NDSU) Library
http://library.ndsu.edu/db/

Several of the links on the State Archives' website actually lead here, to the indexed databases available through the NDSU library. There are indexes for several newspapers and miscellaneous publications, a North Dakota Biography Index, a *Fargo Forum* obituary index, and even naturalization and 1885 Dakota Territory census indexes. A few indexes specific to Cass County are also online.

Digital Horizons
http://digitalhorizonsonline.org/

The digital collections available here aren't necessarily aimed at the genealogical researcher. However, there are collections that may be of interest. Photographic collections, with subjects sometimes identified by name, are abundant. Some old diaries and letters have also been digitized, but you may have to get lucky to find anything that pertains to your ancestors.

NDGenWeb
http://www.ndgenweb.org/

Since some of the resources discussed on the NDGenWeb website have already been discussed here and in other chapters, we won't rehash that information. Information that isn't readily available elsewhere includes territory and early-statehood maps, as well as the expected county-level webpages.

There is also some excellent information on how to locate county-level marriage indexes (i.e., whether an index is online and who to contact if it's not). If indexes aren't online, county contacts are provided and specifically note whether you should contact the county clerk, recorder, or auditor. Some county indexes can also be searched through the State Historical Society of North Dakota, the first North-Dakota resource mentioned above.

Ohio

Date of Statehood: 1 Mar 1803

Neighboring States: Indiana, Kentucky, Michigan, Pennsylvania, West Virginia

Previous Affiliations: Northwest Territory, Indiana Territory, Connecticut

After the Revolutionary War ended and the United States acquired the rest of the British landholdings to the Mississippi River, the Northwest Ordinance was passed to create the Northwest Territory in 1787. This territory included the area west of the new state of Pennsylvania, north of the Ohio River, and east of the Mississippi; as such, it included the entirety of the present-day states of Michigan, Illinois, Indiana, and Wisconsin, as well as portions of Minnesota and Ohio. Portions of this territory had been claimed by several of the original colonies, but most of those claims were settled or ceded prior to the new territory's creation. One notable exception was Connecticut's claim to northeastern Ohio, a claim not given up until 1800 when that land was incorporated into the Northwest Territory.

Although the Northwest Ordinance had defined Indiana's future eastern border, the act establishing the Indiana Territory in 1800 defined a slightly different one. As such, the Northwest Territory (also known as the Territory Northwest of the Ohio River) included a small piece of present-day southeastern Indiana from 1800 until Ohio was admitted as the 17th state in 1803.[**]

Rutherford B. Hayes Presidential Center
http://index.rbhayes.org/hayes/index/

The main reason for the genealogist with Ohio roots to visit this website is to use the obituary index. This index contains more than 2.2-million entries and covers a huge number of newspapers. Even though such a sizeable number of names have been recorded, keep in mind that this index doesn't

---

[**]Congress actually approved Ohio's admittance to the United States on February 19, 1803, but never ratified the state's constitution to finalize the process. Eventually, in 1953, legislation was approved to retroactively ratify the state constitution and set the admittance date at March 1, 1803.

cover every newspaper and county in the state. A list of participating libraries, counties, and the newspapers indexed is available online. Only records held by the Hayes Library are available for purchase online through the website, but links are provided with instructions on how to order from other libraries.

A few other genealogical resources are available, both on the website and in person, but they pertain mostly to Sandusky County and Northwest Ohio as opposed to the rest of the state.

Ohio Historical Society - State Archives

http://ww2.ohiohistory.org/resource/statearc/
http://www.ohiohistory.org/collections--archives/archives-
    library/family-researcher

Regardless of if you're able to find an obituary for your relatives using the above resource, you might be able to find a death certificate through the Ohio State Archives. The online index allows one to search and order death certificates from 1913 to 1944. You can also request a death certificate as early as 1909 or as late as 1953, though you'll have to fill out the request form since there is no online search for these expanded dates.

In addition to the previously mentioned death-certificate index, an online index to the Boys and Girls Industrial Schools (approximately from the 1860s to the 1940s), a list of Ohio's Medal of Honor Recipients, a Civil War database, and War-of-1812 military rosters are all searchable.

By clicking "Archives Library" on the left-hand side of the webpage you'll be presented with information on genealogical resources, available digital collections, and how to request research.

Newspaper indexes and archival holdings are searchable, and other valuable information on vital records and how to request certain documents is provided.

Ohio Memory Project

http://www.ohiomemory.org/

This is a collaborative project to create a digital library that will "provide access to historical treasures of Ohio." Collections range from city directories to land-office records to oral histories and even more obscure records like a roster of owners of purebred livestock. A search tool is available, so if your ancestor was the subject of any particular item, you may be able to locate him/her quite easily. For other collections, like the purebred livestock owners, you'll have to open and visually scan on your own since these aren't fully transcribed and searchable for every individual listed.

State Library of Ohio
http://www.library.ohio.gov/PCS/digitalcontent

The State Library of Ohio's website has external links to several previously mentioned resources as well as a few new ones--the Cincinnati public library has quite a few downloadable Cincinnati area directories and a host of other rare books, for example. By selecting the "Sources for Genealogists" link on the left-hand side of the webpage, one can then move to additional nationwide or Ohio-specific resources. The Ohio-Sources webpage lists numerous county-specific resources and genealogical societies.

Ohio Genealogical Society (OGS)
http://www.ogs.org/

A few of the free databases available here include those pertaining to Revolutionary War soldiers, early settlers, obituaries, and cemeteries. The *Ohio Civil War Genealogy Journal* (an OGS publication) is also searchable.

Quite a few additional databases are available online to Society members. Society holdings are also listed on the website.

OHGenWeb
http://www.ohgenweb.org/

Loads of external links and county-specific webpages are provided at OHGenWeb. Some of my favorites are off-site links to websites that provide county formation maps (www.genealogyinc.com) and a Civil War veterans' burial database (http://www.suvcwdb.org/home/). A statewide table also spells out when birth, marriage, death, probate, land, and court records were first recorded in each county.

Oklahoma

Date of Statehood: 16 Nov 1907

Neighboring States: Arkansas, Colorado, Kansas, Missouri, New Mexico, Texas

Previous Affiliations: Louisiana Territory, Missouri Territory, Arkansas Territory, Spain, Mexico, Texas (Republic and State), Unorganized Territory, Oklahoma Territory, Various Indian Reservations, Indian Territory

Oklahoma is another state whose land has been part of numerous territories and countries at different times. The land that makes up present-day Oklahoma was first acquired by the United States in the Louisiana Purchase, and it was subsequently part of the Louisiana Territory and then the Missouri Territory. When the Adams-Onís Treaty was signed with Spain in 1819, the panhandle went to Spain while the rest of the land remained with the United States; the lower portion of the state was part of the Arkansas Territory, while the upper portion was part of the Missouri Territory. After Missouri became a state and the Arkansas Territory's western border was moved, the United States portion of present-day Oklahoma wasn't in any organized territory. The Spanish portion (i.e., the panhandle) went to Mexico and then the Republic of Texas before the U.S. reacquired it after Texas' annexation and the subsequent Mexican-American War. Although Texas claimed a small portion of southwestern Oklahoma for a time, the rest of the state was unorganized and was set aside for Indian reservations. When the Oklahoma Territory was established, it was approximately half its current size, and the eastern half of the state was a separate territory, the Indian Territory. Although the Indian Territory drew up paperwork to enter the Union as the State of Sequoyah, the two territories eventually combined and entered as a single state, Oklahoma.

Oklahoma State Archives

http://www.odl.state.ok.us/oar/archives/collections.htm

Even though the "Genealogy in the Archives" link brings up information on some of the Archives' holdings, the only online item of interest appears to be an index to Oklahoma's Confederate pension records. The records often include death dates and spousal information, though the original images aren't available online.

Oklahoma Digital Prairie
http://digitalprairie.ok.gov/cdm/

This electronic library is part of the Oklahoma Department of Libraries. Fortunately for state residents, a portion of the website is dedicated to legal forms and recent governmental publications. Unfortunately, this means that the site isn't entirely focused on material that will help the genealogist.

The best collection for the researcher is one for Confederate pension records. Although the currently available collection is merely a set of index cards, it has more information than the index available through the State Archives' website (see above). Remember that pensioners in Oklahoma will have always served in another state since Oklahoma wasn't around during the Civil War. Cards may also have information on the back, so be sure to check both sides. According to the website, Digital Prairie is working on a collection that will make entire pension files available online, so if you find a relative on an index card, check back to see his entire pension file when the collection goes live.

Oklahoma Genealogical Society (OGS)
http://www.okgensoc.org/

The OGS has been around since 1955 and has put together an interesting website. Not only can one search the index of the First Families of the Twin Territories (FFTT), a compilation of settlers who lived in the Oklahoma or Indian Territories before they merged and entered the Union as the forty-sixth state, but a number of other online collections are also available.

Use the search bar to locate your relatives in a variety of sources including bible records, church records, directories, marriages, cemeteries, and much more. Most of these collections are limited to certain counties and/or dates, so whether you're able to locate your relatives may depend on where they lived.

A couple of fairly unique items are a surname index to the *Oklahoma Genealogical Quarterly*, an index of United States Marshalls, and a small transcribed fragment of the 1890 Indian Territory census records. And if you need more than just a fragment of the 1890 Indian Territory census, you're in luck, because our next resource has an index to the Oklahoma territorial census, one of only a few records from 1890 that still exists.

Oklahoma Historical Society
http://www.okhistory.org

An index to the 1890 Oklahoma territorial census is available through the Oklahoma Historical Society. Other online indexes include an early Oklahoma Territory directory, two separate collections of members of the Five Civilized Tribes in the Indian Territory, an index to the 1901 land lottery, divorces, marriages, obituaries, a vertical files index, and more. A collection of historic newspapers is even online. Do yourself a favor. If your ancestors are from Oklahoma, visit this website.

University of Oklahoma - Indian-Pioneer Papers Collection
http://digital.libraries.ou.edu/whc/pioneer/

This is an oral history collection from the 1930s that contains approximately 80,000 entries. A search tool is online, and once you find an interview of interest, the transcript can be opened as a PDF file.

OKGenWeb
http://okgenweb.org/

Along with webpages dedicated to each of the current counties in Oklahoma, there are webpages dedicated to the Indian Territory and many of the tribal nations of which it was comprised.

Links to some of the above-mentioned resources are provided, and OKGenWeb has various projects pertaining to marriages, land records, the military, and a surname registry.

Oregon

Date of Statehood: 14 Feb 1859
Neighboring States: California, Idaho, Nevada, Washington
Previous Affiliations: Disputed Territory, Oregon Territory

Although an 1818 Treaty between the United States and Britain set the 49th parallel as the international border east of the Rockies, it allowed for joint control west of the Rockies. As such, both countries claimed ownership west to the Pacific Ocean and north to the border with Russian America (later Alaska). When the Oregon Treaty was signed in 1846, it set the 49th parallel as the United States' northern border all the way to the Pacific. The Oregon Territory was established in 1848, and at that time it contained the entirety of the present-day states of Washington, Oregon, and Idaho, as well as portions of Montana and Wyoming. The Washington Territory was established in 1853 and Oregon became a state in 1859. The remainder of the Oregon Territory became part of the Washington Territory at that time.

Oregon State Archives

http://arcweb.sos.state.or.us/pages/records/genealogy/

The main items of interest available to researchers online are an Oregon Historical Records Index and an Early Oregonians Database. The former index has records of all sorts and included more than 600,000 entries at the time of writing. Although the State Archives is in possession of many more records than those that have been indexed, this is still an important database if your relatives are from Oregon. The Early Oregonians Database is an attempt to document everyone living in Oregon before statehood. The search is limited to 200 results, so if your ancestors had a common surname, you may have to narrow your search criteria. Finding aids and lists of holdings are also online.

Oregon State Library

http://www.oregon.gov/OSL/GRES/pages/genealogy.aspx

The Oregon State Library has teamed up with the Willamette Valley Genealogical Society to provide the best information it can. Information on how to submit research requests, as well as the holdings of the library, can be found on the website. However, if you want to try and locate your relatives online, you should scroll down until you get to the link for the Surname Index to the Masterfile of Genealogy Resources on Microfilm.

Alternately, click on the "Oregon State Library Vertical File" link and then the "Oregon Vertical File Biography" link to bring up names of individuals located in the Vertical File. Please note that I located another webpage (**http://library.state.or.us/catalogs/obvf.html**) with a biographical list from the vertical files, and this list differed slightly from the previously mentioned one. As such, you may want to check both lists for your relatives.

Family names can also be found through the "Mahonia DAC Records" link, the list of Family Newsletters held by the library, or the Trover Cronise Photograph Index. Links to other resources and to a searchable photographic collection are also online.

Oregon Historical Society (OHS)

http://ohs.org/research/library/genealogy/resources-at-ohs.cfm/

The OHS has a biography index, a DAR index, and numerous others at its research library. Unfortunately, it doesn't appear that these indexes are available online yet.

My favorite online offerings are related to the *Oregon Historical Quarterly*. A complete table of contents beginning in 1900 is online, and an index (including names) for volumes 82 through 110 (1981 to 2009) is also available.

Oregon Genealogical Society (OGS)

http://www.oregongenealogicalsociety.org/

If you can't make it to Eugene, Oregon, worry not, because the OGS will perform research on your behalf for only, at the time of writing, $10 per hour. Perhaps the Society keeps its research fees low by not hosting any large online collections. Or maybe there's just no need since some of the previously mentioned resources already have sizeable indexes online. The OGS has put together various publications over the years and the "Full Publications Catalog and Order Form" PDF file lists some of the surnames found in some of the publications.

Like many other state genealogical societies, the OGS also grants certificates to those whose ancestors were early settlers of the state; an index of these settlers and their spouses is online.

ORGenWeb

http://www.orgenweb.org/

Along with user-submitted information and links to external websites, ORGenWeb also has county-level webpages with all manner of genealogical information. Some highlights include various early settler and Oregon Trail indexes and lists, census records, volunteer lookups, and an external link to a website run by Tom Burrows.

According to ORGenWeb, Tom's website (located at: **http://www.hillbillyblue.com/Oregon/OregonMarriageSearch.php**) has about 11,000 early marriage records with a focus on years and counties not searchable through the State Archives. Tom's site also has Washington County cemetery records and early death records from Morrison County, Minnesota.

Pennsylvania

Date of Statehood: 12 Dec 1787

Neighboring States: Delaware, Maryland, New Jersey, New York, Ohio, West Virginia

Previous Affiliations: Province of Pennsylvania, New York, Province of Maryland, Virginia Colony

As another of the original colonies, Pennsylvania has a complicated border history that is outside the scope of this book to discuss. However, let's hit a few high points, shall we?

The Virginia Colony's charter included part of present-day Pennsylvania and when the Province of Maryland was formed, it, too, included a portion of the area we now know as Pennsylvania. Pennsylvania's charter was worded so that its southern border was meant to meet up with Maryland's northern border at forty-degrees north latitude (just north of Philadelphia) and its northern border should have been closer to Buffalo, New York. With regard to the southern border, the charter made assumptions that turned out to be untrue (i.e., a twelve-mile radius from present-day New Castle, Delaware turned out not to hit forty-degrees north latitude), and border disputes were common until the Mason-Dixon line settled things. Various other colonies claimed certain areas of the state, though the disputes were mostly settled by about 1790.

The state's last important border change was with regard to the Erie Triangle purchase. With the 42nd-degree north latitude set as the final New York/Pennsylvania border, Pennsylvania was going to have minimal access to the Great Lakes (i.e., under five miles of shoreline). It was in order to have better lakefront access that the new state of Pennsylvania purchased the Erie Triangle from the Federal Government. The Federal Government came into possession of that land after several other states ceded control of their western claims.

Pennsylvania Department of Health - Birth and Death Indexes

http://www.portal.health.state.pa.us/portal/server.pt/community/pu
  blic_records/20686

A Senate bill passed in 2011 made birth and death certificates available to the public provided they were at least 105 and 50 years old, respectively. And although 105 years seems like a long time before birth records become public, at least those with Pennsylvania roots don't have to wait 125 years like in Alabama. While people do occasionally live past 105, no one has ever made it to 125--except for Methuselah, land tortoises, and elves, that is. But I digress.

The Pennsylvania Department-of-Health website only has birth indexes from 1906 and 1907 (remember the 105-year rule), but death indexes run from that time all the way through 1962. Original images are in the process of being scanned by the following resource.

Pennsylvania State Archives

http://www.portal.state.pa.us/portal/server.pt/community/state_arch ives/2887

This is another case where the State Archives has so much information that it's necessary to discuss certain portions of it separately. For that reason, we'll discuss the Digital Archives below and focus on the rest of the website's offerings here.

First things first: vital records. As mentioned above, recent vital records are in the process of being digitized and the planned completion date for that work is early 2014. Holdings information is online and some older archival records have already been digitized and made available through third party websites, as described on the State Archives' vital-records webpage. Scans of marriage indexes from the 1880s are also online through the State Archives.

The "Genealogy" link (located on the left-hand side of the webpage) is our next topic. While a lot of information on censuses, county records, prison records, and the like is presented, some of this is holding information and not all of the genealogical subtopics have name indexes online. One interesting collection with a name index is for those individuals involved in coal mining accidents.

Somewhat uniquely, the Pennsylvania State Archives has multiple land-records indexes. Since land records not related to the Federal Government (see the BLM Land Records write-up in the previous chapter for more information on federal land sales) are often difficult to find online (in my opinion), this is a great resource for those with relatives from Pennsylvania.

Military collections from various wars are held by the Archives and some of them have online indexes. Finally, a number of African-American resources related to slavery and the underground railroad have been digitized. Several of these collections are arranged chronologically or alphabetically, though many of them are not arranged in any discernable order whatsoever.

There's a ton of other information on the website, though I think that covers the main genealogical resources, especially those with online indexes or scanned images.

Pennsylvania State Archives - ARIAS

http://www.digitalarchives.state.pa.us/

Pennsylvania's digital archives are known as the Archives Records Information Access System (ARIAS). Currently, these digital records are all military indexes, and online collections include the Civil War, Spanish-American War, Revolutionary War, WWI Service Medal applications, National Guard, Militia Officers, and the Mexican Border Campaign of 1916. Some index cards don't provide much more than a soldier's name and unit, while others have age, residence, and even birth place.

State Library of Pennsylvania

http://www.portal.state.pa.us/portal/server.pt/community/genealogy
   and_local_history/8730

Along with a lot of great background information on different types of records, there are a few places to try and locate your ancestors directly through the State Library's website. Vital records from Elk County are online, and one can also search surname files (the link is on the left-hand side of the webpage). Sadly, the surname index is simply that--an index. Since the index won't tell you anything about your ancestors except that their surname appears somewhere in the State Library's Genealogy section, you'll have to follow up with the library to learn more.

Though many record categories don't contain online indexes, external links to websites that cover the same topics are often provided. And some of those resources, like the Adams Memorial Library Dead-a-Base (http://www.adamslib.org/catalogs/deadabase/), actually do have searchable name indexes.

Genealogical Society of Pennsylvania (GSP)

http://genpa.org/

The GSP has quite a bit of online content--more than most genealogical societies. Although some content is only available to members, other collections are available to the general public. The homepage has a search feature, and some of the public collections include a surname index, conscientious objectors to the Civil War, several burial and funeral home indexes, and alien applications to depart the United States. (That's alien applications, not alien abductions.) Additional online collections and indexes available to members include access to Society publications, marriage licenses, newspaper indexes, church records, and burial records. A disproportionately high number of the online records deal with the Philadelphia area, but then again, a disproportionately high number of Pennsylvanians live in Philadelphia.

Be conscious of the fact that the online search doesn't cover everything on the website with 100-percent accuracy; for example, I found the surname Elston in the GSP Manuscript Archives Surname Index even though the result didn't turn up when I used the online search feature.

One final item is a list of First Families, as you might have guessed. This list contains fewer names than I expected, but hey, it is what it is. It's worth a look if your relatives are from the state.

PAGenWeb

http://www.pagenweb.org/

After you get done looking at the county-level webpages for Pennsylvania, point your browser to the Pennsylvania files that are included in the USGenWeb Archives project. Once there, the researcher will find miscellaneous collections including land records, vital records, ship manifests, naturalizations, and more.

Keep in mind that, as with most USGenWeb sites, many collections cover various years and locations, so data shouldn't be considered all-inclusive. As such, don't despair if none of the PAGenWeb collections include your relatives.

Rhode Island

Date of Statehood: 29 May 1790

Neighboring States: Connecticut, Massachusetts

Previous Affiliations: Massachusetts, Massachusetts Bay Colony, Colony of
Rhode Island and Providence Plantations, Plymouth Colony, Dominion
of New England

Rhode Island hasn't changed its borders much over the years. In fact,
from the time the original charter was granted to the Colony of Rhode Island
and Providence Plantation in 1663, border changes have been minimal.
Disputes with the Massachusetts Bay and Plymouth Colonies were common
in the early years, and in 1686 the colony became part of the Dominion of
New England, a short-lived English colony. After the Dominion's dissolution
in 1689, borders returned to their previous, albeit disputed, states. Due to
conflicting or unclear charters, border disputes and court cases were
common, and the Massachusetts border changed slightly in the mid-1700s
and again in the mid-1800s.

Rhode Island State Archives

http://sos.ri.gov/archives/

According to the Rhode Island Department of Health, birth and marriage
records become public after 100 years and death records become public after
50. Although these records are available through either the State Archives or
the city or town where the event occurred, I was unable to find a searchable
index on the Archives' website. As such, the State Archives will likely be of
more value to the researcher who can visit in person.

Rhode Island Historical Cemetery Commission

http://www.rihistoriccemeteries.org/

The information presented by the Rhode Island Historical Cemetery
Commission is well-intentioned, extensive, and marginally confusing. There
is a list of libraries that have the full cemetery database off-line, and there is
also an online search feature. The online search results have a column for
relationships, so they may be helpful in your genealogical search.

In addition to the online search, the RI Cemetery Database Master Name

Index is accessible through the "Local Database" tab and subsequent link (**http://www.rootsweb.ancestry.com/~rigenweb/Cemetery2/cemindex.html**); the two websites' databases appear to differ slightly so it may be advantageous to search both.

The Rhode Island Historical Cemeteries website (**http://www.rihc.info**) and the American-French Genealogical Society (**http://www.afgs.org**) also have cemetery searches, though the AFGS' index doesn't appear to contain exactly the same set of information either. In addition to the Rhode-Island-cemetery database, the AFGS has a cemetery headstone database, cemetery databases for Massachusetts, and an obituary database from American and Canadian newspapers that contains more than 400,000 entries.

The bottom line is that there are multiple websites that host Rhode Island cemetery databases, though most of them don't appear to be exactly the same.

Rhode Island Genealogical Society (RIGS)
http://www.rigensoc.org/

Much like the State Archives, the RIGS doesn't have many actual databases on its website. That being said, there is some helpful information online. Along with a table showing when major towns were formed, there are links to other societies, libraries, and associations of genealogical importance.

A great FAQ section is also online, and it goes over where to find particular records, as well as providing general information on how to use wills and determine birth, death, and marriage information.

Finally, there is a webpage dedicated to early Rhode Island censuses. Be conscious of the fact that you can't access the census information from the homepage. The reason is that the "Resources" dropdown gets partially hidden by the picture on the homepage. To get to the census information, simply move to another webpage first, and then point your mouse to the "Resources" tab.

Rhode Island Historical Society (RIHS)
http://www.rihs.org/libraryhome.htm

Again we find another Rhode Island resource that's a little short when it comes to online data. Or perhaps I should say one that's short on name indexes and original digitized content. The RIHS does have a lot of finding-aid information online, and if you're lucky this may be helpful.

The Society holds business, governmental, and personal papers in its

Manuscript Collection, and some of those finding aids have individual names. Of note are guides to military records, women's diaries, slave trade papers, and personal correspondence from families and individuals from all walks of life. It's probably easiest to type your relative's name in the search bar and see what comes up. Not every finding aid has a complete name index, so even though you can't find your relative online, he/she might still turn up if you visit the research library in person. The Society also has an online catalog and many links to external genealogical websites.

HathiTrust Digital Library
http://www.hathitrust.org/

HathiTrust is a digital library whose membership is open to groups worldwide. The reason it's being mentioned now is because the RIHS (discussed above) has made some of its print books available here. Many of these books are available in their entirety, though it appears that more recent publications are only searchable and not available online, perhaps due to copyright restrictions. Miscellaneous collections from other states and countries are also searchable, though many of them are not related to genealogy.

RIGenWeb
http://www.rootsweb.ancestry.com/~rigenweb/

Although there are only five counties in the state of Rhode Island, two of the five RIGenWeb county-level pages weren't functional at the time of writing. On the plus side, all sorts of data is accessible through the homepage. For example, there are biographical sketches from out-of-copyright books, several directories and tax lists, and even a minority birth index (mostly from the 1850s, though some earlier records are included). A selection of census images and links to other online resources are also provided.

While USGenWeb state-level websites, like RIGenWeb, don't always have complete name indexes or images of original documents, this is a website worth visiting for its wide assortment of information--and because most other Rhode Island genealogical websites don't appear to have much free content online. In addition to the previously mentioned Cemetery Database, you may have the most luck tracing your Rhode Island roots online with RIGenWeb and larger, more general genealogical sites like FamilySearch.org,

Archives.com, and Ancestry.com.

South Carolina

Date of Statehood: 23 May 1788

Neighboring States: Georgia, North Carolina

Previous Affiliations: Virginia Colony, Province of Carolina, Province of South Carolina

When the Province of Carolina received its charter in 1663, it was formed out of a portion of the Virginia Colony and extended west to the Pacific Ocean and south to 31-degrees north latitude, along the present-day Florida/Alabama border. In 1665, the borders were extended to the north and south, with the northern border moving to the current North Carolina/Virginia border and the southern border moving south towards present-day Daytona Beach, Florida. In the late 1600s, the Province encountered irreconcilable differences, and it eventually became two distinct colonies, namely North and South Carolina. Shortly after splitting from North Carolina, the Georgia Colony was formed, further shrinking South Carolina's land holdings.

Recently the border between North and South Carolina was revisited and found to be slightly inaccurate. Not inaccurate enough to affect most residents, but problematic to the point where some South Carolina residents will find that they no longer live in the state even though they haven't moved. Final surveys to determine the boundary line are supposed to be completed in the spring of 2013.

South Carolina Department of Archives & History

http://archives.sc.gov/onlineresearch/Pages/default.aspx

The best feature of the Archives' website is the Online Records Index. Indexed collections include wills, Confederate records, land records, court records, and more. The Online Records Index includes the Archives' Digital Collections, so if you find your ancestors, there's a chance that you might find a digital version of a source document. Digitized records include Confederate pension applications, colonial land grants, will transcripts, and militia enrollments from 1869.

South Carolina State Library
http://www.statelibrary.sc.gov/

The most interesting items available through the State Library are a webpage on obituary resources, a vertical file index, and another digital collection.

To get to the obituary resources, hover over the "S.C. Information" tab, and then follow the "Obituary Resources" link. The webpage has information from participating libraries state-wide, and some of the libraries have online indexes themselves.

If instead you hover over the "Catalogs" tab, you'll see links for the Vertical File Index and the Digital Collections. The Vertical File Index has a section on biographies, which is where you should search for your relatives. The Digital Collections webpage has links to several different websites with digitized material. The State Library's Digital Collections section didn't have much of genealogical value at the time of writing, since it appears that a lot of the digital content is fairly recent. Items of note are a Tombstone Project and a listing of University of South Carolina alumni who died during the Civil War, though at the moment the former contains mostly weathered stones that won't be of any help to anyone.

Links to other South Carolina digital collections, like the one mentioned below, may prove to be more helpful than the Library's collection itself.

South Carolina Digital Library
http://www.scmemory.org

This is a collaborative effort which includes libraries, archives, universities, and other interested parties from across the state. Though not specifically a genealogical effort, many family records are online, some from the colonial period, and other items include firefighter rosters, Confederate rolls, and even university exams.

Keep in mind that some participating institutions may have separate digital collections of their own, so don't forget to make your way to each set of digital archives listed on the State Library's webpage (see above). For example, the University of South Carolina's library has an online collection of Family Bible Records that I was unable to locate through the South Carolina Digital Library itself, though it's possible that it will be added at some point in the future.

South Carolina Death Indexes - 1915 to 1962

http://www.scdhec.gov/administration/vr/vrdi.htm

The South Carolina Department of Health and Environmental Control has a death index for the years 1915 through 1962. The upper end-date will increase each year, as death records become public after fifty years. You may have to download a free plugin to view death records up until 1949, though records from after that time do not require any special image viewers.

The ages indicated in the death index are three-digit codes, not actual ages of deceased individuals. So if you find someone whose age code is listed as 549, that person wasn't born before Columbus discovered America. The "5" at the start of the code simply indicates that the next two numbers are the deceased's age in years (not hours, days, or months), so our example individual was 49 years old at the time of death. Full details on the numeric code are accessible through the website.

SCIWAY - South Carolina's Information Highway

http://www.sciway.net/hist/genealogy/

Although SCIWAY doesn't host any genealogical collections of its own, it may have the most complete set of links to South-Carolina-specific online resources (aside from perhaps Cyndi's List--see the previous chapter). There are links to genealogical societies, statewide digital collections and repositories, and various links to miscellaneous records indexes. Some of the linked items include Horry County wills, Union County probate records, marriage records, and even a surname list from the 1749 *South Carolina Gazette*.

SCGenWeb

http://sciway3.net/scgenweb/

Some of the more interesting collections online include ship manifests, old census lists, and county-level webpages. Various military rosters and links to other genealogical societies and archives are also provided.

South Dakota

Date of Statehood: 2 Nov 1889

Neighboring States: Iowa, Minnesota, Montana, Nebraska, North Dakota, Wyoming

Previous Affiliations: Louisiana Territory, Missouri Territory, Unorganized Territory, Michigan Territory, Wisconsin Territory, Iowa Territory, Minnesota Territory, Nebraska Territory, Dakota Territory

Being split by the Missouri River, South Dakota's history evolved from several directions. Present-day South Dakota was acquired mostly through the Louisiana Purchase, though a small portion of the state as we know it today was acquired via a treaty with the British in 1818. As such, the state was first located in the Louisiana Territory, followed by the Missouri Territory, before not being a part of any organized territory. In the early 1830s, the portion of the state east of the Missouri River became part of the Michigan Territory, and would eventually be re-designated as a part of the Wisconsin, Iowa, and Minnesota Territories before Minnesota finally became a state in 1858. After not belonging to any organized territory, the western half of the state became part of the Nebraska Territory in 1854 before the Dakota Territory was formed in 1861. Though the territory grew and shrank over the years, its final extent was split in two when it entered the Union as North Dakota and South Dakota in 1889.

South Dakota State Historical Society - Archives

http://history.sd.gov/Archives/genealogists.aspx

Once again, South Dakota's Archives reinforce the notion that many younger states have better information online than states that have been around longer. And although that may have more to do with the fact that fewer inhabitants and younger, larger counties make for easier information compilation, you'll still be happy if your relatives hailed from South Dakota.

Loads of indexes are searchable through the Archives' website, and you'll find collections of all sorts, including naturalization papers (both declarations of intent and second papers), cemetery records, an 1885 Civil War veteran's census (both Union and Confederate armies), a newspaper surname index (mostly recent publications), a biographical index, a Pioneer Daughters collection, several military indexes, and even indexes to the *South Dakota State*

Brand Book and members of the South Dakota Farmer's Alliance. Although these indexes aren't necessarily as valuable as the original documents, if your relatives were from South Dakota you should try to locate them in these collections.

South Dakota Digital Archives

http://sddigitalarchives.contentdm.oclc.org/cdm

It would be helpful if the Digital Archives had images for some of the above surname indexes. Unfortunately, the South Dakota Digital Archives website was only launched at the beginning of 2012, so it doesn't have a ton of content yet. In addition to a photo collection, there are various manuscripts, government documents, and land survey notes online.

Try locating your ancestors with the search feature, but if you don't have any luck, then the guides to county-level records are probably the most broadly helpful documents. While the guides may not have individual names either, they'll let you know what resources are available. More content will, no doubt, be added in the future.

South Dakota State Library

http://library.sd.gov/LIB/ERD/category/news.aspx

Unless you're a South Dakota resident, then the few options listed under the website's Genealogy section probably won't do you any good since you won't be able to access them online. There are, however, a few newspaper indexes that are searchable. A few of them are recent indexes, so the most interesting is probably the Deadwood Historical Newspapers Index (1876 to1905).

A list of tribal libraries and resources is also online.

South Dakota Department of Health - Birth Records Search

http://apps.sd.gov/applications/PH14Over100BirthRec/index.asp

Due to state law, birth records must be 100 years old before they become a matter of public record. Not terribly helpful if your ancestors aren't yet that old, but you should definitely check out the website if you think your relatives were born in the state more than 100 years ago.

Records are searchable by name, date, parents' names, and even mother's maiden name. Keep in mind that although records from the early 1900s and late 1800s exist, records from before 1905 shouldn't be considered complete. So if you have a relative who was born before 1905 and you're unable to find the corresponding birth record, it's possible that it was never filed. According to the website, counties are allowed to put together their own death and marriage indexes for genealogical research, though you'll have to be a member of our next resource to access them.

South Dakota Genealogical Society (SDGS)
http://www.rootsweb.ancestry.com/~sdgs/

The SDGS, like many other genealogical societies, puts out a quarterly publication. In this case, that publication is the *South Dakota Genealogical Society Quarterly*. A name index for the quarterly's first ten years is online, and a county-by-county subject index is available for the first fourteen years of publication. Though indexes for later years aren't online at this time, one can purchase a DVD that includes volumes 1 through 29 as PDF files.

SDGenWeb
http://sdgenweb.com/

From the SDGenWeb homepage, if you're not interested in a particular county, then your best option is to visit the SDGenWeb Archives link on the right-hand side of the page. The reason is because we've already discussed most of the other external links above.

From the Archives' webpage, you can browse more county- and state-specific resources, or you can search for your relatives directly. Some of the statewide resources include biography indexes from early books, miscellaneous church records, land records, military records, and indexes to books and newspapers dedicated to various ethnic groups.

Tennessee

Date of Statehood: 1 Jun 1796

Neighboring States: Alabama, Arkansas, Georgia, Kentucky, Mississippi, Missouri, North Carolina, Virginia

Previous Affiliations: North Carolina, Southwest Territory

Shortly after North Carolina became the twelfth state, it ceded the land that makes up present-day Tennessee to the Federal Government. Later in 1790, that land was organized and incorporated as the Southwest Territory. While the Southwest Ordinance which established the territory didn't expressly define its southern boundary, areas south of present-day Tennessee were claimed by Georgia and Spain at the time. The 35th parallel was set as Tennessee's southern border when it became our nation's sixteenth state in 1796, but when the line was drawn in 1818, it was drawn about a mile too far south. As such, Georgia continues to fight for that extra mile of land in order to give the state access to the water in the Tennessee River.

Tennessee State Library and Archives

http://www.tn.gov/tsla/Collections.htm

Quite a few indexes are available through the Tennessee State Library and Archives: military rosters for various wars; inmate indexes; Confederate pension applications; name index from the Acts of Tennessee for the years 1796 through 1850; indexes for biographical sketches. Nashville City directories are online, Tennessee Supreme Court cases are searchable, and a list of available obituary indexes at public libraries is also provided. Finding aids for Manuscript Collections may yield your ancestor's name, details on Native-American research are online, and uniquely, a list of courthouse fires is online, so you can find out whether the records you desire might have been destroyed. Finally, several death and burial indexes are online for Nashville and a few select areas. A couple of state-level death indexes are also online, and scanned images are on Ancestry.com. If you don't have a subscription and you're a state resident, you can follow the link and access the images through the Tennessee Electronic Library. The Tennessee Electronic Library, and other digital collections, is easily located by hovering over the "Digital Collections" tab and selecting from the dropdown menu.

The bottom line is that the Tennessee State Library and Archives website has quite a bit of content online, so if your relatives are from the state, spend some time searching for them.

Tennessee Genealogical Society (TGS)

http://www.tngs.org/

The TGS has a number of helpful articles and links, but for the online researcher the best resource is probably the section on the *Ansearchin' News*. This is the Society's quarterly journal, and a keyword search and county-level index are both online. At the time of writing, full copies of the journal were online through the year 2000, and it appears that the keyword search covers everything that's online. The county-level index includes more recent copies of the journal.

The Society also has an early settler certificate program, and although these certificates have been compiled and a two-volume set is available for purchase, a surname index isn't online at this time.

Tennessee Valley Authority (TVA) - Cemetery Relocation

**http://www.tva.gov/river/landandshore/culturalresources/cemeteries
.htm**

Construction projects across the state have required that thousands of graves be relocated over the years. Original documentation from the relocations is held by the National Archives, Southeast Region, but a name index, with locations and birth and death dates, can be found on the TVA website.

TNGenWeb

http://tngenweb.org/

Along with a cemetery database and county-level webpages, there are a number of special projects worth checking out. Biographical sketches from the 1911 *Who's Who in Tennessee* have been transcribed, Poor House indexes are online, and a few Native-American and military resources are also available. A few of the latter resources include lists of residents, Indian traders, and the like.

Texas

Date of Statehood: 29 Dec 1845

Neighboring States: Arkansas, Louisiana, New Mexico, Oklahoma, Country of Mexico

Previous Affiliations: France, Spain, Mexico, Louisiana Territory, Orleans Territory, Missouri Territory, Republic of Texas

The United States claimed portions of northern Texas were under its control as a result of the Louisiana Purchase, and these areas were originally incorporated as part of the Louisiana Territory and then the Missouri Territory. However, these claims were given up when the United States signed the Adams-Onís Treaty with Spain in 1819. Mexico would win its independence from Spain shortly thereafter, and eventually Texas won its independence from Mexico in 1836, going on to set up foreign embassies in the United States, Great Britain, and France. Unfortunately, Mexico never ratified the treaty that granted Texas' independence and claimed it was a rebellious state, so when the United States annexed Texas, that sparked the outbreak of the Mexican-American War. During Texas' time as an independent nation and even when Texas was admitted to the United States prior to the war, its borders included portions of present-day New Mexico, Colorado, Oklahoma, Kansas, and Wyoming, although this land was given up as part of the Compromise of 1850. Texas also claimed part of present-day southwestern Oklahoma for a time.

Texas State Library and Archives Commission

https://www.tsl.state.tx.us/arc/genfirst.html

The Texas State Library and Archives Commission has vital-records indexes for use onsite, though they're not online. Actual vital-records certificates aren't held by the Library and Archives Commission, though information on how to obtain copies is provided.

More useful online information includes a Confederate pension application index, Texas Adjutant General Service Records (select military records with digitized images), Republic claim forms from the time of Texas' independence (with images), soldiers' families receiving aid through an 1863 act, and a small collection of individuals who received Republic of Texas passports (with images). Many other valuable resources are available onsite or through interlibrary loan. A few online exhibits (hover over the "For the Public" tab, select "Online Collections," then "Online Exhibits"), like the McArdle Notebooks and Votes for Women!, include various letters and notes, so these collections contain a select number of surnames.

Texas Department of State Health Services - Vital Records Indexes

http://www.dshs.state.tx.us/vs/marriagedivorce/reqindex.shtm

Somewhat unusually, Texas has several recent vital-records indexes online, though no older indexes. Marriage application indexes are online for 1966 through 2010, and divorce indexes are online for 1968 through 2010. The start dates for these two indexes are based on the first year that each type of record was filed with state offices. Birth and death indexes going back to 1903 can be purchased on microfilm.

Texas State Genealogical Society

http://www.txsgs.org/

If your ancestors lived in Texas prior to statehood, then try searching for them in the Texas First Families name index. Next, search the Society's quarterly journal, *STIRPES* (no, that's not a typo). Issues from the year 2000 and before are available through the Portal to Texas History, a project hosted by the University of North Texas Libraries through which partners can contribute digitized material.

Texas State Historical Association (TSHA)

http://www.tshaonline.org

The *Southwestern Historical Quarterly*, TSHA's quarterly, is the oldest continually published scholarly journal in Texas. Each issue can be accessed through the Portal to Texas History website, mentioned above, though the website indicates that online access will eventually be limited to TSHA members.

By clicking the tab for "The Handbook of Texas Online," one will find thousands of entries, many of which pertain to individuals.

Finally, on the Links webpage, there is a section entitled "Digital Publications." A few of these items, like the "Index to Military Rolls of the Republic of Texas 1835-1845" have individual names, so they may be helpful to the researcher.

Discovery Texas

http://www.libraryoftexas.org/

Discovery Texas is a website managed by the Texas State Library and Archives Commission (see above). If you don't have a TexShare login, don't fret because you can also use the website as a guest. This site appears to be more of a card catalog than anything else, but some subject categories include birth, marriage, and death, so you may learn where to find a particular book that covers where your ancestors lived.

Texas Heritage Online

http://texasheritageonline.org/

This is another website administered by the Texas State Library and Archives Commission. Here, one will find digitized newspapers, letters, receipts, bills of sale, yearbooks, and more.

Texas General Land Office

http://www.glo.texas.gov/what-we-do/history-and-archives/research-at-the-archives/surname-index.html

The state's General Land Office (GLO) has a surname index for land grants issued by the Republic and State of Texas. Grantees from the Spanish Collection (i.e., those who received Spanish or Mexican land grants) are also included in the index.

TXGenWeb

http://www.txgenweb.org/

In addition to county-level webpages, one will find census images, 1830s-era muster rolls, Adjutant General's Reports, and miscellaneous user-submitted content online.

Utah

Date of Statehood: 4 Jan 1896

Neighboring States: Arizona, Colorado, Idaho, Nevada, Wyoming, New Mexico (kitty-corner)

Previous Affiliations: Spain, Mexico, Utah Territory

The United States acquired the land that makes up present-day Utah from Mexico in 1848 via the Treaty of Guadalupe Hidalgo. The Utah Territory, which included the entirety of the state as we know it, as well as portions of Nevada, Colorado, and Wyoming, was established in 1850. The easternmost portion of the territory became part of the Colorado Territory, while the westernmost portion became the Nevada Territory. Additional western portions of the territory were annexed by Nevada after statehood was achieved, and small portions of the territory were also added to the Nebraska and Wyoming Territories until the present boundaries of the state were reached in 1868.

Family History Library

The Family History Library is the single largest genealogical library in the world. The Genealogical Society of Utah was founded in 1894 by members of The Church of Jesus Christ of Latter-day Saints, though the library is open to everyone free of charge. The Society expanded and you know it today as FamilySearch.

FamilySearch has millions of rolls of microfilm, and 200 cameras are busy digitizing records. The Library's website is FamilySearch.org (discussed in a previous chapter), and by downloading free software, one can help index these digitized records, a process which makes them much more accessible to the average researcher. If you ever plan a trip to do genealogical research in person, this is the place to go.

Family History Libraries and Centers

The Family History Library (FHL) in Salt Lake City, discussed above, has numerous affiliated libraries located in Utah. The largest of these are located in Ogden, St. George, Logan, Riverton, and at BYU. As with other facilities affiliated with the FHL, their main online presence is on FamilySearch.org, though each center may also have its own website. Holdings for these facilities vary but include thousands of books and rolls of microfilm.

Utah State Archives
http://www.archives.state.ut.us/

Once again, there is a lot of online information available through the State Archives of a young western state. And that shouldn't come as any surprise since the Utah State Archives and FamilySearch are both located in Salt Lake City.

On the website, links to government records, name indexes, land records, vital records, research guides, and digital records are all provided. Everything is arranged in the most straightforward manner if you click on the "Research Our Records" link first (be aware that the homepage was redesigned multiple times while I was writing the book, so the details could change).

From here, there are guides for land, military, naturalizations, court, vital, and even mining records. Not every guide includes an index, though if you click the "Name Indexes" link partway down the webpage, you can search all the indexed collections at once. Alternately, you can browse by category (e.g., birth, death, naturalizations) and use the indexes specific to each collection. At the time of writing, the most recent public-record birth and death certificates were not yet indexed, though digital copies of unindexed years were online and researchers could browse by year and county.

If you move to the "Online Digital Archives" section of the website, you can search or browse through all of the digitized material. Some of the aforementioned collections are located here, and one will also find unique collections like brand books, prisoners' pardon applications, Indian War service affidavits, court case indexes, and a digital copy of *The Book of Pioneers*, a record of 1847 immigrants as recorded in 1897.

Pioneer - Utah's Online Library
http://pioneer.utah.gov/home.html

From the main Utah State Library website, I couldn't find much that was genealogically interesting. However, by pointing your web browser to Pioneer, Utah's Online Library, a few items present themselves.

Available to the general public are portions of the website accessed by hovering over the "Digital Collections" tab and selecting from the dropdown menu. The "Digital Utah" webpage has links to numerous digital collections hosted by various organizations across the state. Some of these collections won't be particularly useful, while others, like the BYU and Weber State offerings, may contain yearbooks, correspondence, newspapers, and more. If instead the user selects "Utah's Newspapers" from the dropdown menu, there are a few other items to note. A number of newspaper databases can be accessed by Utah residents, links to Chronicling America (see previous chapter) are provided, and a collection of digitized Utah newspapers is presented through an external website, Utah Digital Newspapers (**http://www.digitalnewspapers.org**).

Heritage Quest can also be accessed remotely, but only if you have a valid library card.

Utah State Historical Society (USHS)
http://history.utah.gov/historical_society/index.html

The USHS is a state institution and the Society's website is part of Utah State History, a division of the Utah Department of Heritage and Arts. The *Utah Historical Quarterly*, the Society's journal, has been in print since 1928, and one can search and view copies of it online. If you leave the journal's search box blank, your results will contain every available issue of the quarterly. This isn't a genealogical publication, per se, so if you want to search a dedicated genealogical quarterly, you might try our next resource (see below).

By hovering over the "Learn & Research" tab and selecting "Cemetery Records" from the dropdown menu, one can search for relatives buried in Utah.

The final place to visit is the "Research Center & Collections" link (in the dropdown menu from the "Programs" tab). Here, one can search the Research Center's catalog, as well as visit resource pages for family history, yearbooks, newspapers, and even telephone directories. A few of the collections have information online, while others contain only finding aids. More than 65,000 photographs are also online.

Utah Genealogical Association (UGA)
http://www.infouga.org/

The UGA puts out a quarterly publication entitled *Crossroads*. Unfortunately, it's only available online to UGA members. The *UGA Newsletter*, however, is available for free to anyone who cares to subscribe. The Society issues First Families of Utah certificates (for early settlers), but an index was not online at the time of writing.

One can also browse surname queries, though it appears that if anything else is available through the UGA website, then that material is limited to members only.

UTGenWeb
http://www.rootsweb.ancestry.com/~utgenweb/

Scanned copies of the 1850 and 1860 Utah Territory censuses are online, though they aren't indexed by name. Links to other users' GEDCOM files and marriage and death indexes to *Deseret News* publications from the late 1800s are also online. Many other genealogical links are provided, and each county has its own webpage.

Vermont

Date of Statehood: 4 Mar 1791
Neighboring States: Massachusetts, New Hampshire, New York
Previous Affiliations: New York Colony, New Hampshire Colony

For a time in the 1700s, both New Hampshire and New York claimed the area we now call Vermont. Although New Hampshire had already sold land in present-day Vermont (the New Hampshire Grants) to settlers, King George III eventually determined that the land belonged to New York. As one might imagine, this led to numerous disputes. Vermont declared its independence from both colonies in 1777 and eventually entered the union as the 14th state in 1791.

Vermont State Archives and Records Administration

http://vermont-archives.org/

Let's start first with Vermont vital records. Although one can request free informational copies from the vital-records staff, the Archives' website indicates that state vital records are already online through FamilySearch.org and Ancestry.com. A link is provided so that Vermont residents can access the Ancestry.com records for free.

After reading about vital records, visit the "Databases and Indexes" webpage by hovering over the Research tab and selecting from the dropdown menu. From this page one can search the Nye Index, a name index to Manuscript Vermont State Papers, and an additional name index is located at the end of the guide to the Henry Stevens, Sr. Collection. The latter is a collection of miscellaneous manuscripts collected by Stevens principally during the first half of the 19th century, though some items date back to the colonial era.

As with most State Archives, a list of holdings is online and more indexes are available at the State Archives' building in Vermont than on the website. At least one of the military finding aids, the list of Vermont State Guard officers during WWII, has a limited number of names included.

Vermont Department of Libraries

http://libraries.vermont.gov/

If you're a resident of the state, you can access a couple of subscription databases remotely (resources like Heritage Quest). If you're not a resident, there's not much online besides links to some of the resources mentioned here and elsewhere in the book. The State Archives' website (discussed above) indicates that the Vermont Department of Libraries maintains Federal Census records and newspaper obituary information, though it doesn't appear that either collection is online.

University of Vermont (UVM) Libraries

http://library.uvm.edu/

From the UVM-Libraries-and-Collections section of the website, there are a couple of items worth searching. The Vermont Digital Newspaper Project has contributed thousands upon thousands of pages to Chronicling America (see previous chapter), though that project doesn't appear to have any unique digital content online.

On the other hand, the Center for Digital Initiatives (fun name, huh?) does have its own digital content. A couple of family collections, Civil War content, University of Vermont yearbooks, and even a collection of maple sugar and maple syrup recipes are online, though the latter has nothing to do with genealogy. It just seemed fun and worth mentioning.

Genealogical Society of Vermont (GSV)

http://www.genealogyvermont.org/

While Society members have access to additional online content, non-members have access to a few interesting items. The "Vermont Content" link on the left-hand side of the homepage has several PDF files including: an alphabetized version of *Vermont Marriages, Vol. 1*, originally published in 1903; a vital records publication for Weston, Vermont; an index of marriages and baptisms from the 1830s and '40s; name changes and adoptions from 1869.

As far as publications, the Society's newsletter, *Branches and Twigs*, is indexed and online for 1972 through 1974. *Vermont Genealogy*, the Society's regular publication, has topical and name indexes online, and name indexes are provided for both volumes of *Vermont Families in 1791*. Newsletters from 1994 through the present and GSV queries are also online.

Vermont Historical Society (VHS)

http://www.vermonthistory.org/

The most interesting part of the VHS website is a webpage full of unique genealogical indexes and lists. To access the proper webpage, hover over the Library tab, and select Genealogy from the dropdown menu. Some of the items found here include miscellaneous vital-records indexes, Civil War transcriptions, naturalizations, and military photograph indexes from the 1940s.

Vermont French-Canadian Genealogical Society

http://www.vt-fcgs.org/

If your ancestors were French Canadian and from Vermont, you might want to check out this resource. A few French-Catholic church and cemetery indexes are online, along with a marriage index from Burlington, Vermont.

The Society's journal, *Links*, isn't online or indexed in its entirety, though a table of contents is provided for each issue. A small amount of information from *Links* is on the website, including member queries and a "Border Crossings" section which is comprised of data taken from previous *Links* articles.

If you can trace your lineage back to the 1600s, you may be eligible for two different Society programs whereby you can apply to receive a pin or button.

Vermont in the Civil War

http://www.vermontcivilwar.org

Obviously, this is a website dedicated to Vermonters in the Civil War. The researcher can search by name or unit, and information on basically anything related to the war can be accessed through the site. There is even a virtual museum with images of wartime artifacts like flags, uniforms, manuscripts, and pictures of soldiers.

VTGenWeb

http://www.rootsweb.ancestry.com/~vtgenweb/

The most interesting items presented on the VTGenWeb website are an index to the five-volume *Vermont Historical Gazetteer* and the Vermont section of the USGenWeb Archives. The latter contains miscellaneous user-submitted and state-wide content, though my favorite part of the archives is actually courtesy of the Maine State Archives.

Small collections of transcribed records from the Maine Archives are provided for marriages and court records where one or more parties were from the state of Vermont. The marriage records all appear to be from the 1800s, though the court records are from the 1720s through 1760. Remember that Vermont didn't exist at that time, so the court records may indicate that residents were from New York.

Virginia

Date of Statehood: 25 Jun 1788
Neighboring States: Kentucky, Maryland, North Carolina, Tennessee, West
   Virginia, Washington D.C.
Previous Affiliations: Washington D.C.

In the early 1600s, Virginia was a poorly defined British settlement in the New World. Charters in 1609 and 1611 provided land grants to Virginia to the point that it encompassed the vast majority of the present-day United States and even a good chunk of western Canada. Over the years, charters were given out to other colonies until Virginia was bounded (more or less) on the north and south by the colonies of Pennsylvania and North Carolina, respectively (we're ignoring Maryland for the sake of more easily defining a northern border). To the west, the colony's charter indicated that it extended to the Pacific Ocean. France established the Louisiana Colony and after a period of fighting, British holdings were limited to the area east of the Mississippi. The colonies were instructed not to settle west of the Allegany Mountains, and when the British Colony of Quebec was enlarged to include the Ohio Valley, it was one more reason for Virginia and the rest of the original colonies to draft the Declaration of Independence.

In Virginia's new constitution, the state claimed the territory west to the Mississippi; this claim included present-day Illinois, Indiana, Ohio, Michigan, Wisconsin, Kentucky, West Virginia, and part of Minnesota. Virginia eventually ceded much of this territory to the United States Government, a condition that Maryland requested prior to their ratification of the Articles of Confederation. When Virginia became a state, the borders enclosed present-day Virginia, Kentucky, and West Virginia.

Finally, Virginia gave a small area of land to the Federal Government for the establishment of Washington D.C., though it was later given back to Virginia.

That's a gross oversimplification of the colony's historic borders, but it should get the gist of Virginia's border changes across.

Library of Virginia (LVA)
http://www.lva.virginia.gov/index.htm
   The Library of Virginia is "the principal center for genealogical research in

Virginia," and that's coming from the Virginia Historical Society (see below), an institution with its own genealogical library. For the purposes of this discussion we'll focus on material available online, even though far more content is available to those who can visit the library in person.

Under the "For The Public" heading, there are four categories of interest to the researcher, though Virginia Memory is discussed separately below: Using the Collections; Virginia Memory; Search the LVA Catalog; Public Programs and Exhibitions. While many of the links jump between sections and the website's layout feels a bit cumbersome to me, I'll try to discuss available resources in as straightforward a manner as I can muster.

In the "Using the Collections" section of the website, the first item of note is a subsection called "Guides and Indexes." This item principally contains guides to different record types, though links to numerous indexes can also be found. Some of these indexes are more readily accessed via external websites or through other sections of the LVA website itself. As such, those indexes are discussed elsewhere while only a few select indexes are discussed here. Located in this portion of the site, one will find: a marriage collection index, searchable by bride's or groom's name; a Lost Records database, currently being digitized for Virginia Memory (see below); a Burned Jurisdiction database; a Legislative Petitions database, which includes early petitions for the state of Kentucky; military records, like indexes to the Confederate Navy, the Spanish-American War, and those who died in service. The second subsection, entitled "Databases and eBooks," won't be terribly helpful without a Virginia library card. However, if you have one, you can access a "Biography and Genealogy Master Index," Heritage Quest, The American Civil War Research Database, several newspaper indexes, and more.

The "Search the LVA Catalog" section has the most concentrated grouping of indexes and databases. The "Archives & Manuscripts" tab has a search function that will return military, bible, personal, and genealogical documents. Images for thousands of bible records are even online. If you select the "Images & Indexes" tab, you can search collections of wills, military (Confederate, Revolutionary War, and War of 1812), land, photographic, death, and colonial records, as well as a collection of biographical sketches and a few newspaper indexes. Several of these collections have digitized material, though not every collection has scanned versions of source documents.

In the "Public Programs and Exhibitions" section of the website, there is an ongoing project to complete the *Dictionary of Virginia Biography*. Three volumes, covering surnames up to Daniels, are currently in print, and an alphabetical name index is online, though if your ancestor's last name doesn't start with A,B,C, or D, then you'll probably have to wait until additional volumes are released.   Two other programs entitled Virginia Women in History and African-American Trailblazers in Virginia History honor a small number of prominent Virginians annually; honorees may have lived in the colonial era or may still be alive today. These collections are small, but if your relatives were prominent citizens of the state, you might want to see if they're listed here.

Virginia Memory - Library of Virginia

http://www.virginiamemory.com/

Virginia Memory is the vehicle to present the majority of the Library of Virginia's digital content. Collections include chancery records, cohabitation records, religious petitions, military records (Civil, Revolutionary, and War of 1812), a Lost Records collection, colonial records, and photographic records. Some collections link back to the "Images & Indexes" section of the Library of Virginia's website (see above).

Encyclopedia Virginia

http://www.encyclopediavirginia.org/

Encyclopedia Virginia is just what it sounds like--an encyclopedia focused on the state of Virginia. Articles are presented on a wide range of topics, though the submissions contributed by the *Dictionary of Virginia Biography* (see the Library of Virginia section above) may be the most helpful to genealogists.

Colonial Williamsburg Foundation

http://research.history.org/JDRLibrary/Online_Resources/Genealogi calResearch.cfm

The Colonial Williamsburg Foundation is, not surprisingly, an entity focused on history as it relates to 18th-century Williamsburg. On the left-hand side of the webpage, one will find links to finding aids and indexes, searchable databases, special collections, and the CW Digital Library. Some of the indexes are topical and not searchable by name, but a few highlights include digitized copies of the *Virginia Gazette* from 1736 through 1780 (not every year and issue is available); various manuscripts and family papers, and

York County probate records.

By selecting "Special Collections" on the left-hand side of the webpage, one will be presented with a short list of collections. The Family-Bibles collection contains transcriptions and scanned images of family bibles, while the Manuscripts collection brings up a "Guide to Manuscripts" webpage that provides descriptions of the Foundation's manuscript holdings. Many of these descriptions include names of individuals in the title or accompanying notes. More detailed finding aids can also be located online by following the links to the Virginia Heritage Project.

Virginia Genealogical Society

http://www.vgs.org/

Tables of contents for issues of *The Magazine of Virginia Genealogy* are online up until 2010, though the publications themselves aren't; however, the first 40 volumes are searchable through Ancestry.com. The Virginia Genealogical Society newsletters are downloadable online up until 2005. Numerous genealogical links are also provided, but aside from that there's not much free content here. The Society has a number of intriguing publications available for purchase, like the *Index to Virginia Estates: 1800-1865*, among others.

Virginia Historical Society (VHS)

http://www.vahistorical.org/research/genealogy.htm

The VHS website often defers to the Library of Virginia (see above) for genealogical research, even though the Society has a lot of interesting information in its own right. A guide to Civil War manuscripts held by the Society is indexed and contains mostly family papers (**http://www.vahistorical.org/cwg/browse.htm**). A database of slaves called "Unknown No Longer," an index to *Virginia Magazine of History and Biography* (years 2006 through 2012 only), and an index to photographs held by the Society are all online. Additionally, the Society has a number of digital collections, though the website indicates that digitized content comprises less than five percent of the total material available at the library itself.

The Virginia Genealogist

The Virginia Genealogist is a publication put out by John Fredrick Dorman.

It was first printed in 1957, and the first forty years' worth of material is online through the New England Historic Genealogical Society (see the write-up in the Massachusetts section of this chapter). According to the NEHGS, "*The Virginia Genealogist* has a reputation for quality research and genealogical information not available elsewhere."

VAGenWeb
http://vagenweb.org/

As with most state-level websites associated with the USGenWeb Project, the main VAGenWeb resources are the county-level webpages and the user-submitted information. Along with a surname registry, one may find tombstone transcriptions, migrations queries, vital records, and more. Keep in mind that most of these projects aren't inclusive, so if you don't find your relatives, that doesn't mean they weren't from Virginia.

Washington

Date of Statehood: 11 Nov 1889
Neighboring States: Idaho, Oregon, Country of Canada
Previous Affiliations: Disputed Territory, Oregon Territory, Washington Territory

Although an 1818 Treaty between the United States and Britain set the 49th parallel as the international border east of the Rocky Mountains, it allowed for joint control west of the Rockies themselves. As such, both countries claimed ownership west to the Pacific Ocean and north to the border with Russian America. When the Oregon Treaty was signed in 1846, it set the 49th parallel as the United States' border all the way to the Pacific, and the Oregon Territory was established two years later in 1848. At that time, it contained the entirety of the present-day states of Washington, Oregon, and Idaho, as well as portions of Montana and Wyoming. The Washington Territory was established in 1853, and when Oregon became a state in 1859, the remainder of the Oregon Territory was added to the Washington Territory at that time. Portions of the territory were split off to become the Nebraska Territory and the Idaho Territory, leaving the Washington Territory with its present borders in 1863.

Washington State Archives

http://www.sos.wa.gov/archives/

Since the state's Digital Archives are discussed below, for the time being we'll ignore that valuable resource. Arranged by region, one can easily browse the holdings of each branch of the Archives. Alternately, one can search the Archives by keyword.

The main items of interest, however, can be found by selecting the "Genealogy Resources" link. Most of the information here is simply that, informational. However, by searching the "Court & Prison Records" category, the researcher may locate names and/or images of original records. Additionally, by selecting the "Classic Publications" tab at the top of the page, one can browse or search publications that are already online. Some of these publications will be of interest to the researcher, but be conscious of the fact that if you don't have the free plug-in and you attempt to download an entire publication as a PDF file, it might take some time; some of these PDF files can be hundreds of megabytes.

Washington State Library
http://www.sos.wa.gov/library/Genealogy.aspx

In addition to a free obituary request service, there are many other reasons why those with roots in Washington should visit the Washington State Library's website. While some subject categories only note the Library's holdings, others indicate that the collections are available online.

Some collections available online include Thurston County Pioneers, WWI soldiers, and an external link (the Olympia Historical Society) to an index of Olympia area residents from 1845 to 1930. Although some of the more interesting resources--the Biography and Genealogy Master Index and Family Records of Washington Pioneers (a 65-volume DAR publication)--are only available onsite, many other valuable collections have been or are in the process of being digitized and made available at the below website.

Washington State Digital Archives
http://www.digitalarchives.wa.gov/

The Washington Digital Archives is my favorite Washington-specific website for genealogy. The reason I like the website is because loads of collections are searchable by name. The reason I don't love it is because not every record includes a digital version of the source document. I know; I can't believe it either. Although this is the "Digital Archives," not every search result has an accompanying image of the indexed document. That being said, a great many documents of all sorts are available.

The website contains birth, marriage, death, land, census, military, and naturalization records. Coverage varies by county, but this is an excellent collection of digital information and you'll definitely want to search for your Washington ancestors through the Digital Archives.

Washington State Genealogical Society (WSGS)
http://www.rootsweb.ancestry.com/~wasgs/

Like many other state-level genealogical societies, the WSGS provides links to other state and county genealogical groups, as well as external links to other relevant resources, including those discussed above. However, the most unique online feature appears to be related to the Society's publications and certificates.

The Society's bimonthly newsletters and *The Washington State Genealogist* are both online, and while the newsletters have a lot of good information, the journal is more useful. Although it was only printed from 2006 through 2008, each of the three volumes has a name index and is available online in its entirety.

Resource guides for each of the state's counties are online, and one can also search a name index for early settler certificates.

Washington State Historical Society
http://research.washingtonhistory.org/collections/findingaids.aspx

This resource didn't have any vital-records collections that I could find. That being said, there are quite a few names associated with the Women's History Consortium (the Women's-History-Collection link is located at the left-hand side of the webpage) and in the finding aids for the Northern Pacific Hospital Records collection. Other family records and collections are also in possession of the Society, so browse through the list of finding aids or enter your relative's name in the search bar.

WAGenWeb
http://wagenweb.org/

Although it's actually hosted by the Center for the Study of the Pacific Northwest at the University of Washington, one of the most interesting links provided by WAGenWeb is for a full index to the *Pacific Northwest Quarterly*. The journal is focused on history and culture, so it isn't technically about genealogy, but as it's been around since 1906, you should still search the index for your relatives. Plus, it also covers Alaska and western Canada.

Other linked external resources include yearbooks and newspapers, while WAGenWeb itself has county-level webpages and a bibliography page with an index to the 1906 publication, *Sketches of Washingtonians*.

Other special projects that most USGenWeb sites also participate in include tombstone transcriptions, user-submitted records, user queries, military records, census information, and more.

West Virginia

Date of Statehood: 20 Jun 1863
Neighboring States: Kentucky, Maryland, Ohio, Pennsylvania, Virginia
Previous Affiliations: Virginia

Much like Kentucky, West Virginia was formed directly out of the state of Virginia. After Virginia seceded at the beginning of the Civil War, western state delegates established a restored government, and the restored government voted to allow the western counties to form their own state.

West Virginia Archives and History

http://www.wvculture.org/history/archivesindex.aspx

This is a website with a lot of information. So much so, in fact, that I've broken it down into multiple sections, even though they're all linked. This section is about the State Archives in general, the following section is about vital records, and the third section covers the West Virginia Memory Project.

First things first. If you're unable to visit the Archives yourself, a link is provided with information on research assistance. Library staff will do limited research for a fee, but if you need in-depth research, you'll have to contact a third-party; a list of researchers is available on the website.

There are two directions to go at this point, although some of the links and material overlap. The first is the "Genealogy Corner," and the second is the "State Archives" link. While the "Genealogy Corner" has more historical information about the state and genealogy in general, most of the state-records databases appear to be available through both the "Genealogy Corner" and the "State Archives" webpages. Not all collections held by the State Archives are accessible online, though our discussion is limited to those that are.

Of particular note is the fact that West Virginia struck medals to commemorate its soldiers who fought for the Union in the Civil War. Many of the medals were distributed immediately after the war, but the state still has thousands waiting to be given out. A list of soldiers whose medals have not been claimed is on the website, along with instructions on how to apply for your ancestor's medal. After your application is approved, a six-month waiting period commences to allow for any applications from closer relatives to be processed. If a closer relative submits a claim during the waiting period, that application will supersede your claim and prevent you from receiving the medal. I actually had this happen to me, so avoid disappointment and future regret (that sounds like an infomercial) and submit your application in the name of the soldiers' closest living relative. For example, if my father had applied for the medal instead of myself, my claim wouldn't have been superseded by a relative from another line since both he and the other claimant were the same number of generations away from my relative, and the tie goes to the runner, as they say.

The other indexes to check are the Vertical Surname Files and the Genealogy Surname Exchange, both of which are found through the "State Archives" link mentioned earlier. The former is simply a list of surnames that are contained in the Archives' files with no further information given. The latter is a database of individuals who are researching a particular surname.

Lists of newspaper, yearbook, and manuscript holdings are online, as well as county-by-county information on what microfilm data is held by the Archives (e.g., deeds, naturalizations, vital records, etc.).

West Virginia Vital Research Records
www.wvculture.org/vrr

This is the second section of the West Virginia Archives and History website that we're discussing, and it is one of the best state vital-records websites I've found. Not only does it allow the genealogist to search birth, marriage, and death records by name, but every record has a digital version of the source document. Even the oldest records are scanned copies of the original documents, at least in my experience. When you click on a vital record option (i.e., birth, marriage, or death), a search screen comes up, complete with a list of which county records are currently available online. If only every state could provide this sort of information. With the wealth of information on this website, you'll be pleased that your relatives hailed from West Virginia. The only thing that appears lacking from the site is a transcription of each subject's parents. However, since original images are online, this information can be readily obtained by looking at the record itself, provided that the parents were listed in the first place.

West Virginia Memory Project
http://www.wvculture.org/history/wvmemory/index.html

The West Virginia Memory Project, the last section from the West

Virginia Archives and History website to discuss, has several interesting collections and databases online. Searches can be performed for the Vertical Files, Golden Horseshoe recipients, and Veterans' records. While other collections are also located on the website, these appear to be the three that apply most directly to genealogy.

Tri-State Genealogical & Historical Society
http://www.rootsweb.ancestry.com/~wvtsghs/

Since most of West Virginia's genealogical societies pertain only to specific counties or don't have much valuable online content, it seems appropriate to place the Tri-State Genealogical & Historical Society in West Virginia's corner even though it covers the entire tri-state area comprised of West Virginia, Ohio, and Pennsylvania. In all honesty, the Society doesn't have a great deal of online content either, but extensive holdings information is online and the Society will perform research for a fee.

WVGenWeb Project
http://www.wvgenweb.org/

Although numerous links are presented to genealogical societies, resources, and historical data, the information on the county webpages appears to be the most helpful. Some other interesting information on the website is a section on coal mines, complete with user-submitted memorials, and a series of maps showing how West Virginia and Virginia's counties evolved.

Wisconsin

Date of Statehood: 29 May 1848
Neighboring States: Illinois, Iowa, Michigan, Minnesota
Previous Affiliations: Northwest Territory, Indiana Territory, Illinois Territory, Wisconsin Territory, Michigan Territory

After the Revolutionary War ended and the United States acquired the rest of the British landholdings to the Mississippi River, the Northwest Ordinance was passed to create the Northwest Territory in 1787. This territory included the area west of the new state of Pennsylvania, north of the Ohio River, and east of the Mississippi; as such, it included the entirety of the present-day states of Michigan, Illinois, Indiana, and Wisconsin, as well as portions of Minnesota and Ohio. As states were admitted to the Union and new territories were created, present-day Wisconsin was a part of the Indiana, Illinois, and Michigan Territories before the Wisconsin Territory was finally established when Michigan was preparing for statehood. Although the Wisconsin Territory originally included areas as far west as the Dakotas, it grew smaller (if growing smaller is possible) with the establishment of the Iowa Territory. When Wisconsin became a state, the remainder of the Wisconsin Territory was added to the Minnesota Territory.

Wisconsin Historical Society (WHS)

http://www.wisconsinhistory.org/genealogy/

The WHS is both a state agency and a private membership organization, according to the website. Formed prior to statehood and located in Madison, Wisconsin, the WHS is home to the Wisconsin State Archives and, it appears, is the de facto State Library as well, though it wasn't called that in so many words.

A genealogy index is online, and it includes vital records from prior to 1907 as well as name records from newspapers, obituaries, and biographical sketches. Searches return basic information, and there are links to purchase each record directly through the website. Alternately, you could visit the library yourself and copy each document. Prices seemed a bit high to me, so if you need multiple records you may be better off paying for research assistance by the hour as opposed to purchasing individual documents.

Other online searches are for biographical sketches and Civil War veterans. Uniquely, a series of veteran enumerations were completed as part of the Wisconsin state censuses in 1885, 1895, and 1905, and these enumerations have been digitized and made available online. While the Wisconsin Historical Society has many more records than those we've discussed, the rest are, for the most part, not available online. Non-digitized records held on-site include church registers, naturalization and immigration records, and more.

Wisconsin Vital Records Office

http://www.dhs.wisconsin.gov/vitalrecords/genereq.htm

Although many state vital records have been indexed and are available online through the WHS (see above), making an appointment and visiting the Vital Records Office may still be beneficial. The reason is that while the WHS has online vital-records searches from prior to 1907, more recent records are available to the public if one goes through the Vital Records Office.

WIGenWeb

http://www.wigenweb.org/

If you've been reading through each state in order, then you're probably tired of hearing what I'm about to say--or rather, write. But since some readers will jump straight to Wisconsin, let's say it once again. WIGenWeb is part of the USGenWeb Project. While the website has numerous genealogical links and is involved in several transcription projects, my favorite part of the site is the individual county webpages.

Links are provided for genealogical groups, city-directory holdings, tombstone transcriptions, and more.

Wisconsin Veterans Museum

http://www.wisvetsmuseum.com/

The Veterans Museum has quite a few collections online, but the only one I found that was searchable by name (at the time of writing) was a Civil War database. Links are provided for Spanish-American War and WWI databases also, but neither of those databases was online at the time of writing; they are both nearing completion according to the website.

Another neat feature of the website is its "Oral History Collection." This collection contains transcribed interviews, all of which can be opened as PDF files. The project began in 1994 and includes interviews with veterans from WWI up until the present. Needless to say, these interviews were all completed recently, but they may still be helpful with your research.

Wyoming

Date of Statehood: 10 Jul 1890

Neighboring States: Colorado, Idaho, Montana, Nebraska, South Dakota, Utah

Previous Affiliations: Spain, Mexico, Republic of Texas, Texas, Louisiana Territory, Missouri Territory, Unorganized Territory, Oregon Territory, Utah Territory, Nebraska Territory, Washington Territory, Wyoming Territory

Wyoming has a convoluted history based on the fact that its location was at the border of not only the Louisiana Purchase, but also the Oregon Country and the Mexican Cession of 1848. As far back as the Louisiana Purchase, present-day Wyoming was split into three areas. After the Louisiana Purchase, the eastern part of the state became a part of the Louisiana Territory, the Missouri Territory, and then an unorganized territory.

The southwestern portion of the present-day state was first under Spanish control and later Mexican control after Mexico won its independence. (Prior to Mexico's independence, the border between the United States and Spain, which ran through present-day Wyoming, was slightly altered as a result of the Adams-Onís Treaty of 1819.) After Texas won its independence from Mexico, the south-central portion of the state was part of the Republic of Texas and then the state of Texas after it was annexed by the USA. Following the Mexican Cession of 1848 and the Compromise of 1850, Texas gave up its Wyoming land holdings and the southwestern corner of the state became part of the newly established Utah Territory.

The same year as the Mexican Cession, the Oregon Territory was established; the west-central portion of present-day Wyoming was part of this new territory.

Beginning in 1854 when the Nebraska Territory was formed (it included present-day Wyoming east of the continental divide), border changes started coming fast and furious. Not only did the land that makes up present-day Wyoming belong to, at various times, the Nebraska Territory, the Idaho Territory, the Washington Territory, the Dakota Territory, and the Utah Territory, but many of those changes took place in the 1860s.

Eventually the Wyoming Territory was formed when it acquired its last missing piece (its southwest corner) from the Utah Territory in 1868. It's much easier to visualize with maps, so if you were interested enough to read all the way through this disgustingly complicated and difficult-to-follow description, do yourself a favor and find a few maps. Everything will make a lot more sense.

Wyoming State Archives
http://wyoarchives.state.wy.us/

You finally made it to the last state-level write-up--unless your relatives are from Wyoming and you started here, in which case, you finally made it to your first state-level write-up. Either way, the Wyoming State Archives' holdings are a big part of the website's appeal, and even though entries don't include individual names, they might be helpful.

Although the Archives has vital-records indexes on-site, the only one online is an in-progress death certificate database (At the time of writing, the website stated that the database was complete for last names A through E, though I did find some F surnames). If you use the search bar, you need to click the button to initiate the search. Just pressing enter won't perform a valid search. The website also suggests last names based on what you've entered in the search bar, but the suggestions, at least on my computer, were at the bottom of the webpage, not immediately below the search bar as might be expected.

A few oral histories are online, and links are provided to some of the following resources.

Wyoming Newspaper Project
http://www.wyonewspapers.org/

Funding was provided by the Wyoming Legislature so that the state's newspapers could be digitized and made available online. Newspapers that are no longer protected under copyright law are currently being digitized, and at the time of writing more than 800,000 pages of content were online.

Wyoming State Library
http://will.state.wy.us/exhibits/
http://gowyld.net/subj.cfm?subject=genealogy

It appears that most of the State Library's genealogical information is actually located on the GoWYLD.net website. Through GoWYLD.net, residents can access some of the library's subscription services like Heritage

Quest, and links to external websites are provided. Some links to external websites take users to items like an Albany County obituary index and an index to the *Pinedale Roundup*. Other links are to the previously mentioned Wyoming Newspaper Project and the following resource, Wyoming Memory.

Wyoming Memory

http://www.wyomingmemory.org/

Some of Wyoming Memory's best content is located under the "History & Geography" link on the left-hand side of the homepage. From there, one can view Campbell County's and Niobrara County's vital-records indexes through their respective county-library websites. Other picture collections and even an Inventors database are also online.

Wyoming State Historical Society (WSHS)

http://www.wyshs.org/

The *Annals of Wyoming: The Wyoming History Journal* has been the official publication of the WSHS since 1953, though it had already been in existence for thirty years at that point. An index is now available, and copies of the journal itself are also online.

American Heritage Center Digital Collections - University of Wyoming

http://digitalcollections.uwyo.edu:8180/luna/servlet

The University of Wyoming's American Heritage Center doesn't appear to have any large collections of vital records online, but this website still has a lot of unique information: old letters; newspaper clippings; photographs; sports-related documents; passports; wedding pictures. While many collections are small, there are so many collections overall that you might find something related to your ancestors anyhow. You can browse the collections individually or use the search bar instead.

WYGenWeb

http://rootsweb.ancestry.com/~wygenweb/

After the county-specific webpages, the most interesting item here (in my opinion) is a transcribed list of Civil War pensioners from 1883. Other

WYGenWeb special projects and links to some of the aforementioned websites are also provided.

Chapter Summary

Whew, that was a long chapter. While the odds are that you can't trace your ancestors to every single state discussed, hopefully the information on your state(s) of interest has been beneficial.

Remember that the Internet is ever changing, and it's possible that websites will be reconfigured and material will be moved, added, or even taken down. It's even possible that sites will acquire new URLs, and the links throughout this chapter and book won't work into perpetuity. If a link doesn't work for some reason, try typing the title of the website or association into a search engine and see if a new URL pops up in your search results.

Another thing to remember is that I've tried to present all of the main collections and surname indexes that I could find online, though there are definitely other valuable resources and their absence here doesn't mean they aren't worthwhile. As such, this should be considered a non-inclusive starting point for your research. As an example, there are far more genealogical societies than those I've listed here. However, I tried to limit the discussion to state-level societies that had valuable content online. Try using a search engine to find additional genealogical societies and resources for your area of interest. Or check the more general websites discussed in the previous chapter, as many of them have collections that are specific to certain regions and states. And don't forget to recheck websites you've already visited as new collections are always being added.

A few of the State Archives and State Libraries discussed throughout this chapter have resources online that are meant only for state residents. This can be problematic if you have ancestors from a state that you don't actually live in. Often your local library or State Archives will have access to some of the same databases, so try your own State Archives or your local library to see what they offer. If you don't have access to something you need, try clicking on the database you're interested in and see what credentials you need to access it. Sometimes you'll need a library card from the state, and in this case, I don't have any suggestions for you besides visiting in person or hiring a researcher. However, sometimes these collections simply want to authenticate your residency by asking for your phone number and zip code. If this is the case and you really need access, look online for some state-level zip-code and area-code maps. It's possible that if you get the details right, you can gain access to restricted databases even if you're not a resident. Since I can't imagine that states want non-residents using their databases, I can't condone or recommend this course of action. I merely mention it here for the sake of completeness and because I believe it might be one way to gain access to a restricted collection.

Finally, I have spent a lot of time with each of these websites trying to understand what information is available online and how each website is laid out. I have tried to make each write-up accurate, though it's possible that erroneous statements, either through changing websites or mistakes on my part, still exist.

Wrapping Things Up

Now that you've read the book, or at least the portions you were interested in, you should know a lot about genealogy and using the Internet to research yours.

First, you learned a few genealogical basics, tips, and tricks, and how to get your family tree started. Next, you learned the types of resources that might contain the names and dates you're looking for. Third, we went over different types of nationally available source documents, their content, and how best to use them. We then covered national and worldwide Internet resources, with write-ups on each website and library discussed. Finally, you were presented with an extensive list of state-by-state Internet resources, including digitized material, name indexes, and any other collections of genealogical importance. Now you're reading the book's summary chapter, which, perhaps obviously, was written to give you a summary of the book.

Be mindful that different areas of the country (and the world, though we haven't gone into a high level of detail on the genealogical world stage) make different types of records available through different channels (e.g., on-site only, through a dedicated website, through a third-party website). If the collection you seek isn't online, try searching the holdings of the associations discussed in the previous chapter on state-specific resources. If a collection jumps out at you, you'll either have to visit the library, archives, or society in question, have a researcher visit on your behalf, or wait until the material is digitized and made available online.

If the material you're looking for is online, or might be, but you don't have a subscription to the website that hosts said material, you should again try your local library, archives, or genealogical/historical society. These groups may have subscriptions that their patrons can use free of charge. Should these options not work for your particular situation (perhaps you live hours away from the state capital or any genealogical society), try your State Library or Archives' website. They may allow state residents to use some of their subscription collections remotely. And if none of that works, you could always subscribe to the website you need access to.

Hopefully by using the resources, tips, and tricks provided throughout the book you'll be able to break through that sticking point of yours. If so, then congratulations on a fine bit of detective work. If not, try not to get discouraged. That final bit of information that ties everything together is probably still out there, even if it's not on the Internet yet. Remember that there is far more material available than that which has been digitized and put online.

When you've looked at every single pertinent resource listed in the previous chapters, you've identified additional county and regional resources that pertain to your particular search, and you've tried all the alternate spellings you can come up with and you still can't scrounge up anything new online, it may feel like you're spinning your wheels without getting anywhere. If this is the case, it may be time to focus on the genealogical holdings of different associations as opposed to searching for your ancestors specifically online. This might require an extra step or twelve, since you'll be using the Internet as a card catalog (for those who are unaware, card catalogs were the old way of finding books before Internet- or computer-based searches) to locate holdings, collections, and books of interest. Once you find them, you'll have to set the computer aside to visit the host institutions or hire a researcher to visit on your behalf. This might not be as convenient as simply opening your laptop, but there will likely come a point when this is your only route forward. Unless you want to wait for more material to become digitally available.

Genealogical research is a giant jigsaw puzzle, and the information pertaining to your relatives could be located anywhere. How easily you locate your relatives is partially based on luck (did the local courthouse burn down?), but patience and determination can yield results even if those results don't come easily. When patience and determination come up empty and even setting your computer aside to read historical accounts and browse microfilm doesn't seem to help, you might consider DNA testing to give your research a kick start.

Although I've attempted to be thorough with regard to the data presented here, there are literally millions (billions?) of source documents that aren't yet available online and millions of places to look for those records. You now have the knowledge you need to put the pieces together, so don't get discouraged if you can't immediately find the record you want. Simply get off the computer to search the pertinent record repository, take a DNA test, or recheck your favorite websites when you feel the urge. After all, the final clue in your puzzle might already be online. And you might just find it tomorrow.

ABOUT

About the Author

Ryan Elson, the 31-year-old transplant from the Midwest, is a relative newcomer to the genealogy game. Living in Nevada, Ryan had to rely largely on the Internet for researching his ancestors and realized that this was true for genealogists the world over. As a result, he decided that an easy-to-read book that gave researchers the basics, tips, and tricks they needed to get started, as well as a lengthy list of websites to consult would be an invaluable resource.

When Ryan isn't researching his family history, he enjoys traveling, camping, bouldering, skiing, and all manner of outdoor activity. Ryan has camped everywhere; from the cornfields of the Midwest to the desert that is West Texas; from the mountains of Colorado and California to the frigid shores of Antarctica. Perhaps his propensity for enjoying sub-zero outdoor activities stems from the fact that he was born during one of the most brutally cold Januaries that Chicago has ever seen. Or perhaps not.

In his youth, Ryan lived in the suburbs of Chicago, outside of Dallas, and finally followed his parents to the great state of Indiana where, in high school, he played football and ran track, even trying his hand at pole-vaulting, something he probably should have had a coach for. Afterwards, he graduated from Iowa State University with a black belt in Taekwondo and an electrical engineering degree.

Before quitting his job and moving to Nevada to enter the world of writing full-time, Ryan had relocated to California to work as the electrical supervisor at a cement plant and after being laid off, for a defense contractor. These maintenance positions put Ryan in a location where he could camp regularly and gave him a unique perspective on the world that one only acquires after years of early morning call-outs and rocket-fuel coffee.

In his free time, Ryan enjoys ignoring his girlfriend's cats, rock climbing, hiking, camping, traveling, genealogical research, reading, skiing, beer (both drinking and brewing), solving crossword puzzles, spreadsheets, and pretty much anything in the great outdoors. Although Ryan's interests have changed over the years, some hobbies from his youth included eating far too many eggs and mixing the pieces from several puzzles together before proceeding to solve each one--at the age of two.

Having previously visited Ecuador and Antarctica using the scant vacation a maintenance position afforded him, Ryan now desires nothing more than the time and ability to experience new places and see new things. Oh, and beer. He also desires a tasty beer.

Connect with the author online:

Homepage:
http://www.ryan-elson.com

Facebook:
https://www.facebook.com/RyanElsonAuthor

Twitter:
https://twitter.com/authorryanelson

WordPress Blog:
http://ryanelson.wordpress.com/blog/

SAMPLE

Free Sample Chapter

Don't Step on the Dirt
Chapter One - Introduction

Fishers, Indiana... Fishers, Indiana... Fishers, Indiana...

We had been telling the cows where we were headed for almost three weeks now, and as we got closer to our final destination, they were becoming steadily less interested. Not only had their interest declined, but it seemed to have done so exponentially. I hadn't previously been aware of the inverse square law of bovine interest, but I made a mental note to write up a paper and submit it to a reputable journal as soon as I made it home.

To be honest, I wasn't even aware that roadside cows wanted to know where I was headed until last year. Although this may sound a bit racist (although speciesist may be a more appropriate word if I may coin a new term; one that we'll certainly need if we ever meet an alien race), I never considered the cows along the highway to be anything more than milk-giving, meat-providing, cud-chewing, and methane-producing large mammals (the milk-giving or meat-providingness of the cow being largely dependent on the breed). I had always considered cows to be well-mannered; they don't talk back to you, they don't honk at you in traffic, they don't drink the last beer or eat the last slice of pizza. But I never considered they would have intellectual interests as well. On the whole, I would equate their temperaments with that of a strawberry sundae; deliciously relaxed.

Of course, this all changed when my girlfriend informed me the previous year that roadside cows do, in fact, want to know where the thousands of cars that drive by each day are headed. Since most cows never get to travel, it seems that they like to live vicariously through the road warriors that zip past their bit of pasture. And being supremely knowledgeable about geography, they don't even need to consult maps for the most obscure of towns. You could just as easily be headed for Chugwater, Wyoming as Chicago, Illinois and nary a bovine would ask you to point out your destination on a map.

We discussed this phenomenon at length and although neither one of us spoke cow, we felt safe in assuming that they were less and less excited as our destination became more and more humdrum and boring. Whereas a happy cow in California might be genuinely interested in a trip to Fishers, Indiana, or the neighboring towns of Noblesville or Carmel (pronounced like the candy and not the Californian city of the same name, in case you care to go back and reread this sentence with proper pronunciations), a cow from Indiana would be about as excited as a worm at the prospect of being up early.

We were on the last leg of our road trip to Indiana for my youngest sister's wedding. We would also be attending the wedding of her soon-to-be husband which, conveniently enough was being held at the same time and place. Of course, we hadn't just flown into Northwestern Indiana to road trip through the country's 6th most tornado-prone state. Our road trip started three weeks ago when I departed from Santa Cruz, California and improved rather immensely when I picked up my girlfriend, Dondra, in Denver six days ago.

The idea for the road trip all started back in November of 2010 when Tom, the groom-to-be, proposed to Heather, the bride-to-be and future Mrs. Hagenberg. Although, without rather strict qualifiers, the start date of the trip, or anything for that matter, is highly debatable. Since I wasn't actually employed at the time of the proposal and didn't plan on having regular employment when the wedding took place, you could say that the start date for me was when I left my previous job, an act which would give me the time for the road trip. Or perhaps the circumstances which led me to that job in the first place would be more appropriate. In that case, we could say that my trip began at a career fair approximately seven years earlier when a recruiter for a cement company asked if I could snag him a beverage koozie from another company's table (which I did), which led me to give him a resume, which led to a series of interviews, and a job offer, which I would ultimately accept, move to California, and get laid off when the economy tanked. And if we take it even farther, I only ended up at Iowa State due to another series of life happenings which I won't go into because we could continue down this road all day. But were we to do that, then you would be reading something more akin to a biography of a particularly handsome and likable chap whom you don't even know, which is probably not what you set out to do when you picked up this book (if it is, then I'm sorry to disappoint, but perhaps we can meet up for a beer sometime). For the rest of you who set out to read a hilariously tangent-filled book about a cross-country road trip, national parks, and the outdoors, in order not to pull a literary bait and switch on you, we'll define the start of the trip planning and subsequent road trip as the moment when the happy couple became the happily-engaged couple.

Needless to say, I wasn't actually present for the proposal either, taking voyeuristic pictures from a nearby bush for example, as my best friend's brother was during his proposal (I'm looking at you, Mike). So it would probably be more accurate to say that it all started when I heard that they were getting married and they booked the venue. Waiting for the venue booking was critical because I had been pushing for a destination wedding and hoped that I would be flying somewhere exotic, say, anywhere but Indiana.

Not that there is anything wrong with Indiana, of course. It's an eminently agreeable state; full of fields of corn, soy beans, and cows; professional sporting teams; some great college and high school athletics; and a rather well-known race track, not to mention the world's largest children's museum. We even have several ski resorts in Indiana. It's true. The largest one offers one hundred skiable acres and 400 vertical feet. And no, I didn't leave out any digits in those statistics. Go ahead... Take a moment to regain your composure... It does seem a rather modest tract of land to house a ski resort, and I'll admit that if you like skinning up mountains and hucking yourself off of perfectly good cliffs, then skiing in Indiana may not be for you. Powder hounds and heli-skiers should probably also resist the urge to vacation on the glorious alpine slopes of Indiana. On the plus side, you'll probably never need an avalanche beacon. And best of all, you'll get very good at skiing on very bad snow. I should know. When we have icy conditions in the Sierras, those are the only days when I can bomb down the mountain and leave Dondra, an admitted speed junkie, in my dust (or ice crystals as it were). I have the great state of Indiana to thank for that.

And so I decided that I was going to take some time off from my normal routine of reading, planning for other business ventures, and trying not to sneeze at the cats with whom we rented a room and whom I was allergic to, in order to drive cross-country for a spring wedding in the great state of Indiana.

****

Since the date for the wedding had been set, I used it as the starting point for our road trip. It would be held on Friday, May 13, 2011.

Yes, the wedding would be held on a Friday. Yes, the wedding was going to be on the 13th. A fear of Friday the 13th, a condition so common that we actually have a term for it, friggatriskaidekaphobia, would not be tolerated at this wedding.

An estimated seventeen to twenty-one million Americans suffer from this fear, a figure that equates to roughly five to seven percent of the population. That seems like an awful lot of people to be afraid of a particular day which doesn't even occur every month. Heck, it doesn't even occur every six months. On average, Friday the 13th occurs approximately every 212 days, or about every seven months. There are longer stretches of Friday the 13th-less bliss, however. Every once in a while, we can make it a whopping fourteen months between these dreaded days. However, sometimes we have to endure the scariness two months in a row when February happens to have a Friday the 13th in a non-leap year. In that case, the 13th of both February and March will fall on a Friday. Heaven help us if one of those days is also a full moon…

Since the 13th of any particular month will not fall on a Friday every year, our fear is really based on the day itself, how we were brought up, and our calendar conventions. There's nothing mystical about the point in our orbit when we flip days of the calendar from Thursday the 12th to Friday the 13th. In fact, our calendar conventions are the only way we can even determine when Friday the 13th will occur. In that way, the day differs from most of our other holidays or meaningful days. Any day that falls on the exact same day every year (i.e., Christmas, the 4th of July, your birthday, my birthday, etc…) will take place at the same point in the Earth's revolution around the sun. By carefully observing the positions of the stars, precession of the equinoxes, and accounting for the differences between our calendar and the actual time it takes us to orbit the sun, differences that we attempt to correct for through the addition of February 29th every four years, you could be certain when any day would occur.

Of course, most of us don't even know as much about leap years as we think we do. In school, you were probably taught that leap years occur every four years, and we add a day to the end of February. Were we still following the outdated Julian calendar, you could remain secure in that bit of knowledge. One extra day, February 29th, every four years. End of story.

However, the average time for a trip around the sun is not exactly 365.25 days. Instead we travel around the sun approximately eleven minutes faster than that every year. As a result, all of these eleven minute blocks started adding up and eventually the Vernal Equinox, when nighttime and daytime are equal in the spring (assuming you're in the Northern hemisphere) started getting earlier and earlier. In fact, by the time Pope Gregory XIII instituted what would become our standard calendar in 1582, the Vernal Equinox was taking place on March 11th, not March 21st. We were off by ten whole days! Since the date for the celebration of Easter is based in part on the date of the Vernal Equinox, or a tabular approximation thereof, this affected when the holiday was held. By losing so many days, Easter had to be celebrated earlier and earlier, which was entirely unacceptable in the eyes of the church.

The new Gregorian calendar was established to ensure that the Vernal Equinox remained on (or around) March 21st and was soon adopted by several Catholic countries; Spain, Portugal, and Italy. The British Empire (and the future United States, which was not yet a free country) adopted the new calendar in 1752, but in order to bring the Vernal Equinox back in line, eleven days needed to be skipped. In 1752, in the United Kingdom, the American colonies, and all across the British Empire, Wednesday, September 2nd was followed by Thursday, September 14th. So the next time you're reading an Encyclopedia Brown mystery based on a 1752 artifact or document of some sort, just remember that September 3rd through September 13th never happened. Similarly, when the United States purchased Alaska in 1867, the new owners were on the Gregorian calendar while Russia was still using the Julian calendar. As a result, it was necessary to skip twelve days to bring Alaska into sync with the rest of the country. Since it was also decided that the International Date Line would be moved from Alaska's eastern border to its western border, the ingenious solution was to skip eleven days and repeat Friday. So in Alaska, Friday, October 6th, 1867, was followed by Friday, October 18th, 1867.

The Gregorian calendar keeps the Vernal Equinox situated on, or near, March 21st by skipping three leap years in every four-hundred-year period, which provides a far superior method for keeping dates. With respect to the mean tropical year, it's accurate to about one day in 3300 years.

The bottom line is not to worry about losing a day somewhere along the line. We'll all be dead and gone by the time that happens. In fact, by the time we lose a day under the Gregorian calendar, possibly around the year 4000 or so, it will be so disparate from the Julian calendar that any remaining Julian calendar devotees will be celebrating Thanksgiving while their Gregorian counterparts open presents on Christmas morning.

The agreed-upon dates to skip leap years, and thus keep ourselves from opening presents on Thanksgiving, are every year ending in '00 that is not evenly divisible by 400. So while we observed leap year in 2000, as per our normal experiences, we'll skip the coming leap years in 2100, 2200, and 2300. The last skipped leap year was in 1900 and since the average age at which a person starts remembering their life is three and a half years, even Besse Berry Cooper, born on the 26th of August, 1896, and verified as the oldest living person by the Gerontology Research Group in 2012, would likely not remember the last non-leap-year leap year.

It so happens that no one knows the true origin of our fear of Friday the 13th. For different reasons, the number thirteen is considered to be an unlucky number, and Friday is considered to be an unlucky day. The number twelve is considered to be an important and complete number in many religions, and thus the number thirteen is considered to be irregular and unlucky; twelve apostles, twelve gods of Olympus, twelve signs of the zodiac, the Norse god Odin had twelve sons, twelve Imams in Islam, twelve full lunar cycles in a year, and so on and so forth. In one calendar year there are always twelve full lunar cycles, but occasionally we have thirteen full moons in one calendar year. In the same way that the Julian calendar was problematic for the celebration of Easter, having an additional full moon was problematic for other church celebrations, which may be one reason that thirteen is considered an unlucky number. At the Last Supper, counting Jesus and the twelve apostles, there were thirteen people around the table; Loki is the thirteenth, uninvited, guest in a Norse myth when Balder is killed; there are thirteen witches in a Wiccan coven; on Friday, October 13, 1307, the Knights Templar were arrested by King Philip.

Of course, not all cultures find Friday the 13th to be an inauspicious wedding date. In Greece, Spain, and many Latin American countries, Tuesday the 13th is known as a day of bad luck. And in Italy, Friday the 17th is unlucky. So a wedding held on Friday the 13th in those countries would likely be taken in stride.

Regardless of anyone's misgivings about the date of the wedding, this meant we would have to be in town by Thursday, May 12th, 2011, in order to attend the rehearsal dinner and take advantage of the free food and drinks that accompanied the event. With Dondra currently attending graduate school, we didn't have the luxury of meandering across the country at our leisure. She was able to take a week off from her research, but that hardly left us time to cover the 2300-plus miles and see much of anything along the way.

As a result, we decided that the best way to plan our trip was to see how far we could drive in a week while still leaving ourselves time to camp, hike, and play the tourist. It turned out that if we pushed it, we could start as far west as Denver. Since we didn't live in Denver, Dondra booked a flight for May 6th. And to make sure I was there to pick her up on time, I decided it was necessary to leave the Republic of Santa Cruz and set out for California on April 22nd. It was time to start packing.

****

Don't Step on the Dirt is available in print through Amazon.com and can also be ordered by your local bookstore and library. It is available on a variety of eReaders.